DISCIPLINING THE STATE

Virtue, Violence, and State-Making in Modern China

Harvard East Asian Monographs 283

DISCIPLINING THE STATE

Virtue, Violence, and State-Making in Modern China

Patricia M. Thornton

Published by the Harvard University Asia Center
Distributed by Harvard University Press
Cambridge (Massachusetts) and London 2007

© 2007 by the President and Fellows of Harvard College

Printed in the United States of America

The Harvard University Asia Center publishes a monograph series and, in coordination with the Fairbank Center for East Asian Research, the Korea Institute, the Reischauer Institute of Japanese Studies, and other faculties and institutes, administers research projects designed to further scholarly understanding of China, Japan, Vietnam, Korea, and other Asian countries. The Center also sponsors projects addressing multidisciplinary and regional issues in Asia.

Library of Congress Cataloging-in-Publication Data

Thornton, Patricia M.
  Disciplining the state : virtue, violence, and state-making in modern China / Patricia M. Thornton.
      p. cm. — (Harvard East Asian monographs ; 283)
  Includes bibliographical references and index.
  ISBN-13: 978-0-674-02504-2 (cl : alk. paper)
  ISBN-10: 0-674-02504-0 (cl : alk. paper)
    1. China—Politics and government--History. 2. Political corruption—China--History. I. Title.
  JQ1510.T48 2007
  320.951--dc22

                              2006038683

Index by David Prout

Designed and typeset by Pinnacle Design, New York City

♾ Printed on acid-free paper

Last figure below indicates year of this printing
17 16 15 14 13 12 11 10 09 08 07

To my family,
especially Eugene Paul Peplinsky and MaryAnn Peplinsky
Lindgren, Teresa Padavano, and Richard S. Jardine

Acknowledgments

Research for this project was funded by a Fulbright Foundation grant under the auspices of the Institute for International Education, and a Henry Robert Braden Fellowship offered through the University of California, Berkeley. To these institutions, as well as to the Academia Sinica in Taiwan and the Fairbank Center for East Asian Research at Harvard University, I wish to express my gratitude for their generous support.

The scope of this project is such that I cannot begin to acknowledge properly all of the individuals to whom I owe thanks. In particular, I have been extraordinarily fortunate to have had wonderful teachers, beginning with Lillian Li and Mary Poovey at Swarthmore College, James Townsend and Christine DiStefano at the University of Washington in Seattle, and Shannon Stimson, Lowell Dittmer, and Frederic Wakeman, Jr., at the University of California at Berkeley. I am profoundly grateful to Elizabeth J. Perry, whose incisive analysis and firm mentoring over the course of many years has simply made all the difference in the world. I could not have asked for finer role models, and their example continues to inspire me, many years later.

In Beijing, my research would not have been possible but for the assistance of Jiang Tao of the Chinese Academy of Social Science's Institute of Modern History and Yin Tongyun of the Institute of Qing History at National People's University. Zhu Shuyuan and the staffs of the Number One Historical Archive and of the Rare Book Room at Beijing University Library were generous with their time and expertise. My time in Beijing fortuitously overlapped with the research visits of Iwo Amelung, Beatrice Bartlett, Mike and Dorothy Chambers, Cheung Sui-wai, Brian Dott, Joseph Esherick, Tom Reilly, and Janet Theiss; I benefited enormously from their advice and support while in Beijing.

My visit to Nanjing was sponsored by Zhang Xianwen and Shen Xiaoyun of Nanjing University's Institute of History. The staff of the Number Two Historical Archive was very helpful in locating appropriate materials; during my stay, I had the good fortune of overlapping with Julia Strauss and Mary Buck, and am grateful to both for their companionship and advice.

In Taibei, Chen San-ch'ing, Chen Yung-fa, Hsiung Ping-chen, and Huang Ke-wu (Max Huang) of the Institute of Modern History at the Academia Sinica all provided much-needed guidance and support. Yen Chen-shen and I Yuan of the Institute of International Relations, and Shao Ming-huang and Jiang Jing of the Central Committee of the Kuomintang's Historical Commission, all kindly offered assistance in locating materials. While in Nangang I overlapped with the research visits of Robert Antony, Paulo Frank, Jennifer Rudolph, Elizabeth Scully, Julia Strauss, and R. Bin Wong, all of whom contributed, in various ways, to the shaping of this project. Bao Taihang and his family made my stay there immeasurably more entertaining than it would have otherwise been. To Christian DePee, with whom I also crossed paths at the Academia Sinica, I owe a special debt of gratitude: his wonderful book and his wisdom on so many topics over the years have transformed my perspective on Chinese historiography.

During the writing process, which continued at the Fairbank Center for East Asian Research, I benefited from yet another cadre of scholars from whom I learned a great deal, including Guo Xiaolin, John Hermann, and Michael Schoenhals. Elizabeth Remick at Tufts University kindly read through an earlier draft of the chapters and offered excellent suggestions and advice, as did anonymous readers at Harvard's Asia Center Publications Program. Finally, my colleagues and students at Trinity College in Hartford, Connecticut, where I teach political science, have supported me through numerous revisions. I owe particular thanks to Christopher Nadon, not only for keeping his razor honed to precision, but also for wielding it with surgical skill.

At home I owe a debt of gratitude of a different order altogether. I wish to thank Linda Liu (Liu Guoyun) of Berkeley, Mrs. Ma of Weigongcun in Beijing, the teachers and staff of the Daosheng Nursery School in Nangang, Cindy Amdur of Juneau, the Oxford Street Daycare Center in Cambridge, Massachusetts, and the staff of the Auerbach Center for Early Childhood Learning in Hartford for the wonderful and loving care that they provided for my three children while I completed my research and writing.

Finally, I wish to thank my family, to whom this book is dedicated. I owe thanks to my parents, Eugene Peplinsky and MaryAnn Peplinsky Lindgren, my maternal grandmother, Teresea Padovano, and my paternal uncle,

Richard S. Jardine. My daughter Mariah, who endured long separations from her father and daily fingernail inspections at her Taiwanese nursery school, was a tremendous source of comfort and entertainment for me during the year and half we spent in China and Taiwan together. My son Liam precociously developed a remarkable range of traits that made the job of writing and rewriting the early drafts of this manuscript endurable for me: a wide and easy smile, a propensity for long afternoon naps and, later, a tremendous fondness for his younger brother Roan, whose birth has brought me more joy than I can express. Last, my greatest debt is to Thomas Thornton, a wonderful father and partner, who has patiently endured both long periods of separation and togetherness with equal fortitude, countless midnight monologues on any number of obscure and fruitless topics, and without whose wisdom, understanding, and forbearance this project could never have been conceived, let alone completed.

P.M.T.

Contents

DISCIPLINING THE STATE

Virtue, Violence, and State-Making in Modern China

Introduction

No one remains dominant politically for very long who cannot in some way promise violence to recalcitrants, pry support from producers, portray his actions as collective sentiment, or justify his decisions as ratified practice. Yet to reduce the negara to such tired commonplaces, the worn coin of European ideological debate, is to allow most of what is interesting about it to escape our view. Whatever intelligence it may have to offer us about the nature of politics, it can hardly be that big fish eat little fish, or that the rags of virtue mask the engines of privilege.

—Clifford Geertz, *The Theatre State in Nineteenth Century Bali*

What are states, and how are they made? In his broad survey of state-formation in Western Europe, Charles Tilly argues that modern nation-states evolved, first and foremost, as war machines: the architecture of governance we now know as the state originally appeared as the historical by-product of various rulers' attempts to acquire the means to make war. The coercion-or capital-intensive strategies employed to achieve that end gave particular shape to both extant and emerging political organizations, resulting in the variety of state structures found within Europe today.[1] Western European state-building—which involved the elimination or subordination of internal political rivals on the one hand and the creation of differentiated, autonomous, centralized organizations designed to mobilize and extract resources for war on the other—incurred significant and sustained social resistance from subject populations at every step in the process.[2]

This study of state-making in modern Chinese history offers a different perspective, one that highlights the normative dimensions of the state-building process. Without denying that mobilization for war has played a role in the extension and deepening of the power of the Chinese state,

---

1. Charles Tilly, *Coercion, Capital, and European States, AD 990–1992* (Cambridge, MA: Blackwell, 1990); see also Charles Tilly, "War Making and State Making as Organized Crime," in *Bringing the State Back In*, ed. Peter B. Evans, Dietrich Rueschmeyer, and Theda Skocpol (Cambridge, Eng.: Cambridge University Press, 1985), pp. 169–91.
2. *The Formation of National States in Western Europe*, ed. Charles Tilly (Princeton: Princeton University Press, 1975).

I argue instead that in modern China, state-making strategies—defined as concerted efforts toward administrative centralization, increased social penetration, bureaucratization, and rationalization—have been shaped at least as decisively by normative agendas as they were by military goals. As was the case in Western Europe, such strategies frequently employed coercion- or capital-intensive methods to achieve state-building ends. However, insofar as the state-making process in modern China was not driven by the nearly continuous competition for trade and territory within a field of neighboring states of unequal size, Chinese state-making has not centered on the mobilization of troops and material resources for war.[3] Rather, the geopolitical challenges associated with governing the imperium over the *longue durée* produced a trajectory of state-building shaped in large part by the increasingly elaborated drive for moral regulation and social control. In the chapters that follow, I argue that the process of Chinese state-making has long been shaped by the recurring need to define and redefine the center as a moral agent—in fact, *the* moral agent—in modern Chinese history.

The key finding of this study is that the socio-ethical agendas of modern Chinese leaders were central to the state-making process, not because they served to cloak more fundamental material or political interests behind a mask of legitimation, but because state-making and moral regulation are in fact co-constituting historical processes. Most studies of state-formation rely explicitly or implicitly either on Max Weber's axiomatic definition of the state as "a compulsory political organization with continuous operations" in which an "administrative staff successfully upholds the claim to the monopoly of the legitimate use of physical force" within "a given territorial area,"[4] or adopt a Marxist perspective that casts the state as an instrument of repression wielded by the ruling class. This paradigmatic focus on the repressive or coercive capacities of modern states not only serves to de-emphasize the importance of alternative forms of power in the process of state-formation but also presumes that it is the monopolization of power that produces legitimacy rather than

---

3. Tilly notes that "although China had once lived through an era of Warring States that had much in common with the international anarchy of Europe, and if insurrections and invasions from the frontiers recurrently threatened imperial control, most of the time a single center dominated much of Chinese space, a zone that was unimaginably large by European standards. Empire was long China's normal condition; when one empire declined, another seized its place." See Tilly (1990), p. 128.
4. Max Weber, *Economy and Society*, volume 1, ed. Guenther Roth and Clause Wittich (Berkeley: University of California Press, 1978), p. 54.

the possibility that the monopolization of legitimacy might in turn produce power.

Some have argued that when viewed outside the historically anomalous context of war-making in medieval Western European history, the process of state-formation finds its fullest expression in the construction of a particular social order, and in the collective observance of specific codes of behavior shaped by underlying normative precepts. Norbert Elias's account of the "civilizing process" also begins with the monopolization and centralization of physical force in the hands of European feudal princes. However, Elias proposed that over time, the formation of progressively larger collectivities and pacified social spaces forced ever greater numbers of individuals to restrain the expression of their own violence and gratification. The resulting evolution of new codes of conduct and increasingly differentiated control organizations culminated in what Elias refers to as "the sociogenesis of the state": the historical emergence of a centralized regulating and coordinating organ from a tangle of disorganized and highly differentiated social interests.[5] In a related vein, Philip Corrigan and Derek Sayer argue that the process of English state-formation was in fact a bourgeois cultural revolution, carried out through an extended process of collective moral regulation.[6] Citing Emile Durkheim on the cultural and normative dimensions of state activity, they propose that the state should be viewed as "above all, supremely, the organ of moral discipline."[7] In the Chinese case, Chen Chi-yun notes that the etymological origins of the word "orthodoxy" (*zheng*) represent a notion of power in which coercive might, political dominion, and moral justification are inextricably linked together in a causal chain, with each giving rise to the other. He proposes that, in its earliest and most pristine formulation, the Confucian dictum *zheng zhe zheng ye* likely meant "to govern is to coerce with force or authority"; however, over time, the related homophones for coercive power, formalized governance, and moral rectification have blended into the more frequently adopted gloss of the phrase: "To govern is to rectify."[8] It is this complex and interrelated

---

5. Norbert Elias, *The Civilizing Process: The History of Manners*, trans. Edmund Jephcott (New York: Urizen Books, 1978); and Norbert Elias, *Power and Civility*, trans. Edmund Jephcott (New York: Pantheon Books, 1982).

6. Philip Corrigan and Derek Sayer, *The Great Arch: English State Formation as Cultural Revolution* (Oxford and New York: Basil Blackwell, 1985), p. 4.

7. Emile Durkheim, *Professional Ethics and Civic Morals*, trans. Cornelia Brookfield (London and New York: Routledge, 1957), p. 72.

8. The latter gloss appears in James Legge's translation of the Confucian Analects, 12:17. See James Legge, *The Four Books* (Shanghai: China Book Company, 1923), p. 208. See also Chen Chi-yun, "Orthodoxy as a Mode of Statecraft," in *Orthodoxy in Late Imperial China*, ed. Liu

process, involving simultaneous state-making, moral regulation, and social control, that I seek to map over three historical Chinese regimes.

By focusing on the normative dimensions of the state-making process, I do not imply the existence of an unchanging moral core at the center of the Chinese state, nor do I suggest that central state-makers invariably, or even generally, triumphed in their quest to impose and enforce their particular moral visions on a passive populace. To the contrary, the normative dimensions of the state-building process shifted dramatically across the three regimes under consideration in this study, ranging from the late imperial model of statecraft that prevailed during the reign of the Yongzheng emperor to the conservative or proto-fascist republican vision embraced by Jiang Jieshi during the Nanjing decade to the revolutionary Maoism that prevailed during the early 1960s. The depth, breadth, and coherence of these moral visions varied significantly, as did their reception by those not in the service of the regime. All were contested, sometimes violently, both from within the core of centralized political leadership as well as from those perceived to be on the margins of state control. Yet state-making is, in China as elsewhere, a profoundly normative and normalizing process, which seeks not only to impose a particular moral order within which the state can claim primacy but also to make the presence of the state at the center of that totalizing vision appear both natural and necessary. These activities rely on what I refer to here as the boundary-drawing capacity of the state: the ability of a regime to construct itself as an autonomous moral agent simultaneously separate from and embedded within an imagined political community.

This study focuses on the state-making process during three periods of key reform in modern Chinese history: the reign of the Yongzheng emperor (1723–35); the Nanjing-based rule of the Guomindang (1927–37); and the Socialist Education Campaign as it unfolded under the direction of the Communist Party (1962–66). During each of these time periods, central authorities introduced considerable institutional change designed to extend the reach of central control over local political life: the Yongzheng-era fiscal reform program of "return[ing] of the meltage fee to the public coffers" (*huohao guigong*), and the extension of funds for "nourishing virtue" (*yanglian*) to each official yamen, as well as the emperor's concerted attempt to expand state control over the county-level granary system;[9] the Nanjing-

---

Kwang-ching (Berkeley: University of California Press, 1990), pp. 27–52. Chen's essay seeks to recover the roots of coercive state power in the history of the Chinese state.

9. Pierre-Etienne Will and R. Bin Wong, *Nourish the People: The State Civilian Granary System in China, 1650–1850* (Ann Arbor: University of Michigan Press, 1991), pp. 30, 38.

based Nationalist government's attempts to set up new county government organizations and to depose local leaders in the drive to consolidate its rule in the early 1930s under the auspices of new administrative, constitutional, and criminal legal frameworks; and the Chinese Communist Party's (CCP) shift to production-team accountability, smaller communes, and the guarantee of private plots and local control over domestic industries to peasants in the early 1960s.[10] As in Western Europe, Chinese state-makers employed capital-intensive and/or coercion-intensive strategies in pursuing fiscal rationalization, administrative professionalization, and economic planning. Yet a closer examination of how such activities were actually carried out— the multitude of practices that were central to the rearrangement of bureaucratic power, as well as the specific technologies of administrative investigation, discipline, and control that were employed in each of these three cases—strongly suggests that beyond the more immediate goal of implementing new policies at the local level, central authorities aimed to redefine the realms of normative and normal political behavior by way of constituting the realm of the pathological in particular ways.

At the core of such efforts was the problem of political corruption, defined in imperial law dating back to the Tang as illicit official behavior that spanned the border between the "public" (*gong*) and "private" (*si*). The three rounds of concerted state-building described in the chapters that follow included ambitious anti-corruption campaigns designed to fortify the boundary between "state" and "social" forces in the aftermath of critical institutional changes that redefined the nature of public and private responsibility. Correlatively, by locating the source of moral deviance outside the newly delineated boundaries of state control, central leaders sought to circumscribe the scope of the regime's own legitimation project by defining those institutions, practices, and activities for which the state would claim responsibility, as well as those for which it would not. Over the long term, the identification and punishment of particular bureaucratic practices within the edifice of state power produced surges of power that seeped beyond the newly articulated boundaries, saturating and, ultimately, reconfiguring realms of local practice.

Yet the imperfect fit between the moral formulations of central authorities and the complex socioeconomic realities of local communities

---

10. The post–Great Leap period witnessed an increased emphasis on production-team accountability (as opposed to the larger commune structure), but the increased use of agencies outside or above the basic production units nullified the trend toward decentralization. R. J. Birrell, "The Centralized Control of the Communes in the Post-'Great Leap' Period," in *Chinese Communist Politics in Action*, ed. A. Doak Barnett (Seattle: University of Washington Press, 1969), pp. 401, 442.

on the periphery left room for interpretation, improvisation, and, in some cases, subversion and resistance. Local agents who operated on the fringes of central state control were neither uniformly compliant nor uniformly hostile to the designs of central authorities; rather, the deployment of state-making designs in the local context established limits to the hegemonic expansion of state power, often serving perceived local interests by subtly contesting the boundary-drawing capacity of the center. This account serves to highlight the ways in which the fixing of the imagined boundary between state and society emerged as a technique of wielding normative power as central to Chinese state-making strategies as war-making was in the case of Western Europe.

CHINESE STATE-MAKING IN COMPARATIVE CONTEXT

Recent studies of state-making in China have highlighted fundamental departures from the historical trajectories of state-formation that unfolded in Western Europe. Research on the Republican era has attempted in a variety of ways to account for the simultaneous successes and failures of the state-building efforts under the Nationalist regime, including a consideration of the various units and levels of analysis involved and ultimately pressing for a more nuanced understanding of the process.[11] Elizabeth Remick's comparison of taxation and public finance during the Nanjing Decade and post-Mao reform eras argues that the state-building efforts of local governments succeeded in some cases even while the power of the central state declined.[12] Julia Strauss's study of four Republican-era central administrative organizations maps the various institution-building strategies pursued under the rubric of the larger state-making process pursued by the regime, detailing organizational successes unfolding alongside institution-building failures.[13] R. Keith Schoppa finds that even as Republican state-making efforts succeeded at rationalizing and bureaucratizing government processes and maintaining social order, the regime's ability to penetrate

---

11. Kenneth Pomeranz argues that Nationalist rule involved both "state-making and unmaking," and urged students of the Republican era to look beyond simple models that predict unilateral political and economic change on a national level. See Kenneth Pomeranz, *The Making of a Hinterland* (Berkeley: University of California Press, 1993), p. 271.

12. Elizabeth Remick, *Building Local States: China During the Republican and Post-Mao Eras* (Cambridge, MA: Harvard University Asia Center, 2004).

13. Julia C. Strauss, *Strong Institutions in Weak Polities: State-Building in Republican China, 1927–1940* (Oxford: Clarendon Press, 1998).

local society eroded, resulting in a growing separation between state and society that manifested itself on several different levels.[14]

Other studies of Chinese state-making have emphasized the inadequacy of categories and concepts drawn from European history to explain or adequately describe the process of state-formation in China. In his influential study of state-making in twentieth-century China, Prasenjit Duara argues that the distinction drawn by many Europeanists between state-making—the process by which states increase their penetration and control over the societies that they govern—and nation-building—the process by which states seek to build loyalty and commitment to the regime—was inappropriate in the Chinese context. Proposing instead that "the Chinese pattern of state strengthening [was] closely interwoven with modernizing and nation-building goals," Duara argues that the potent combination of simultaneous state-making, modernization, and nation-building efforts pursued by late imperial and Republican-era authorities represented a new and crippling challenge to the pre-existing "cultural nexus of power." This nexus encompassed all "hierarchical organizations and networks of informal relations that constantly intersected and interacted with one another" linking together the imperial Chinese state, gentry, and other classes in a "common frame of reference . . . of shared symbolic values . . . [that] worked to legitimate authority in local society."[15] As officials attempted to penetrate rural society by alternately circumventing and destroying the nexus, the state itself was ultimately undermined and its legitimacy eroded. Despite increases in the functions, size, and costs associated with the state over the period covered by his research, Duara notes that the state-making process became "involutionary," and central authorities received a declining proportion of the total revenues collected.[16]

R. Bin Wong's impressive survey of state-formation begins by contrasting initial conditions in Europe and China from their respective early-imperial periods onward. Wong notes that whereas the Holy Roman Empire failed to create the types of ideological and institutional legacies that could sustain an imperial successor state, imperial consolidation under the Qin and Han created a solid foundation for the expansion of rule. Thus, the challenges and capacities of Chinese and European polities as both entered their respective periods of state-formation differed widely, with European state-makers facing multiple internal challenges from both clergy and nobles,

---

14. R. Keith Schoppa, "State, Society, and Land Reclamation on Hangzhou Bay During the Republican Era," *Modern China* 23:2 (April 1997): 246–71.

15. Prasenjit Duara, *Culture, Power, and the State* (Stanford: Stanford University Press, 1988), pp. 2, 15, 24.

16. Ibid., p. 247.

and from external competitors that required them to develop and hone their military might. The central challenge for Chinese rulers, by contrast, was not the development of a radically new and more effective polity in a competitive geopolitical field but rather the maintenance and reproduction of a vast agrarian state that expanded to include increasingly heterogeneous populations. The resultant political dynamic gradually gave rise to a state that was often far weaker militarily than many of the groups along its frontiers, but one that not only succeeded but thrived. The survival of the Chinese empire was due less to its reliance on coercive power, and rather more to its elaborate administration of systems of tribute, taxation, and social order.

The comparatively higher level of internal heterogeneity within the emerging Chinese state, along with a traditional ideological commitment to material and moral control, produced a polity that admitted only an uncertain and shifting boundary between so-called "state" and "social" forces throughout the imperial period and beyond. The construction of state power in Europe frequently involved the forcible extraction of material resources and begrudging political inclusion of resisting elites over the highly contested border between the state and society. In China, by contrast, Wong notes that the Confucian agenda for maintaining moral and material order possessed a distinctively "fractal" quality that allowed for the replication of authority relations at any level of government, producing overlapping networks of state and social forces.[17]

Each of the preceding accounts calls attention to the central problem of locating a supposed unitary and coherent center of political and coercive power—the "state"—in juxtaposition to the relatively disorganized and fragmented "society" in which it is said to operate. In his attempt to bridge the historical experience of Chinese state-formation with the binomial framework of analysis provided in Western European scholarship, Duara presses into service what he refers to as a "mediating concept" that "negotiates[s] the area between the structural regularities of social systems and the contingency of history, between high culture and popular culture, and between other oppositions we face; [a concept] capable of persuading those realms to speak to each other without reducing the one to the other."[18] Duara's "cultural nexus," like Rankin's "managerial public sphere," Rowe's "civil society," and Huang's "third realm," represents a conceptual innovation designed to overcome or sidestep the structural

---

17. R. Bin Wong, *China Transformed: Historical Change and the Limits of European Experience* (Ithaca, NY: Cornell University Press, 1997), especially chaps. 4 and 5.
18. Duara (1988), p. 262.

limitations inherent in the dichotomous "state-society" paradigm of Western European historiography.[19]

Others focus attention instead on the manner in which power circulated between the state and social realms, as suggested by Wong's reference to the "fractal" quality of the Confucian polity in late imperial and Republican China. Vivienne Shue argues that the new systems and practices associated with the post-Mao reform-era policies produced a web-like net of power relations, overlaying the older, honeycomb pattern of cellular organizations established in the wake of the Communist revolution. The fluidity of these two patterns of political relations necessitated what she referred to as a "politics-as-process orientation" that would lead us "to explore for pattern of flux and flow among those internal elements, arrayed in tension, that constitute and animate the polity itself . . . [and] press us into recognition of all those mutually conditioning interactions that occur among elements of the polity that we are accustomed to think of as rather distinct and often, therefore, as rather static."[20]

These important insights seek to capture the complexity inherent in modern Chinese political transformations while circumventing the bifurcated tools of analysis (state/society) that arise from the Western European experience. Neither the Weberian concept of the state, with its association with the monopolistic control of coercive power, nor the Marxist understanding of the state as the instrument of the ruling classes, sits easily or well on the social fabric of late imperial or early-Republican China, which suggests a more fluid circulation of both political power and practice among agents operating within a polity not easily defined by such categories of analysis.

It is therefore clear that the elusive and fluid nature of the state-society boundary, which is by no means exclusive to the Chinese case, is central to our understanding of the state-making process. Some propose that the relative invisibility of this boundary in normal times is itself a resource of power for the regime, allowing it to mask its reliance on practices and organizations that, if viewed directly, might threaten the regime's claim to

---

19. On the "state-society" paradigm in Western studies of Chinese politics, see Elizabeth J. Perry, "Trends in the Study of Chinese Politics: State–Society Relations," *China Quarterly* 139 (September 1994): 704–13. Discussions of the "managerial public sphere," "civil society," and "third realm" appear in the Symposium " 'Public Sphere'/'Civil Society' in China? Paradigmatic Issues in Chinese Studies, III," *Modern China* 19:2 (April 1993).

20. See the chapters "Honeycomb and Web: The Process of Change in Rural China" and "State, Society and Politics Under Mao: Theory and Irony in the Study of Contemporary China," in Vivienne Shue, *The Reach of the State: Sketches of the Chinese Body Politic* (Stanford: Stanford University Press, 1988); the quotations occur on pp. 130–32 and 25–26.

legitimacy.[21] However, it is when this perceptual boundary is on the move, as it clearly is during periods of intense state-making, that it is thrown into high relief and the state's involvement with the process of moral regulation is more easily discerned. As central authorities seek to bring particular practices under the institutional umbrella of regime control, they are pressed to articulate in precise terms what on a day-to-day basis often remains inchoate and ill-formed: the normative basis of the regime's claim to power. I argue, therefore, that the process of fixing the boundary in conceptual space is key to the projection of the state as a coherent and autonomous moral agent in history.

BOUNDARIES OF STATES AND EMPIRES

In the modestly entitled "Notes on the Difficulty of Studying the State," Philip Abrams proposed that the modern nation-state actually incorporates two distinct objects of analysis: the "state system," which he defined as "a palpable nexus of practice and institutional structure centered in government and more or less extensive, unified and dominant in any given society," and the "state-idea," "projected, purveyed and variously believed in in different societies at different times." Scholarly analysis of the former reveals that such institutions "conspicuously fail to display a unity of practice—just as they constantly discover their inability to function as a more general factor of cohesion. Manifestly they are divided against one another, volatile and confused." Yet it is precisely these political institutions that nonetheless comprise "the real agencies out of which the idea of the state is constructed. Those institutionalized forms of coercive power—armies and prisons . . . as well as the whole process of fiscal exaction . . . are all forceful enough. But it is their association with the idea of the state that silences protest, excuses force and convinces almost all of us that the fate of the victims is just and necessary." Thus, Abrams argues, the state

is first and foremost an exercise in legitimation . . . [and] in every sense of the term a triumph of concealment. It conceals the real history and relations of subjection behind an a-historical mask of legitimating illusion; contrives to deny the existence of connections and conflicts which would if recognized be incompatible with the claimed autonomy and integration of the state. . . . [It] is at most a message of domination—an ideological artifact attributing unity, morality

---

21. Timothy Mitchell, "The Limits of the State: Beyond Statist Approaches and Their Critics," *American Political Science Review* 85:1 (March 1991): 90.

and independence to the disunited, amoral and dependent workings of the practice of government.[22]

He concludes that the projection of a coherent "state-idea" from the manifestly disorganized institutional maze of the "state system" is at least as fundamental a technique for maintaining the power of the regime as is the application of coercive force. It is the "state-idea" that "presents politically institutionalized power to us in a form that is at once integrated and isolated and by satisfying both these conditions it creates . . . an acceptable basis for acquiescence."[23]

At the same time, the act of withholding the imprimatur of official sanction from particular institutions and practices can provide another source of power for a regime. Timothy Mitchell argues that the Arabian American Oil Company (Aramco), the consortium of American oil corporations that holds the exclusive rights to Saudi Arabian oil, is one such case. In the late 1940s, the Saudis demanded that their royalty payment from Aramco be increased from 12 percent to 50 percent of profits. The US State Department, eager to continue to subsidize the pro-American Saudi monarchy, arranged for Aramco to exploit a loophole in US tax law by treating the royalties as a foreign direct tax. In so doing, Aramco was permitted to deduct the total royalty paid from the taxes it owed to the US Treasury and therefore to retain a higher percentage of its generous profits; and the State Department was able to subsidize a conservative Saudi regime largely without the oversight of Congress or the American public. The point of the Aramco case, according to Mitchell, is not merely to reveal

that the state is something surrounded by parastatal or corporatist institutions, which buttress and extend its authority. It is to argue that the boundary of the state (or political system) *never marks a real exterior*. The line between state and society is not the perimeter of an intrinsic entity, which can be thought of as a free-standing object or actor. It is a line drawn internally, *within* the network of institutional mechanisms through which a certain social and political order is maintained.[24]

Like Abrams, Mitchell proposes that when the arrangements that create the apparent structural difference between state and society are effective, the state is commonly perceived as an external and autonomous agent that directs and manipulates society, and this perception in fact extends and deepens the power and efficacy of a regime.

---

22. Philip Abrams, "Notes on the Difficulty of Studying the State," *Journal of Historical Sociology* 1:1 (March 1988): 75, 79, 76–77, 81.
23. Ibid., p. 68.
24. Mitchell (1991), p. 90. Italics in the original.

Clearly, then, the projection of unity, coherence, and autonomy of the regime is a core task of the state-making process. If Duara, Wong, and others are correct in asserting that historically, Chinese regimes have operated with a broad dispersion of power and functions among "state" and "social" forces, it is also worth noting that the histories of these regimes were punctuated by bursts of state-making activity during which central leaders periodically sought to wrest control over particular spheres of practice at the margins of regime control. The process by which such transformations were realized involved the imposition of a boundary demarcating "state" from "social" forces, or the "public" from the "private" realms, and the articulation of respective norms of conduct for each.

The boundary-drawing capacity of the state thus emerges as a technique of modern power in which the center asserts itself over a complex and interwoven social reality in order to bring it to heel within a larger normative—and normalizing—agenda. While it is certainly the case that imperial authorities had long sought to organize various social forms to render them more legible and responsive to central control,[25] the power to define broad norms of conduct became increasingly salient as a method of statecraft from the late imperial period onward. The gradual process that Mark Elvin calls the "democratization of virtue" involved the increasing use of Qing political institutions in order to recognize and reward moral conduct in the private, everyday lives, not merely of elites, but increasingly, of commoners as well.[26] As central authorities turned their attention to defining social and bureaucratic mores, state institutions expanded in part through policies designed to normalize and control the conduct of increasing numbers of people by repositioning them relative to the imagined boundaries of the state.

State-formation in late imperial and republican China therefore involved the gradual displacement of imperial technologies of rule, diplomacy, and social control by the more rationalized, homogenized, and bifurcated forms of power associated with the modern nation-state. Emerging as it did from long centuries of cohesion, contraction, and expansion, the late imperial state was itself the product of a complex series of political and economic arrangements designed both to administer and to exploit internal heterogeneity in service to a centralized "imperial project."[27] In

25. James C. Scott describes the fuller fruition of these trends in the modern era in his *Seeing Like a State: How Certain Schemes to Improve the Human Condition Have Failed* (New Haven: Yale University Press, 1998).

26. Mark Elvin, "Female Virtue and the State in China," *Past & Present* 104 (1984): 111–52.

27. Thomas J. Barfield, "The Shadow Empires: Imperial State Formation Along the Chinese-Nomad Frontier," in *Empires: Perspectives from Archaeology and History*, ed. Susan E. Alcock,

broadly comparative terms, the administration of the imperium involved the arrangement and manipulation of multiple foci of power set within a larger totality, a process that in turn relied heavily upon the ritual creation of social order as well as the production and management of imperial subjects. This was effected in part by the careful inscription and manipulation of boundaries "through a series of macrocosmic/ microcosmic resemblances," a process rather unlike the exercise of binomial power associated with the modern state, "wherein a sovereign subject (king/state) oppresses a passive object (people/society)."[28] As Benedict Anderson notes,

In the modern conception, state sovereignty is fully, flatly, and evenly operative over each square centimeter of a legally demarcated territory. But in the older imagining, where states were defined by centers, borders were porous and indistinct, and sovereignties faded imperceptibly into one another. Hence, paradoxically enough, the ease with which pre-modern empires and kingdoms were able to sustain their rule over immensely heterogeneous, and often not contiguous, populations for long periods of time.[29]

Traditional imperial technologies of governance, which sought to successfully manage internal heterogeneity in service to an orthodox etho-political agenda,[30] began a shift during the Qing to the techniques of more centralized rule that we associate with the modern nation-state: a totalizing projection of power that aims in large part at the suppression of internal difference within the rubric of a rationalized social and political order.[31] The gradual displacement of imperial modes of governance by the techniques and practices of state administration was partially the result of a

---

Terence N. D'Altroy, Kathleen D. Morrison, and Carla M. Sinopoli (Cambridge, Eng.: Cambridge University Press, 2001), pp. 29–33.

28. Angela Zito, *Of Body and Brush: Grand Sacrifice as Text/Performance in Eighteenth-Century China* (Chicago: University of Chicago Press, 1997), p. 216. See also James Hevia, *Cherishing Men from Afar: Qing Guest Ritual and the Macartney Embassy of 1793* (Durham, NC: Duke University Press, 1995).

29. Benedict Anderson, *Imagined Communities: Reflections on the Origins and Spread of Nationalism* (London: Verso, 1991), p. 19.

30. Pamela Crossley, *A Translucent Mirror: History and Identity in Qing Imperial Ideology* (Berkeley: University of California Press, 1999).

31. Western European state-formation was also coterminous with the process of empire-building, but, insofar as European colonies tended not to be contiguous to the states themselves, the two processes blended differently. At the same time that the absolutist states of late feudal Europe were begrudgingly giving way to elite pressures for inclusion, the distinctly bifurcated practices of colonial rule produced the "Manichean" divides described by Franz Fanon and others. See Ann Laura Stoler and Frederic Cooper, "Between Metropole and Colony: Rethinking a Research Agenda," in *Tensions of Empire: Colonial Cultures in a Bourgeois*

convergence of several larger historical trends in the seventeenth century, including population growth, rising commercialization, and increased interaction with emerging states elsewhere in the world. The fall of the Ming to the Manchus ushered in a new, highly centralized administration that maintained an ethnic, as well as a ritual, distance from Han society.[32] Even more significant for the emergence of the nascent Qing state was the migration of wealthy landowners from rural villages during this period, which created a power vacuum in the countryside. Control over key functions—law enforcement, tax collection, and the maintenance of irrigation systems—was gradually assumed by local administrators and sub-bureaucratic personnel. Although such functions would shift back to local elite control in the mid-nineteenth century,[33] the early Qing responses to these pressures resulted in a wave of centralization, rationalization, and the expansion of bureaucratic control similar to processes of state-making noted elsewhere in the world.

As the multiple boundaries that administered the "realms within the realm" of the imperium eroded,[34] they were replaced by a newly fortified boundary between "state" and "society." Yet as Shue's description of the reform-era polity reminds us, this process is never fully actualized: older forms of power coexist with, compete with, and sometimes undermine even the most concerted efforts of central state-makers to transform them.

WRITING AND READING THE CHINESE STATE

Thus far, I have argued that the projection of the state as a moral actor—a historical agent claiming internal unity, coherence, and autonomy—has played a central role in the Chinese state-making process. It is the perceived association between local agents and the central state that legitimates a wide range of interventions by local actors and minimizes overt resistance; the justification for such actions arises directly from the normative agendas of central authorities, and in the process, discourages dissent. Nonetheless, the boundary-drawing efforts of Chinese state-makers have by no means gone

---

World, ed. Frederic Cooper and Ann Laura Stoler (Berkeley: University of California Press, 1997), p. 1.

32. Mark Elvin, *The Manchu Way: The Eight Banners and Ethnic Identity in Late Imperial China* (Stanford: Stanford University Press, 2001); Crossley (1999).

33. Philip Kuhn, *Rebellion and Its Enemies in Late Imperial China: Militarization and Social Structure, 1796–1864* (Cambridge, MA: Harvard University Press, 1970).

34. The concept of the "realms within the realm" is discussed by Christopher P. Atwood in his "National Questions and National Answers in the Chinese Revolution," *Indiana East Asian Working Paper Series*, no. 5 (Winter 1994).

unchallenged by those operating in the peripheral regions of state control. The discursive construction of the Chinese state as a moral agent, and the institution of new practices among local agents, incurred myriad forms of countervailing pressure and, sometimes, overt resistance from such agents and their supporters.

The complexity of these struggles is part of the written historical record itself. As Hayden White points out, Hegel long ago noted the relationship between the state and the production of a particular type of historical narrative: "it is only the state which first presents subject-matter that is not only adapted to the prose of History, but involves the production of such history in the progress of its own being."[35] The extraordinary investment of the Chinese state in the production of texts—historical, literary, and ritual—arguably is unparalleled in human history. From its roots in distant antiquity down through the present day, the act of writing not only defined those who wielded power but also generated the significant political resources at their disposal.[36] The kings and nobles of the archaic states of the Shang and Zhou enjoyed political authority largely by virtue of their participation in ancestral cults that practiced divination and other forms of spirit communication. The oracle inscriptions ritually produced by these cults served as both the vehicle and verification of their political status and, over time, evolved into a more elaborate mechanism of power. The ability to note the genealogies of state elites to keep population registers, to record oaths and covenants, and to inscribe territorial maps was not merely a manifestation of power, but the medium through which political power was consolidated, exercised, and realized in early China. The collective commitment of elites both inside and outside the official state structure gradually tied the imperial center to its localities in a subtler, more complex, and ultimately, more enduring manner than was the case with the relatively modest bureaucratic apparatus designed to govern them.[37]

The persistent power of the written word as a technique of rule is evident in the commitment of successive Chinese regimes to the careful compilation of canonical texts and standard histories (*zheng shi*), as well as the suppression of unofficial and alternative accounts. States fashioned

35. Hayden White, *The Content of the Form: Narrative Discourse and Historical Representation* (Baltimore: Johns Hopkins University Press, 1987), p. 12.
36. On the power of writing in modern Chinese politics, see Richard C. Kraus, *Brushes with Power: Modern Politics and the Chinese Art of Calligraphy* (Berkeley: University of California Press, 1991).
37. Mark Lewis, *Writing and Authority in Early China* (Albany: State University of New York Press, 1999), pp. 14–15.

histories not merely to preserve those events that must not be forgotten but also to obliterate that which should not have occurred. The nexus of writing and authority, in early China as well as elsewhere, serves to conceal, to reveal, and above all, to reproduce the power of the state in a broad array of documents compiled and authorized by central authorities down to the contemporary period.

Yet even as the archaic state sought to monopolize the power of the written word, a parallel discursive tradition emerged that originated in schools and local academies not directly under official control. Economically linked to powerful families outside the inner court circle, these scholarly traditions managed to maintain themselves in a condition of perpetual tension with respect to the central state, never wholly free of its influence but remaining within its orbit, interacting with those at the center of political power through patronage, mimicry, and, at times, overt opposition. Like the state, such groups deployed literacy as a tool to project their influence, create new social roles, and generate forms of authority that generally overlapped with those of the state. Bound to the center through a shared commitment to classical texts, those working from within this parallel discursive tradition helped to define, transform, and recreate the political center over time.[38]

These shared conceptions of state power were, as Mark Lewis argues, "based on an imaginary realm created within texts."[39] Reading the Chinese state across time requires attention to the shifting parameters of these social imaginaries, ranging over the cases under consideration in this study from the concept of *tianxia* ("all under heaven" or "world") during the imperial era, to the *minguo* (generally glossed as "republic" in English, but more precisely translated as "commoner-realm") under the Nationalists, and *gongheguo* ("people's republic") under Mao.[40] Broadly speaking, these collectively imagined realms served as fields on which the highly contested process of state-making unfolded, often within the framework of key scholarly debates concerning the various arrangements of power between center and periphery: the bureaucratic (*junxian*) and feudal (*fengjian*) debates of the imperial period; the competing models of state tutelage (*xunzheng*) versus mass-based democratic local self-government (*zizhi*) during the Nanjing decade; and revisionist and radical versions of mass-

---

38. Ibid., p. 53.
39. Ibid., p. 4.
40. See, for example, *Imagining the People: Chinese Intellectuals and Concepts of Citizenship 1890–1920*, ed. Joshua A. Fogel and Peter G. Zarrow (Armonk, NY: M. E. Sharpe, 1997); Michael Schoenhals, "'Non-people' in the People's Republic of China: A Chronicle of Terminological Ambiguity," *Indiana East Asian Working Paper Series*, no. 4 (Summer 1994).

line politics in post-1949 China.[41] Local actors competing for power and influence often framed their claims for legitimacy in terms of these larger debates but were also frequently cast, in official discourse, as threats to the normative order of the state: as "evil folk" (*diaomin*), "local bullies" (*tuhao*), or "counter-revolutionary elements" (*fangeming fenzi*). These highly formalized constructions therefore became sites of political contestation, struggle, and resistance. While central leaders deployed such categories to demarcate certain groups of individuals as objects of state concern and control, those so interpellated frequently contested such labels and the normative agendas that shaped them.[42] Local interpretations of such terms varied, sometimes radically, from the models offered in the formulations of central leaders.

Reading resistance to the discursive projection of central state power is by necessity a genealogical project, one that "operates on a field of entangled and confused parchments, on documents that have been scratched over and recopied many times."[43] The imbrication of largely overlapping discursive traditions—one centered in the administrative structure of the state, the other subsisting largely in its shadow—amits no easy division between the two textual orders. Local gazetteers and the more recent collections of published historical and literary materials (*wenshi ziliao*), for example, both originated in central state mandates to collect and record available information either about or from within the various administrative units under central control, but over time have come to represent and express a

41. *Conflict and Control in Late Imperial China*, ed. Frederic Wakeman, Jr., and Carolyn Grant (Berkeley: University of California Press, 1975); Philip A. Kuhn, *The Origins of the Modern Chinese State* (Stanford: Stanford University Press, 2002); Chester C. Tan, *Chinese Political Thought in the Twentieth Century* (New York: Doubleday, 1971); Lowell Dittmer, "Public and Private Interests and the Participatory Ethic," in *Citizens and Groups in Contemporary China*, ed. Victor C. Falkenheim (Ann Arbor: University of Michigan Press, 1987); Lowell Dittmer, *Liu Shao-ch'i and the Chinese Cultural Revolution* (Berkeley: University of California Press, 1974).

42. Louis Althusser suggests "that ideology 'acts' or 'functions' in such a way that it 'recruits' subjects among individuals (it recruits them all), or 'transforms' individuals into subjects (it transforms them all) by that very precise operation which I have called *interpellation* or hailing, and which can be imagined along the lines of the most commonplace everyday police (or other) hailing: 'Hey, you there!'" (italics in original). My use of the term here underscores the manner in which individuals were recognized (or misrecognized) by agents of the state and targeted for specific handling and action. Louis Althusser, "Ideology and the State," in *Lenin and Philosophy and Other Essays*, trans. Ben Brewster (New York: Monthly Review Press, 2001), p. 118.

43. Michel Foucault, "Nietzsche, Genealogy, History" in *Language, Counter-memory, Practice: Selected Essays and Interviews*, ed. D. F. Bouchard (Ithaca, NY: Cornell University Press, 1977), p. 139.

broader range of what Carlo Ginzburg refers to as "evidential paradigms," carrying traces of opposing narratives.[44] Such sources, along with clan and family genealogies, so-called "wild histories" (*yeshi*), and other unofficial writings, have all served as intermittent vehicles for the narrative expression of local interests and other claims that challenge the moral primacy of the central state.[45]

Localist narratives are themselves products of collective struggle, and ought not to be read as an expression of shared moral consensus centered in local communities united against the state-making efforts of central authorities. Unofficial sources are as likely as official narratives to suppress and deny the existence of fissures that divided local communities, internal rifts as potentially destabilizing as the extractive and invasive incursions of the state. As Elizabeth Perry has demonstrated, the politics of localism was "a two-edged sword that both opened possibilities and set boundaries to the development of collective action."[46] Local identities and institutions were not necessarily counterposed to those of the regime, and, over time, such groups were as prone to boundary-drawing as were those in control of the central state.[47] The central concern of this study is the manner in which specific identities were expressed, manipulated, and invested with moral power through discursive practice in the process of state-making, both by those who wielded official power and those who did not. As central leaders in all three periods forcefully projected the state as a unitary, coherent, moral agent, a multitude of often-conflicting voices responded in kind from newly targeted sites at the margins. The narrative forms that these responses took were themselves political tools used to nurture a sense of the local community as a distinct entity on the one hand and at the same time legitimate a range of local political, social, and cultural resistances on the other.[48] The point of this study is neither to establish whether the counter-

---

44. Carlo Ginzburg, *Clues, Myths, and the Historical Method*, trans. John Tedeschi and Anne Tedeschi (Baltimore: Johns Hopkins University Press, 1986).

45. James M. Hargett links the emergence of the local gazetteer as a genre of historical writing to the history of maps and illustrated compendia (*tujing, tuji*, or *tuzhi*), but notes that Sui officials during the Daye reign (605–17) mandated that all commanderies throughout the empire submit accounts of local customs, products, and maps to the Department of State Affairs to assist in the administration of the realm. See James M. Hargett, "Song Dynasty Local Gazetteers and Their Place in the History of *Difangzhi* Writing," *Harvard Journal of Asiatic Studies* 56:2 (December 1996): 409–10.

46. Elizabeth Perry, *Shanghai on Strike: The Politics of Chinese Labor* (Stanford: Stanford University Press, 1993), p. 30.

47. Bryna Goodman, *Native Place, City, and Nation: Regional Networks and Identities in Shanghai, 1853–1937* (Berkeley: University of California Press, 1995).

48. Lynn Hunt, *The New Cultural History* (Berkeley: University of California Press, 1989), p. 17.

claims made by such respondents were true, nor to evaluate the strength of the interests that may have motivated them. It is to demonstrate how the normative and normalizing effects of the state-making project defined particular agents and practices and rearranged them, by placing them either within the conceptual boundary of the state or outside the realm of state control, and to record the broad range of countervailing responses to such efforts.

The chapters that follow offer a reading of the state-making process as a contest between central and local regimes of bureaucratic practice. A focus on practices as opposed to formal institutions or ideologies reveals how central state-makers in each time period perceived the range of issues and goals associated with the problem of governance: what, in each time period, was to be done in order to govern, and how was this to be accomplished? How were the limits of the state apparatus perceived, by central authorities working from within that structure, and by the intended targets of their actions? In short, what technologies of governance drove the state-making project at these critical historical junctures, and what types of political projects did such knowledge make possible? By juxtaposing, for each time period, official practices and discourses regarding the state-making project with the wide range of local responses to such efforts, the chapters that follow can be read as a historically grounded "ethnography of the state": an examination of the everyday practices of the state through an analysis of how central authorities and local residents evaluated the conduct of those who were charged with carrying out the quotidian practices of political domination and control at three critical junctures in the history of Chinese state-making.[49]

Finally, in my conclusion, I consider the nature of corruption discourse in China today. Clearly, the process of state-making is limited, both in its scope and duration. The three periods under consideration here were selected because they represent phases of intense state-making activity under three different regimes that had already successfully seized and consolidated political power. State-building efforts and normative discourses framed in the earliest years of a regime frequently target those perceived to be loyal to the previous government; central leaders of regimes in decline are less capable of mobilizing the resources necessary to enact state-making reforms. In contrast to the three cases analyzed here, the post-Mao reform era represents a reversal of the state-making dynamic, characterized by a steady withdrawal of central state power from local communities. What

---

49. Akhil Gupta, "Blurred Boundaries: The Discourse of Corruption, the Culture of Politics, and the Imagined State," *American Ethnologist* 22:2 (May 1995): 375–402.

happens to the process of moral regulation when the center retracts, and the boundary-drawing capacity of the state cedes to the interpenetration of public and private forces? As numerous studies of the reform-era polity attest, the erosion of the normative authority of the regime in recent years has created considerable moral anxiety and expressions of popular concern about the practices of the state and its agents. In the absence of a centralized leadership that is collectively willing to assert itself as a unitary and coherent moral agent, the capacity of the state to draw and maintain normative boundaries has been largely neglected in the pursuit of economic reform. The simultaneous softening of multiple boundaries during the reform era—public/private, state/society, plan/market—and the steady erosion of those organizational structures in the state's ambit that exert normative and normalizing pressures has produced a vacuum of both moral authority and power.

With the moral primacy of the central state in question, and awash with the haphazard forces and products of privatization, I conclude that popular culture in the reform era has witnessed the emergence of a pathological public sphere, a collective space characterized not by the rational exchanges and reasoned debates described by Jürgen Habermas, but instead by public appeals to and expressions of fear, suspicion, and desire. The proliferation of corruption discourse in the contemporary media, and the graphic depictions of violence, debauchery, and sexual excess that frequently accompany it, is designed to simultaneously titillate and repel the reading public by provoking a welter of unfulfilled longings that ultimately lead back to the political center. Narratives that detail outrageous abuses of coercive power by local officials, or the diversion of public assets by rapacious cadres, serve as implicit reminders of the state's capacity to exercise violence and to control the flow of material resources in a society in which "comrades have become consumers without necessarily also developing into citizens."[50] The collective conviction that contemporary society is poised on the brink of moral collapse has fueled popular nostalgia even for the more muscularly interventionist, and more uniformly repressive, state of the Maoist era.[51] Ironically, the constant spectacles of reform-era corruption perpetuated in

---

50. Geremie Barmé, *In the Red: On Contemporary Chinese Culture* (New York: Columbia University Press, 1999), p. xiv.

51. See Kevin O'Brien and Li Lianjiang, "Campaign Nostalgia in the Chinese Countryside," *Asian Survey* 39:3 (May/June 1999): 375–93; Li Lianjiang, "Support for Anti-Corruption Campaigns in Rural China," *Journal of Contemporary China* 10:29 (November 2001): 573–86; Patricia M. Thornton, "Comrades and Collectives in Arms: Tax Resistance, Evasion and Avoidance Strategies in the Post-Mao Era," in *State and Society in 21st Century China: Contention, Crisis, and Legitimation*, ed. Peter Hays Gries and Stanley Rosen (London and New York: Routledge, 2004), pp. 87–104.

the popular media may serve to legitimize existing power arrangements by conjuring a social world saturated with danger and moral ambiguity. The pathological public sphere thus recursively reproduces the power of the reform-era state by drumming home the singular observation that in the stormy seas of economic reform, the big fish can and do eat little fish, and the rags of virtue mask only the engines of privilege.

TWO

Virtue and Venality in the Qing

The reign of the Yongzheng emperor represents a significant departure in the history of Chinese state-making, a key transitional period during which the general pattern that characterized traditional imperial modes of governance was briefly overlaid with the more distinctly centralized and bifurcated technologies of power associated with modern statehood. The more muscular and robust expressions of state control pursued by Yongzheng, characterized by economic historian Gao Wangling as an "unfinished experiment" in big government,[1] stand in marked contrast to the more minimalist tradition of governance observed during the long centuries that preceded his ascension to the throne. The nature and substance of these reforms—including the creation of the Grand Council, significant revisions to the main system of official communication in the empire, the centralization of control over the censorial system, and the rationalization of local fiscal administration—have been richly documented by scholars of the late imperial period;[2] viewed as a whole, the depth and breadth of state-building reforms introduced during this period arguably rank Yongzheng as "the greatest centralizer and stabilizer of the Qing dynasty,"[3] despite the relative brevity of his reign.

Late imperial statecraft negotiated an uneasy balance between the

---

1. As cited by William T. Rowe, *Saving the World: Chen Hong-mou and Elite Consciousness in Eighteenth-Century China* (Stanford: Stanford University Press, 2001), p. 46.

2. Beatrice Bartlett, *Monarchs and Ministers: The Grand Council in Mid-Ch'ing China, 1723–1820* (Berkeley: University of California Press, 1991); Silas Wu, *Communication and Imperial Control in China: Evolution of the Palace Memorial System* (Cambridge, MA: Harvard University Press, 1970); Madeleine Zelin, *The Magistrate's Tael: Rationalizing Fiscal Reform in Eighteenth-Century Ch'ing China* (Berkeley: University of California Press, 1984).

3. Huang Pei, *Autocracy at Work: A Study of the Yung-cheng Period, 1723–1735* (Bloomington: Indiana University Press, 1974), p. 21.

minimalist style of governance that some scholars have characterized as the systematic "under-administration" of the empire,[4] and the vastly more ambitious rhetoric of the all-inclusive civilizing project to which the concept of the mandate of Heaven laid claim. As Kate Leonard and John Watt recently pointed out, "For the Qing, the term 'state' conveys both less and more than the Western referent. While its bureaucratic functions, centering narrowly on tax collection and security, were more limited than those of modern governments, its overarching moral-cosmic functions far exceeded those of the secular state in the West."[5] The legitimation of the dynasty rested not merely on the successful negotiation of strategic tasks such as the collection and redistribution of resources and the maintenance of internal security but also on the "ordering of the world" (*jingshi*), the civilizing and nourishing (*jiaoyang*) of the common people, and the transformation of human affairs by harmonizing social interactions in accordance with heavenly principles (*tianli*).

Yet, as William Rowe recently argued, the administrative tradition inherited by the Manchus generally viewed the necessity of the imperial bureaucratic state as "an embarrassment." At best, "when it was functioning especially well, as it was in the mid-eighteenth century, it was an embarrassment that most within the official elite could live with."[6] For the most part, models of good governance that prevailed after the bureaucratic retrenchment during the Song eschewed the centralization of power in favor of granting maximum latitude to local elites in the hope—once articulated by the Ming founder—of using "good people to rule good people."[7] Yongzheng's more tightly centralized and interventionist policies, characteristic of *junxian* (bureaucratic) models of statecraft, therefore immediately encountered both the institutional and philosophical resistance of those committed to maintaining the longstanding commitment to limited central control, a position associated with the *fengjian* (feudalist) tradition.[8]

---

4. Robert J. Antony and J. Kate Leonard, "Dragons, Tigers, and Dogs: An Introduction," in *Dragons, Tigers, and Dogs: Qing Crisis Management and the Boundaries of State Power in Late Imperial China*, ed. Robert J. Antony and Jane Kate Leonard (Ithaca, NY: Cornell University Press, 2003), p. 4.
5. Jane Kate Leonard and John R. Watt, "Introduction," in *To Achieve Security and Wealth: The Qing Imperial State and the Economy, 1644–1911*, p. 2. In a similar vein, H. Lyman Miller characterized the late imperial polity as a "minimalist state" that reigned without truly ruling local society. See H. Lyman Miller, "The Late Imperial Chinese State," in *The Modern Chinese State*, ed. David Shambaugh (Cambridge, Eng.: Cambridge University Press, 2001).
6. Rowe (2001), p. 326.
7. As cited by Wakeman (1975), p. 6.
8. Min Tu-ki, "The Theory of Political Feudalism in the Ch'ing Period," in *National Polity*

The institutional legacy of this inherited tradition resulted in what some have referred to as the systematic "under-administration" of the empire: a lean bureaucratic framework that, at the lowest levels of the department (*zhou*) and county (*xian*), provided for little more than the collection of relatively modest taxes and basic public security needs.[9] The robustly activist policies of the Yongzheng-era state quickly reverberated down through the ranks of Qing officialdom, with profound consequences for local bureaucrats poised at the boundary between the late imperial state and society. The philosophical balancing act between minimalist administration and maximalist aims translated into a practical conundrum for the county or department magistrate (*zhixian* or *zhizhou*), who was charged with an extraordinarily wide range of duties that encompassed both the sacred and the mundane. Within his assigned jurisdiction, the magistrate was responsible for settling legal cases, meting out disciplinary action and punishments, investigating criminal cases, and maintaining social order. His other duties included fostering agriculture in his district, overseeing public works, and maintaining the institutions and mechanisms that provided disaster relief in dire times. He provided charity to the poor and assisted the elderly, oversaw the moral education of county residents by scheduling regular public lectures and readings of the Sacred Edict, and enacted rituals paying homage to the imperial family and local deities. To accomplish these myriad tasks, magistrates relied heavily on sub-bureaucratic staff, including clerks, runners, secretaries, and personal servants,[10] as well as upon a range of extra-bureaucratic actors and groups, including local militias, clan and lineage associations, and members of the local gentry. If the formal exercise of Qing political power at the lowest levels extended only as far as the skeletal official bureaucracy, then it was the sub-bureaucratic yamen staff and extra-bureaucratic order that put flesh on the bones of the Manchu state in its local incarnation.

The connective tissue of social forces that spanned the nexus between minimalist administrative structure and maximalist goals was one site upon

---

and Local Power: The Transformation of Late Imperial China, ed. Philip Kuhn and Timothy Brook (Cambridge, MA: Harvard-Yenching Institute Monograph Series, 1989), pp. 100–105. The term *junxian* is sometimes also glossed as "prefectural" in English.

9. Antony and Leonard (2003), p. 4.

10. Bradley Reed, *Talons and Teeth: County Clerks and Runners in the Qing Dynasty* (Stanford: Stanford University Press, 2000); Melissa MacAuley, *Social Power and Legal Culture: Litigation Masters in Late Imperial China* (Stanford: Stanford University Press, 1998); Philip C. C. Huang, *Code, Custom, and Legal Practice in China: The Qing and Republic Compared* (Stanford: Stanford University Press, 2001); and Robert J. Antony, "Subcounty Officials, the State, and Local Communities in Guangdong Province," in Antony and Leonard (2003).

which Yongzheng sought to operate. Underfunded and understaffed by design, the yamen of the local magistrate evolved into a locus of complex political and economic exchanges that supported the quotidian maintenance of social order. Magistrates, who were barred by law from serving in their home districts, orchestrated a series of exchanges with the local elites who comprised the yamen's sub-bureaucratic staff and extra-bureaucratic affiliates in the intendance of their daily duties. The potential interplay between the magistrate's formal exercise of authority and these local agents ran the full range from cooperation to overt conflict, and distinctive socioeconomic and ecological trends in various locales did shape regional patterns of elite dominance.[11] Yet insofar as magistrates and local gentry belonged to the same privileged class, early Qing political structures inclined toward collaboration, recognizing the necessity of what Susan Mann has referred to as "liturgical governance" at the local level.[12] Magistrates relied on wealthy elites to fund and organize public works projects, to make contributions of grain or money for famine relief, and to adjudicate minor conflicts among members of the community; in return, gentry were exempted from participating in corvée labor projects and corporal punishment, paid taxes at a lower rate than commoners did, and were often accorded considerable influence on the administration of local affairs.[13] With the exception of an early crackdown on gentry tax evaders in Jiangnan during the Oboi regency, the Kangxi emperor's aversion to "causing trouble" and his apparent preference for continuity in provincial and local government affairs smoothed the way for a generally accommodative alliance between officials and gentry over the latter decades of his rule.[14]

The reforms of Yongzheng's era cut deeply into the comfortable fabric of local power, reversing the trend of his father's long reign. Unlike both his father, Kangxi, and his son and successor, Qianlong, who tended to adopt less rigid and legalistic operational boundaries regarding corruption, from the very outset of his reign Yongzheng sought to impose clear normative boundaries for official conduct at all levels of administration.[15]

11. *Chinese Local Elites and Patterns of Dominance*, ed. Joseph W. Esherick and Mary Backus Rankin (Berkeley: University of California Press, 1990).

12. Susan Mann, *Local Merchants and the Chinese Bureaucracy, 1750–1950* (Stanford: Stanford University Press, 1987).

13. Ch'ü T'ung-tsu, *Local Government in China Under the Ch'ing* (Cambridge, MA: Harvard University Press, 1961), p. 169.

14. Jonathan D. Spence, "The K'ang-hsi Reign," in *The Cambridge History of China*, vol. 9, pt. I, *The Ch'ing Empire to 1800*, ed. Willard J. Peterson (Cambridge, Eng.: Cambridge University Press, 2002), esp. pp. 147–48 and 174–75.

15. Tang Xiyong, "'Dafa xiaolian' lun yu Qing Kangxi di dui guanli caoshou de yaoqiu" (On the adage "When high officials are loyal, low officials are dutiful" and Qing emperor Kangxi's

By asserting the power of the central government to evaluate, control, and normalize the myriad practices that characterized the highly fluid realm of local governance, Yongzheng redefined the parameters of state control and repositioned a wide variety of agents—magistrates, yamen personnel, local elites, residents—on either side of a newly fortified boundary projected by the center, an undertaking that began with his attempt to rationalize local fiscal administration.

QING ADMINISTRATIVE DISCIPLINE AND CONTROL

Seldom was a magistrate's practical skill in negotiating the political agendas of his superiors in milieux dominated by local elites openly acknowledged by his superiors, and rarely, if ever, by central authorities in Beijing. Administrative control over the conduct of a local magistrate was primarily exercised by his immediate superiors at the prefectural and provincial level, whose reports were submitted to Board officials in Beijing. The routine task of disciplining the Qing bureaucracy fell to the Board of Civil Office, in the case of minor administrative infractions, or to the Imperial Board of Punishments, which had the option of subjecting wayward magistrates to penal regulations prescribed by Qing administrative and criminal law.[16] The system of routine evaluation used by the Board of Civil Office involved two primary mechanisms of control: the annual "examination of results" (*kaocheng*), and the triennial "great reckoning" or "grand accounting" (*daji*) system. Each year, under the auspices of the former, a magistrate's superior officer evaluated his efforts at tax collection and the maintenance of social order. Failures to collect some portion of any taxes due by the stated deadline, or to solve a significant crime occurring within the jurisdiction, incurred a negative evaluation by the magistrate's superior officer, ranging from the recording of a demerit, the institution of a fine, a demotion in rank, or dismissal from office.[17]

The triennial "great reckoning" system involved the governors and governors-general of each province in a review of the administrative accomplishments and conduct of all local administrators, as recorded

---

insistence on personal integrity among bureaucrats), *Renwen ji shehui kexue jikan* (Taibei: Zhongyang yanjiuyuan Zhongshan renwen shehui kexue yanjiusuo) 7:2 (September 1995): 43; Nancy E. Park, "Corruption in Eighteenth-Century China," *Journal of Asian Studies* 56:4 (November 1997): 967–1005.

16. Philip A. Kuhn, *Soulstealers: The Chinese Sorcery Scare of 1768* (Cambridge, MA: Harvard University Press, 1990), p. 191.

17. *Da Qing huidian* (Yongzheng edition), *juan sishi er, hubu ershi*, pp. 33–41. See also Watt (1972), pp. 295–96; 175.

in a personnel report prepared by the official's immediate superior and amended by the provincial treasurer and provincial judge. These were approved or modified before being passed along to the Board of Civil Office, which then sorted them into three categories: "outstanding and distinctive" (*zhuoyi*), "satisfactory" (*gong zhi*), and those whose conduct was unsatisfactory for any number of reasons.[18] "Outstanding and distinctive" magistrates qualified for an audience with the emperor (*yinjian*), and, not infrequently, an immediate promotion. "Satisfactory" magistrates were generally retained at their posts and continued to have their conduct evaluated in "four-column registers" which listed individual ratings for "integrity" (*caoshou*), "administrative performance" (*zhengshi*), "talent" (*caiju*), and "age" or "physical fitness" (*nian, nianli*). For each category, each magistrate was rated on a three-point scale: integrity was rated from "incorrupt" to "careful" to "ordinary"; administrative performance from "assiduous" to "diligent" to "ordinary"; and talent as "exceptional," "good," or "ordinary."[19]

Magistrates whose conduct was deemed unsatisfactory at the "Grand Reckoning" were subject to further investigation. Those who violated the administrative sanctions (*chufen zeli*) set by the Board of Civil Office had their cases reviewed and classified under one of eight legal categories (*bafa*) for which an official could be impeached.[20] These categories included both administrative failures and criminal deeds: avarice (*tan*); cruelty (*ku*); nonfeasance of duty (*piruan wuwei*); impropriety (*bujin*); old age (*nianlao*); infirmity (*youji*); instability (*fuzao*); and incompetence (*caili buji*). Officials found guilty of impropriety were impeached; those found guilty of nonfeasance of duty were cashiered; and the aged and infirm were retired. Those judged incompetent were demoted one grade and transferred to another post. "Unstable" officials were demoted three grades and transferred, without appeal, and if they were subsequently recommended for promotion, the additional compensation normally due them would be withheld. Officials found guilty of avarice or cruelty, if they absconded, were to be impeached in absentia. Once located and interrogated, those

---

18. Huang Liuhong [Huang Liu-Hung], *A Complete Book Concerning Happiness and Benevolence: A Manual for Local Magistrates in Seventeenth-Century China*, trans. and ed. Djang Chu (Tucson: University of Arizona Press, 1984), pp. 508–09; Ch'ü T'ung-tsu, *Local Government in China under the Ch'ing* (Cambridge, MA: Harvard University Press, 1961), p. 33.

19. Kuhn (1990), pp. 193–94; Ch'ü (1988), p. 35.

20. During the Jiaqing reign, two of these eight legal categories—cruelty and avarice—were removed from the list, and officials found guilty of either of these crimes were subject to immediate impeachment. Thus, from Jiaqing onward, the Board of Civil Office list was commonly known as the "six proscriptions" (*liufa*). Ch'ü (1988), pp. 33–35.

found innocent of charges were immediately dismissed and barred from government appointment (*yong bu xu yong*).[21] Those found guilty had their cases turned over to the Board of Punishment for sentencing under criminal law.[22]

The Qing penal code, which was originally adopted with some modifications from the preceding Ming, theoretically drew a distinction between the so-called "public" and "private" crimes committed by state officials. This distinction, which first appeared in the Tang legal code, applied only to ranked officials (officials of the eighth rank or higher) in the commission of particular types of offenses.[23] "Public crimes" (*gongzui*) generally carried lighter penalties than did "private offenses" (*sizui*), and discipline was overseen by the Board of Civil Office rather than by the Board of Punishments. The decision to observe this inherited distinction was prompted by a collective concern, shared by the Manchu ruling elite, to preserve "the order and dignity of the state" (*guoti*) by observing the long-standing dictum that "criminal punishments do not reach up to the officials."[24] Violations committed by ranked officials were classified as "public crimes" (*gongzui*) if such errors were committed "owing to errors in the commission of public duties, or if such errors occurred in handling such matters, providing that the official's private interests were not involved, or if the errors were unintentional." "Private crimes" (*sizui*), on the other hand, were transgressions committed "owing to [the pursuit of] private interests, or if the act were intentional in nature, and not due to an administrative oversight."[25] The severity of the violation also served to separate "public" from "private" crimes: nonfeasance of duty and incompetence were considered "public offenses," provided that local residents had not been seriously harmed by the non-action of the magistrate in question.

However, in actual juridical practice, the distinction between crimes (*zui*) punishable under penal law (*xingfa*) and those administrative failures (*gongshi shicuo*) that incurred disciplinary sanctions (*chufen*) was not

---

21. *Yongzheng Liubu chufen zeli, libu lei*, National Library Rare Book Collection (Taibei, Taiwan), p. 37.

22. *Da Qing Huidian, Yongzheng, juan* 150, xingbu 2, p. 24. See also Thomas Metzger, *The Internal Organization of Ch'ing Bureaucracy* (Cambridge, MA: Harvard University Press, 1973), p. 278.

23. Dai Yanhui, *Tang lü tonglun* (A comprehensive discussion of Tang dynasty law) (Taibei: Zhengzhong shuju, 1965), p. 264.

24. Metzger (1973), pp. 276–77. This distinction, along with the so-called "eight considerations" (*bayi*), constituted a preferential form of legal treatment for imperial scholars and officials.

25. *Da Qing lüli huitong xinzuan* (Taibei: Wenhai chubanshe, 1966), p. 269.

rigorously observed,[26] often for the simple reason that magistrates were rarely found guilty of a single violation. Local officials were held legally responsible not only for the activities of their private and yamen staffs but also for the omissions of their predecessors, even when they were not aware that any violations had taken place. This fact, along with the systematic underfunding and understaffing of county and department yamens, virtually guaranteed that even the most conscientious local officials operated on the fringes of Qing administrative law in the performance of their duties. The modest resources allotted to local governments during the early Qing were simply insufficient for the extensive and far-ranging projects they were obliged to perform. As Etienne Balazs once observed, if a magistrate were capable of fulfilling all expectations of him, "he would be a genius. Instead, he was an all-around blunderer, a harassed Jack-of-all-trades, an easy-going member of the mediocracy, eternally worried as to how to steer clear of Scylla and Charybdis—the people below and the authorities above."[27] As a result, even a relatively cursory investigation of yamen affairs could yield evidence of bureaucratic malfeasance that ran the gamut from minor infractions to criminal violations. The routine memorials of Board of Punishment officials to the Grand Secretariat (Neige *tiben*) during the Yongzheng reign reflect the structural limitations of the early Qing state that made both administrative failure and criminal behavior endemic among local magistrates, while discursively shifting the responsibility for such failures away from the center of the regime toward the outer margins of state control. By handling cases of "tax arrears" (*kuikong yinliang*) as criminal violations associated with political corruption (*tanwu, tanlie,* or *tanzang*), deficits in treasuries and granaries were effectively redefined as moral failures and were placed squarely at the doorstep of the local yamen.

CONSTRUCTING THE CRISIS

Within days of his father's death, Prince Yinzhen, who would shortly become the Emperor Yongzheng, expressed his concerns about the state of the imperial treasury. An audit of the Board of Revenue's funds disclosed a balance of 8,000,000 taels, an amount that totaled just over a fourth of

---

26. Metzger (1973), pp. 235–36*n*; Ch'ü T'ung-tsu (1961), p. 194. The lack of clarity apparently extended back to the original provision in Tang law. See Denis Twitchett, "The Fragment of the T'ang Ordinances of the Department of Waterways Discovered at Tun-huang," *Asia Major* 6 (1957–58): 23–79.

27. Etienne Balazs, *Political Theory and Administrative Reality in Traditional China* (London: School of Oriental and African Studies Press, 1965), Lecture III, p. 54.

the central government's annual tax quota. Audits of provincial and local government accounts that followed shortly after revealed that deficits were widespread throughout the empire, a situation the prince interpreted as dire.[28] By contrast, decades of war in Europe had left many of his contemporaries in far more dire straits: upon the death of Louis the XIV in 1715, the French national debt totaled some 2,800,000 *livres*, the face value of which was roughly equivalent to the total of the country's annual output at the time. The British national debt that same year was only somewhat less onerous, totaling 38,000,000 pounds compared to an output of roughly 60,000,000.[29] Nonetheless, Prince Yinzhen's early formulation of treasury and granary deficits as a political crisis necessitating direct and immediate action signaled a dramatic shift from the relatively lenient fiscal policies characteristic of his father's reign, in favor of a more robustly interventionist approach.

Significant treasury shortages had proved an intermittent, if not endemic, hazard during the Kangxi reign without provoking major institutional reforms. A precipitous rise in military expenditures caused by the Three Feudatories rebellion and pacification of Taiwan in the early years of the Kangxi reign strained the treasury, resulting in a reallocation of military expenses to the head-tax burden of counties and departments.[30] Kangxi modified the centralized system of annual accounting (*zouxiao*) during the eleventh year of his rule to ensure that annual budgets of local governments tallied with the records that magistrates submitted to the financial commissioners of their respective provinces, as well as with the amounts listed in the tax rolls sent to taxpayers. Later changes required financial commissioners to conduct routine audits of treasuries and granaries, and prefectural authorities to supervise county and department tax collection, the accumulated reports of which were to be submitted to provincial governments. Keeping abreast of the accounts under their jurisdiction, provincial governors or governors-general were ordered to memorialize the throne whenever deficits arose.[31]

---

28. Feng Erkang, *Yongzheng zhuan* (Biography of Yongzheng) (Beijing: Renmin chubanshe, 1985), p. 139; Madeleine Zelin, "The Yung-cheng Reign," in *The Cambridge History of China*, vol. 9, pt. I, *The Ch'ing Empire to 1800*, ed. Willard J. Peterson (Cambridge, Eng.: Cambridge University Press, 2002), p. 203.

29. François R. Velde, "Government Equity and Money: John Law's System in 1720 France," *Federal Reserve Bank of Chicago Working Papers*, WP-2003-31 (April 2003), pp. 7-9.

30. *Qingchao wenxian tongkao, juan* 19, *hu kou* (*yi*), as cited by Nie Hongqin, "Qingdai qianqi de huji yu fuyi" [Census registers, taxes and corvée during the early Qing] *Shilin* [Historic review] 2001:1: 81.

31. Zelin (1984), pp. 14-15.

Yet despite such reforms to the supervisory process, by all accounts the Kangxi emperor adopted a lenient approach to matters of public finance. The benevolence for which he is known was manifested in frequent and sweeping dispensations of tax forgiveness. According to the calculations of the Board of Revenue, tax amnesties granted by the emperor from his first through his forty-ninth year represented a total loss in central revenue that exceeded 100,000,000 taels. Apparently undeterred by the trend of fiscal insolvency set by his administration, to mark his fiftieth year in power Kangxi decreed an empire-wide general amnesty that excused each province in turn from remitting its annual land tax once in a three-year cycle, further stipulating that future tax relief be apportioned between tenants and landowners as a 30/70 split.[32] Finally, in the last decade of his reign, Kangxi froze the head tax (*ting*) at its 1711 level in a magnanimous declaration of the prosperity of the realm.[33] Thus, under the rule of Kangxi, the normative order of the imperium was characterized by paternalistic tolerance.

Kangxi's successor wasted no time in reversing the pattern set by his father. Before formally assuming the throne, Prince Yinzhen ordered the Board of Revenue to conduct a complete audit, and provincial governors to carry out a thorough investigation of all treasuries within their respective jurisdictions. A three-year extension was granted for the remission of outstanding taxes, after which, he warned, on no account would any outstanding deficits be tolerated. Furthermore, within a month, he established a new office, the Audit Bureau (Huikaofu), to correct widespread abuses in the existing *zouxiao* system. The annual audit procedures had originally been designed to give the Board of Revenue authority over local spending by requiring board approval prior to the allocation of tax revenue for yamen expenditures. However, in practice, the board's approval and clearance of local government accounts had long been based upon the payment of illegal fees (*bufei*), resulting in the granting of approval for projects and expenses of dubious value, and an estimated total deficit of 2,500,000 taels in the Board of Revenue's treasury in the second year of Yongzheng's rule.[34]

With respect to the deficits uncovered in provincial, prefectural, and county treasuries and granaries around the empire, the prince clearly suspected a similar causal mechanism was at work: bureaucratic malfeasance.

---

32. Fu Zhiyu, "Kangxi caizheng sixiang jiexi" (An analysis of Kangxi's ideas on public finance), *Xiandai Caijing* (Modern finance and economics) 153 (November 2002): 63.

33. Spence (2002), p. 178.

34. Feng (1985), p. 141; see also Bartlett (1991), pp. 41–43.

In a strongly worded edict issued only days after his father's death, Yinzhen accused mid-level officials of turning a blind eye to the accumulated deficits in local funds and grain stores, recording such funds as having been "shifted" (*nuoyong*) for legitimate purposes, and delaying the repayment of arrears indefinitely. Whereas incoming officials were supposed to guarantee the soundness of local granary and treasury accounts before assuming office, the prince observed that their superiors frequently intimidated new magistrates into falsely certifying such accounts; the same superiors, who feared being exposed for their earlier laxity, covered up subsequent shortfalls. In the end, although the official who originally incurred the deficit was technically responsible for repayment, prevailing bureaucratic practice held no one accountable. According to Yinzhen's analysis, the self-perpetuating cycle of corruption and abuse that originated in the ranks of officialdom resulted in endemic deficits in the imperial treasury. To end the cycle of official peculation, the prince decreed that while no one would be punished for uncovering pre-existing shortages, all deficits would have to be remanded within three years, without the levying of any additional illegal surcharges or fees on taxpayers. Recognizing that superior officials frequently sought to make up their own deficits by compelling their underlings to "contribute" their own wages (*juanfeng*), or voluntarily provide "food silver" (*fanyin* or *fanshiyin*) for yamen clerks, or any number of "customary fees" (*lougui*) when conducting routine business with government offices, the emperor banned such practices as well. On the day of his formal ascension to the throne, Yongzheng steadfastly refused the suggestion that deficits in county and department accounts be replenished by drawing upon the "meltage fees" (*haoxian*) routinely collected by magistrates in order to compensate for losses in the weight of silver taels when they were melted down into larger ingots for transport to the capital. These wastage allowances, which were also sometimes levied on taxes collected in grain to make up for loss and spoilage during transit, had long provided magistrates a fiscal margin of safety within which they might fund their daily operations, public works projects, or their own private needs. Widely regarded as the private prerogative of the individual magistrate and not previously regulated by the throne, they customarily ranged from 10 to 20 percent of the official tax due, but in some areas rose to 50 percent or more. While tolerated by early Manchu leaders as a necessary evil, Yongzheng resolutely prohibited their collection, arguing that such practices only added to the burden of the common people, and thus violated the throne's long-standing commitment to probity and frugality.[35]

---

35. Zelin (1984), pp. 79–81, 88.

Provincial governors and governors-general initiated comprehensive reviews of all financial accounts within their respective jurisdictions in accordance with Yongzheng's directives, and reported their results both through the established channel of routine memorials addressed to the Grand Secretariat (Neige), as well as through a new system of secret palace memorials originally utilized by Kangxi. Yongzheng immediately expanded the scope of the palace memorial system, in part to check the potential intransigence of the outer court, but also because such memorials provided him with an invaluable source of information. Financial and judicial commissioners below the rank of provincial governor were encouraged to submit memorials directly to the emperor on matters that fell outside the scope of administrative routine and precedent, and censors were barred from discussing with their colleagues the substance of any matters transmitted via secret palace memorial. By contrast, the routine memorials submitted to the Grand Secretariat were seen by comparatively large numbers of officials, and, as such, reflect not only how the routine matters of audits and administrative practices were handled by the outer court but also the process by which imperial decisions were translated into administrative policy and overseen by the Six Boards.[36]

The routine memorials to the Grand Secretariat (Neige *tiben*) detailing the investigation into public finances during the Yongzheng reign tended to conform to the emperor's initial analysis of the problem. The emperor's skepticism regarding oft-cited causes for local deficits—the "shifting" of public funds (*nuoyong*) to pay for public works projects or other expenses, "people's arrears" (*minqien*) allegedly caused by the inability of local taxpayers to meet their tax obligations, and the intimidation of incoming magistrates by superior officials—was echoed in the reports. Investigating officials duly noted such causes, but did not consider them extenuating factors when recommending punishment. Rather, following the model set by the emperor's assessment of the situation, Board of Punishment officials held magistrates strictly accountable for any and all deficits not reported when they assumed office, on the grounds that their willingness to conceal deficits may have reflected a hope of some future illicit gain. Cases of alleged "people's' arrears" and "shifting funds" were rigorously scrutinized for evidence of potential engrossment on the part of the officials involved, but on no grounds were deficits simply excused, and the magistrates in question were ordered to make restitution within three years of incurring the original deficit.

In a few cases, investigators uncovered extensive webs of corruption,

---

36. Wu (1970), esp. pp. 115–23.

extortion, and misappropriation of public funds of the sort suspected by Yongzheng. For example, one early investigation uncovered a deficit in Hubei's Tongcheng county that dated back to the final years of the Kangxi reign. The estimated total amounted to 3,745 taels, including 314 taels of bona fide "people's arrears" (*minqien*), which were immediately repaid upon commencement of the audit. Of the remaining amount, Tongcheng Magistrate Wu Wenji confessed that a former provincial commissioner (*buzhengshi*), Mo Qiyuan, had extorted 1,760 taels by threatening to impeach him for the arrears. When Wu readily agreed to pay, two of Commissioner Mo's personal servants also demanded 40 taels. A third employee of the commissioner and a personal servant of Magistrate Wu witnessed the transaction and thereupon demanded a total of 180 taels to keep quiet. However, word of the bribes soon spread, and the runner of yet another provincial commissioner extorted 40 taels. This was followed by the visit of a former Hubei provincial administration commissioner, Jiang Shengbi, who saw fit to "confiscate" 382 taels of the collected land taxes for some unnamed purpose before taking leave of Magistrate Wu.

The following year, when the hapless magistrate again found himself in arrears in county land taxes (3,807 taels, 2,329 taels of which was "people's arrears"), a new round of extortion began. Former Hubei Provincial Administration Commissioner Jiang Bi again paid Magistrate Wu a visit, and "confiscated" another 442 taels of the collected taxes. Retired Huguang Governor-General Zhang Liandeng then decided to pay his respects to Magistrate Wu and insisted upon collecting 600 taels before departing. Hearing that the annual round of payoffs had begun again, another personal servant of Magistrate Wu extorted 975 taels in order to keep the entire affair under wraps.

Following an extensive investigation of the arrears, which took place nearly four years later, Board of Punishment officials charged him with corruption (*tanwu*) and recommended beheading for the hapless Wu, but agreed to commute the sentence to three years in prison if the missing sums were repaid in full to the imperial treasury. Wu's personal servants, as well as those employees of Commissioner Mo who had also extorted funds from Magistrate Wu, all received the sentence of a 100 blows of the heavy bamboo and were furthermore banished to a distance of 3,000 *li*. Former Commissioner Mo received 80 blows, followed by two years of hard labor. Former Hubei Provincial Administration Commissioner Jiang Bi and the retired Governor-General of Huguang, Zhang Liandeng, were both charged with extortion (*lesuo*) and were originally sentenced to receive 100 blows and a banishment of 3,000 li. However, as investigators discovered that both had been involved in similar schemes to extort funds from other local officials, Board of Punishment officials recommended beheading for both of them.[37]

Whereas complex webs of bureaucratic malfeasance of this sort were occasionally uncovered during the massive audit, the causes of county and department deficits generally tended to be both more mundane and more pernicious than Yongzheng's early assertions suggested. The culture of Qing officialdom did support a shadow political economy of exchanges between bureaucrats that exacted a toll against the balance of the central treasury. However, private engrossment among magistrates clearly played a role in only one-fifth of the cases submitted for Grand Secretariat consideration during the Yongzheng reign. The majority of investigations uncovered deficits that had either been transferred to incoming magistrates by their predecessors, or that were due to various public works projects or military needs that could not be funded by the meager resources accorded to counties and departments by the central state.

FROM THEORY TO PRACTICE

Because of the reforms of the annual auditing (*zouxiao*) system initiated by Kangxi, any deficits not reported by magistrates, either intentionally or unintentionally, should have been caught by their immediate superiors at the prefectural level or by the financial commissioner of the province within the year in which they occurred. Magistrates had no administrative authority to "shift funds" (*nuoyong*) between accounts, or to withhold for any reason, without the consent of higher authorities, any taxes collected. Thus, unreported deficits technically involved violations of law (*wanfa*), regardless of their cause. Initial reports submitted in routine memorials frequently noted the removal of magistrates for deficits (*kuikong*), but in most provincial inquiries, a genuine attempt was made to ascertain the original cause of such shortfalls, and to assign to particular officials legal and moral responsibility for them. In cases in which the official in question or his subordinates or family members intentionally withheld grain or money from the public coffers, the original report of arrears generally yielded a charge of corruption (*tanwu*); if an official or his subordinates misused their authority in order to obtain such resources forcefully, or violated social norms, the charge was often depravity (*tanlie*). Other charges stemming from the deliberate commission of crimes include the appropriation or embezzlement of resources from the public (*tanzang*), extortion (*lesuo*), and bribery (*shouhui*).

---

37. *Neige Tiben* (hereafter *NGTB*), *tanwu lei*, case #30 (dated YZ 2/9/14).

However, more frequently, losses were not connected to private engrossment, and the charge levied against such magistrates was the simple "shifting" of funds or grain. In several cases, county tax arrears were clearly related to expenses for county public works projects that needed to be undertaken within a given tax year. One 1725 investigation of land-tax arrears in Anhui's Tongling county revealed that of the nearly 2,000 taels missing, 353 taels represented people's arrears. The remaining sum was spent on a variety of projects and routine expenses: salary for yamen runners and for the purchase of supplies necessary for carrying out routine yamen business, purchase of pigments to make paint for temple gates that needed repainting, and repair of sections of the city walls that had collapsed. Magistrate Lu Shouren was ordered to replace the missing amounts within three years or face sanctions.[38] Investigators in Shandong's Changba county the same year uncovered an accumulated arrears of nearly 26,000 taels in land taxes that spanned the reigns of three magistrates. More than half of this amount was used to purchase horses for the army in 1716 and to pay for repairs to the granary storage buildings and other county-owned buildings. Four years later, a massive famine swept the county, and more funds were "shifted" to purchase firewood and grain to feed famine victims. The following year, the local school required repairs, and two years later, sections of the city wall again required repairs.[39] None of the missing money had been stolen or used for "private" purposes, yet the projection of the moral agency of the central state habitually redirected responsibility for such failings downward in the ranks of officialdom, with the heaviest burdens falling at the bottom rung.

In 1723, two cases from Shanxi uncovered even more significant deficits that were due largely to the "shifting" of funds to pay for legitimate public works projects. Datong Magistrate Wu Zongli borrowed collected taxes in order to repair the county granary when he discovered that nearly all of its contents had rotted away as a result of structural deterioration. To make the repairs and replace the rice, beans, wheat, millet, and hay that were lost required more than 13,500 taels, just under half of which he was able to repay within two years of his dismissal for tax arrears. In the preliminary report submitted to the Grand Secretariat, Board of Punishment officials warned that if Wu was unable to repay the remaining 7,500 taels within the year, the outstanding balance would be used to calculate his final punishment. Similarly, when Taiping county magistrate Zhang Xuedu fell short more than 22,000 taels in land taxes, it was discovered that 7,600 taels

---

38. *NGTB, tanwu lei*, case #44 (dated YZ 3/7/14).
39. *NGTB, tanwu lei*, case #48 (dated YZ 3/10/4).

had been confiscated by his superior in order to pay soldier's wages; the remainder had all been used for a variety of public works projects. When he was cashiered for tax arrears, Zhang sold his family home and lands to make up the deficit, but was unable to pay the final 12,000 taels of the county's debt and so was sentenced to hard labor.[40]

Military expenses were frequently at the root of such deficits. One early investigation of arrears in Shaanxi's Yichuan county is typical. An audit of the Yichuan granary revealed a shortage of nearly 3,000 piculs (*dan*) of grain. Magistrate Zhang Dexiu confessed that the deficit originated in an order he received from his superior to acquire 181 camels for the military commander at Liangzhou to assist in the defense of the northwestern frontier. Despite having just arrived at his new post, Zhang procured the requisite number of camels and set off for the treacherous journey to Liangzhou. Upon his arrival, the commander's staff accepted only 39 of the camels, claiming that they had no need for the rest. Zhang immediately sent word back to his superior, but, fearing that the military commander might reverse his staff's decision, Zhang remained in Liangzhou with his camels for four months awaiting further instructions. During his wait, each of the camels needed to be fed and cared for at a cost of 60 taels a day; in order to provide fodder for the camels, Zhang instructed one of his yamen runners to sell 2,000 piculs of grain from Yichuan's granary, hoping to replace the grain after the harvest, and recording it in the meantime as people's arrears. After returning to Yichuan four months later, Zhang's misdeed was discovered, and he was charged with "shifting funds" in the matter of the camels. Although Zhang had managed to replace nearly half the amount he had taken from the granary, he was immediately cashiered and initially sentenced to receive 100 strokes with the heavy bamboo. The fate of the camels is not recorded.[41]

In a similar case, investigators discovered that the annual land tax was short nearly 6,000 taels in Shaanxi's Yang county in the last year of Kangxi's rule. Magistrate Chi Yin confessed he had "borrowed'" nearly 5,000 taels of collected land taxes to cover the costs of transporting 30 mules with saddles and reins to a military outpost in Gansu. When 24 of the mules died in transit, Chi sold off nearly a third of the county's stored grain in order to pay for replacements, representing a net loss to the county funds of more than 7,500 taels. When investigators arrived, Assistant Magistrate Qu Gun admitted that he had attempted to "shift" 5,657 taels from land taxes to cover up the arrears, which he admitted had been mounting since a

---

40. *NGTB, tanwu lei*, cases #42 and #43, both dated YZ3.

41. *NGTB tanwu lei*, case #7 (dated YZ 1/5/6).

demand to supply the military outpost in Gansu with 180 donkeys during the fifty-fourth year of Kangxi's reign. Both men were sentenced to 100 blows with the heavy bamboo, banishment of 3,000 li, and ordered to restore the missing funds within three years.[42]

Magistrates could also be cashiered for misfeasance with respect to granary supplies. In a 1726 edict on the granary situation, Yongzheng argued that any shortages in granary supplies were, from the point of view of the throne, even more reprehensible than tax arrears. Accordingly, his ministers proposed that the punishments for granary shortages be brought into line with those for tax arrears, although they did distinguish between losses due to embezzlement and those due to mismanagement. However, Yongzheng overruled their suggestions, stipulating that losses due to spoilage or rodents be calculated on the same scale as those caused by misappropriation, on the grounds that spoilage losses were the direct result of official negligence. This policy was adopted as administrative law, and was quickly pressed into service by audit investigators.[43] For example, Shanxi Datong county magistrate Wu Zongli was cashiered when an investigation revealed that the granary buildings in his county had fallen into disrepair, and that some of the stored supplies had subsequently spoiled.[44]

Frequently, the investigation into account and granary deficits uncovered a variety of unrelated bureaucratic misdeeds. As the pressure for prompt repayment of tax arrears mounted, some officials scrambled to raise funds in a hasty attempt to conceal deficits. Roughly one-tenth of the cases against magistrates involved the much-reviled system of "customary fees" (lougui), the collection of illegal taxes and surcharges or "voluntary contributions" from local residents, all of which had been banned by Yongzheng on the date he formally assumed the throne. For example, in 1723, the Zhili Qingyuan county magistrate Jiang Renxiu was cashiered for imposing no fewer than eleven illegal forms of fees and surcharges on various local residents, including: an illegal tax on sellers of cotton cloth; rent collected from a salt merchant for a small plot of unused land that did not belong to the county, and rent collected on a piece of land the county had actually sold to a family years before when the family misplaced the deed of sale; the illegal sale of offices; additional and sporadic excess sales taxes; "contributions" solicited for a public project that was never

---

42. NGTB tanwu lei, case #39 (dated YZ 3/4/18).

43. Will and Wong (1991), pp. 124–25.

44. Investigating officials maintained that the amount of spoiled grain was equivalent to just over 13,541 taels of silver. Wu Zongli had been able to repay 6,000 taels' worth of his debt within two years, and so was given another two years to make good on the remainder before a harsher punishment would be assessed. NGTB, tanwu lei, case #43 (dated YZ 3/5/3).

undertaken; various sums illegally extorted from individuals convicted of minor crimes, including one against a Buddhist nun whom Magistrate Jiang claimed had committed an unmentionable act.

However, during their inquiry, Board of Punishment officials uncovered evidence that Jiang's levying of illegal fines and taxes had caused the deaths of three residents. The first victim was a farmer who was beaten to death by runners when he refused to pay an illegal tax. The other two victims resulted from a case in which Jiang had two monks arrested as poachers for tending a garden on land previously owned by the yamen that had been donated to a local temple by Jiang's predecessor. Jiang had the two monks beaten and imprisoned for a short period of time. Upon their release, one committed suicide by throwing himself into a well. When the other returned to the temple and reported the incident, the temple master was purportedly so infuriated that he also collapsed and died of anger. In their memorial to the Grand Secretariat, the investigating officials recommended that Jiang be immediately cashiered for corruption (*tanwu*), and that both Jiang and his yamen runners be severely punished for their excessive cruelty (*cannue*) as well.[45]

In 1727, Magistrate Fu Zicheng of Henan's Guangshan county was accused of having embezzled 1,468 taels of meltage fees collected during the first three years of Yongzheng's reign. Additional investigation into Guangshan's accounts led to a discovery of granary arrears as well, which occasioned a series of interviews with local residents. Investigators learned that Magistrate Fu had opened the granaries the previous spring to allow residents to borrow grain on the condition that it be paid back after the fall harvest. However, one group of residents told investigating officials that the magistrate had demanded the original amounts be paid back with interest, collecting an additional 425 *dan* in this manner.[46] Two other groups came forward with separate accusations of "voluntary contributions" they claimed the magistrate had in fact coerced from them: a group of wealthy elites alleged that two years earlier, Magistrate Fu invited them to a banquet to celebrate his own birthday, compelling each of those in attendance to give him one or two silver taels as a present; a group of tobacco growers came forward to say that on the same occasion, they had been collectively extorted by the magistrate to turn over 135,000 copper cash. While investigators were unable to corroborate these allegations, they found that Magistrate Fu had illegally collected one surcharge in order to repair the county's examinations halls and had mishandled two criminal cases. In the

---

45. *NGTB, tanwu lei*, case #22 (dated YZ 2/6/17).
46. One *dan* is equivalent to a hectoliter of grain.

matter of the missing grain, Fu Zicheng was immediately cashiered, and for his other criminal violations, including the original embezzlement charge, he was sentenced to 100 heavy blows.[47]

Local officials could also be held accountable when yamen runners levied illegal surcharges during the tax-collection process, even without the consent or awareness of their superior. For example, in 1724 Zunyi Subprefect Sun Qianfeng came under investigation because his yamen underlings had secretly raised the amount of salt-transport taxes in order to provide themselves with salaries and "food silver" while engaged on official business. For every picul of salt collected for transport, Sun's functionaries added a four-penny (*fen*) surcharge under the guise of "transport fees," three of which were actually used to cover their own expenses. In this manner, they managed to collect illegally a total of more than 63 taels of "food silver" without the knowledge of Subprefect Sun. The yamen employees involved were sentenced to 100 blows with the heavy bamboo, followed by three years of hard labor; Subprefect Sun was originally sentenced to one light stroke of the whip. However, subsequent interrogation of his staff revealed that Sun had dispatched one of his personal servants to escort a local prostitute named "Fourth Lady Lu" (Lu Siniang) back to his yamen, where he openly cohabited with her for over a month, showering her with gifts of silk and satin. For her part in the matter, "Fourth Lady Lu" was also sentenced to receive 30 blows with the light bamboo, and spent a month in jail. Sun was cashiered and his sentence was revised to 100 heavy blows.[48]

YONGZHENG AND THE STATE OF VIRTUE

Within a year of initiating the massive audit of local finances, Yongzheng ruthlessly pursued deficits by holding even high-ranking commissioners personally responsible for any missing funds. He confiscated the private residences and lands of key officials in various provincial administrations, including Huguang Provincial Administration Commissioner Zhang Shengbi, Hunan Surveillance Commissioner Zhang Anshi, and Jiangsu Provincial Governor Wu Cunli. In several such cases, if the individual responsible for incurring the deficit in question was unable to make restitution, the debt was transferred to his family. Private homes were searched for coins or goods that may have been pilfered, extorted, or accepted as bribes by the official in question or by his family members;

---

47. *NGTB, tanwu lei*, case #52 (dated YZ 5/3/16).
48. *NGTB, tanwu lei*, case #17 (dated YZ 2/4/4).

in a few cases, family members were sold into servitude.[49] The penalties for magistrates were equally severe. Magistrates who recorded deficits in either taxes or granary supplies were immediately cashiered and returned to their home districts, where they were ordered to make restitution on the entire outstanding debt. If the missing funds could be quickly repaid, no further penalties were levied against them. If, however, they were unable to pay within the time frame allotted them by the Board of Punishments, any outstanding debt was used to determine the level of punishment they would receive.

Yet delays in repaying funds were common, and the logistics of managing the repayment process strained political resources. Three years into the audit of county and department accounts, Henan provincial officials described the numerous difficulties encountered in the repayment of local deficits, which frequently involved the cooperation of officials from more than one jurisdiction. In one case, the Jiangxi Ningdu county magistrate, Liu Can, was immediately cashiered for arrears of more than 25,000 taels and was ordered to repay the money within three years. He returned to his home in Henan, where his personal effects were auctioned off. However, the sale of the property yielded a mere 4,500 taels; Liu died within a few months, so the remaining debt was transferred to his son. The son offered the family home and lands for sale, at an estimated worth of over 24,000 taels, but two successive years of drought had so drained the local economy that no buyer could be found before the deadline for repayment. To make matters worse, the local magistrate pilfered 387 taels of the returned funds in order to make good on his own arrears; he, too, was immediately cashiered, and ordered to make good on his outstanding debt.[50]

Sometimes repayment was not possible because the official who incurred the original arrears had already passed away, either from natural causes or by his own hand. In 1726, when the Guangdong provincial governor reported that a local circuit intendant named Li Bin was in arrears, Li immediately killed himself. The same year, when the military governor of the Fujian-Zhejiang region and the Fujian provincial administrative commissioner recommended that Xingquan Circuit Intendant Tao Fan be dismissed, Tao committed suicide even before a hearing could be held. When apprised of these developments, Yongzheng ordered that the debts in question be passed on to the sons and grandsons of the former officials and had the military governor subject their wives and descendants to rigorous interrogation to locate any embezzled property.[51]

---

49. Feng (1985), pp. 143–44, 147.
50. *NGTB, tanwu lei*, case #24 (dated YZ 2/5/12).
51. Feng (1985), p. 155.

The pressure of investigation itself proved extreme and adversely affected the health of some officials. In 1724, an exhaustive investigation into the accounts of Sichuan's Suining county yielded a stunning range of accusations against Magistrate Zhuang Chengzuo, but little hard evidence of wrongdoing. Various residents accused him of demanding an oppressively high meltage fee during tax collection, levying surcharges for bogus town improvement projects, extorting funds from residents by falsely accusing them of crimes, and even falsely imprisoning the wife and son of a local landowner. After weeks of careful investigation, none of these charges could be corroborated. The only evidence of potential wrongdoing uncovered by the team of investigators was that one yamen runner had tentatively hatched a plot to extort some money from a local resident, and that a local woman had attempted suicide when she was married off against her will, a case in which the magistrate had declined to intervene. For these two infractions, the investigating officials fined Zhuang and demanded that he temporarily turn over his official seal to the magistrate of the neighboring county until Board of Punishment officials could review the facts of his case. However, Zhuang resisted, protesting his innocence and repeatedly expressing his personal antipathy for his replacement. When pressed, he pulled a small knife from the sleeve of his gown and purportedly ran through the streets of the county seat, screaming that he would kill anyone who approached him. The standoff lasted the better part of the day, but ended without bloodshed. Board of Punishment officials noted in their memorial to the Grand Secretariat that his crimes were not serious, and while he would not be returned to office on account of his apparent mental instability, all criminal charges against him would be dismissed.[52]

Yongzheng's uncompromising stance clearly exacted a heavy toll on the ranks of Qing officialdom. Shortly after assuming the throne, Yongzheng ordered the Board of Personnel to immediately impeach officials with arrears, and not to allow them to remain at their posts until the cycle of investigation, hearing, and sentencing was complete. The emperor argued that, in the case of deficits caused by bureaucratic engrossment, allowing an official to remain at his post until proven guilty simply extended his opportunities to engage in wrongdoing, further burdening the common people. Officials who were immediately able to repay missing funds could continue to serve if a request were submitted on their behalf by their supervisors. As a result of such policies, by the third year of Yongzheng's reign, Hunan Provincial Governor Wei Tingzhen complained that

---

52. *NGTB, tanwu lei,* case #26 (YZ 2/8/15).

the majority of district and department magistrates in Hunan had been cashiered, and, as the audit was still ongoing, he expected that even more would be dismissed in the coming year. Seven years later, the military governor of Zhili noted that of all the magistrates in his province, only a small handful had managed to serve more than three years without being dismissed.[53]

The steep attrition within the ranks of local magistrates was not an insignificant price to pay for the amelioration of the national debt, but, nevertheless, progress toward fiscal solvency had been made within the emperor's original time frame. By his third year on the throne, every province in the empire had made good on at least some portion of the funds owed the central treasury, and a few had repaid nearly in full. In 1724, just over a year after Yongzheng assumed power, Zhili Governor-General Li Wei memorialized to report that of the province's original arrears of over 400,000 taels, roughly half had already been repaid. The remaining 200,000 would be replaced by the end of the following year. Henan had also repaid all arrears within provincial treasuries, and the 30,000–40,000 taels missing from county and department accounts were quickly made up.[54]

Other provinces were less successful for a variety of reasons in carrying out the audit in a timely fashion. As reports of granary deficits and tax arrears continued to flood in from the provinces, a reluctant Yongzheng extended the original three-year deadline for an additional three years. Despite the relative success achieved in Zhili and Henan, information uncovered in the audit process suggested that the problem of deficits was considerably more complex than Yongzheng's initial framing of the issue stipulated. As investigators patiently probed the state of local finances throughout the empire, the structural dilemma implicit in the throne's dual commitment to low and stable rates of taxation and its ambitious ideal of benevolent governance was laid bare. Investigating officials sorting through county and department tax records uncovered evidence of long-standing debts amassed by successive local officials, compounded by deficits incurred by the land-holding elites and public tax arrears that dated back generations. Many counties and departments suffered financial setbacks due to extraordinary circumstances, such as natural disasters or military demands, which ultimately resulted in significant tax arrears. However, the problem of deficits was also widespread in other areas, often caused either by tax evasion, the cost of routine repairs to public facilities, or the simple mismanagement of scant material and administrative resources. The

53. Feng (1985), pp. 142–43.
54. Feng (1985), pp. 144–45.

scope of the problem, as well as its persistent manifestation, indicated that structural limitations were at least partly to blame.

The emperor's determination to root out corruption and at the same time to hold individual magistrates accountable for any and all deficits effectively shifted the responsibility for such shortcomings away from the central regime, and redefined fiscal shortages as the moral failures of those on the margins of officialdom. The normative framework undergirding the Qing state's commitment to light taxation in order to "store wealth among the people" (*cangfu yu min*) and its concomitant pursuit of vast strategic and social-welfare goals, gave shape to Yongzheng's efforts to build and extend central state power, but at the same time produced significant strain on the resources of the late imperial state. Thus, while Yongzheng's initial formulation of the problem resulted in significant transfers of wealth from the office-holding members of the elite to the central treasury, it failed to redress substantively the root of the problem. As the pressure to find an acceptable solution mounted, the compromise that eventually emerged involved a redefinition of public and private responsibility, and an ambitious reconfiguration of local bureaucratic practice that temporarily extended the reach of the state into the web of social relations.

THREE

Localist Critiques of Corruption and Virtue

The Yongzheng emperor's hard line on corruption was part of a larger agenda by which he sought to reconfigure Qing bureaucratic practice. As noted in the previous chapter, the strict standard he advocated of holding individual officeholders personally responsible for deficits placed local magistrates in a quandary. The bans on collecting "customary fees" (*lougui*) and appropriating the salaries of one's subordinates through the "contribution of wages" (*juanfeng*) severely delimited the fiscal margins within which early-Qing officialdom routinely operated. His steadfast refusal on moral grounds to permit the customary practice of using "meltage fees" or "wastage allowances" (*huohao* or *haoxian*) to make up existing deficits effectively criminalized the modus operandi of the local yamen. By treating budgetary shortcomings as individual moral failures, Yongzheng shifted responsibility for the structural dilemma created by the throne's dual commitment to minimal taxation and maximalist aims outside the perceived boundaries of the state itself.

However, the massive investigation into arrears not only strained scarce bureaucratic resources but also caused a steady attrition of experienced personnel in the lowest ranks of officialdom, which potentially threatened the stability of the empire perhaps even more directly than had the deficits that initially prompted the investigation. Unlike the audit of the Jiangnan region during the early years of the Kangxi reign, which focused on tax-evading wealthy landowners, Yongzheng concentrated his efforts on uncovering patterns of official peculation and the mismanagement of resources within the ranks of the state bureaucracy. His extensive examination of government accounts, along with the expansion of the secret palace memorial system, yielded a wealth of raw information on the workings of the outer court. The overt goal of this enhanced scrutiny was, in the emperor's own words, to rehabilitate the Qing state by "putting officials under surveillance" (*chali*).[1] Indirectly, however, the instability such measures introduced created a window of opportunity that allowed Yongzheng to effect two institutional shifts that reoriented bureaucratic practices on the margins of the state: increased government control over financial resources that did not result in raising taxes; and a curtailment in the activities of local gentry, who largely made up the sub-bureaucratic and extra-bureaucratic staffs upon which local administrations relied. The net effect of these changes weakened, at least temporarily, the institutional basis of the alliance between landed elites and local bureaucrats and enhanced the lines of communication and control between county and department magistrates and the hierarchy of officialdom that supported the throne.

It is hardly surprising, given the vast and imposing edifice of these newly refined "machineries for autocracy,"[2] that proponents of decentralized governance opposed such measures. Resistance to the local implementation of both initiatives—the "return of the meltage fees to the public coffers" (*huohao guigong*), as well as to the curtailment of elite privileges—took a variety of forms, ranging from dissimulation and subversion to collective action against state agents. As the examination of county and department arrears wore on, teams of investigating officials found themselves the target of obstructionist tactics, endless obfuscation, and even overt violence. In official communications, opposition to enhanced state control was cast in moral terms, and challenges to the emperor's reforms were frequently described as the work of "evil people" on the margins of the state.

Popular resistance to the centralization of political power and material resources also found its way into local historical narratives during the Yongzheng reign, giving particular shape to unofficial records of county and department magistracies. Local gazetteers, some of which were compiled at the direction of regional officials and some of which were written by local literati, frequently included for didactic purposes biographical and other accounts of local magistrates, describing both virtuous and venal officials. Family, surname, and clan histories also highlighted the government service of their members, most often in hagiographical terms. The careers and policies of local magistrates were also a popular topic in anecdotal "wild histories" (*yeshi*), where they were often either extolled or reviled at length, sometimes on the basis of apparent hearsay or rumor.

---

1. Vermillion endorsement on a memorial dated YZ 5/2/10, *Zhupi yuchi* (Vermillion endorsements of the Yongzheng emperor), as cited by Wu (1970), p. 69.
2. Huang (1974), p. 111.

While such accounts vary widely in terms of their historical reliability, collectively they represent an alternative account of local bureaucratic conduct to those expressed in palace memorials during the mid-Qing. Insofar as memorials were generally composed by officials at the rank of the province or above, they provide a view of bureaucratic conduct from within the structure of the state itself, situated with respect to the policy agenda of the central court. Unofficial accounts, while written by a range of authors with a variety of aims, differ from palace memorials insofar as their intended audience was not members of the imperial bureaucracy. Whereas memorials tended to measure official performance in terms of legal standards or instrumental political ends, unofficial records provide a perspective on official conduct that was oriented toward the locale, away from the concerns of the central court.

Such unofficial accounts were not, however, characteristically anti-state: the imbrication of local literati, gentry families, and the official bureaucracy during the late imperial era produced overlapping spheres of shared interests in the maintenance of social and economic stability. Within this context, localist genealogies of virtue and venality aimed not to oppose the state but, rather, to effect a more favorable balance of power and resources between the center and the margins. When their interpretations of policies and bureaucratic conduct differed from those found in official sources, they tended to advocate arrangements that would allow local elites enhanced autonomy within a stable social order maintained by the regime. While no single "localist" agenda can be discerned from such documents, collectively they espouse an activist role for local elites in taking the initiative to organize institutions and practices beyond the purview of the local yamen. The models of bureaucratic virtue and vice offered in such sources presented an image of the local literati as more responsive to local needs than were the remote and legalistic imperial authorities, and furthermore suggested that ethical conduct was not something that could be coerced or imposed on local communities from above. Rather, local hagiographies collectively sought to demonstrate that public-spiritedness could be cultivated only from within, and it was most effective where local elites were permitted to exert their influence freely within the public sphere as exemplars of Confucian learning and decorum.

TRANSFORMING LOCAL PRACTICE

Although Yongzheng banned the collection of so-called meltage fees by county and department magistrates on the day he formally assumed the throne, an alternative plan began to take shape within the first year of his reign. As noted in the previous chapter, local administrations were notably underfunded during the early Qing, requiring magistrates to devise sufficient streams of revenue on their own. One common method of making up deficits was the levying of an inflated surcharge ostensibly designed to offset the loss in the weight of silver during the melting process. Disdained by Yongzheng's father as a necessary evil, meltage fees had long provided local yamens with much-needed monetary resources, but in some areas climbed as high as 80 percent of the total tax due, the brunt of which was borne by commoners.[3]

Five months after Yongzheng imposed the ban, Huguang Governor-General Yang Zongren submitted a secret palace memorial requesting permission to allow magistrates to retain a portion of the meltage fees already collected that year in order to defray public expenses, and to remit the remainder to the province. Notwithstanding the ban, the emperor privately approved the new arrangement with enthusiasm, commending Yang's plan as "utterly flawless" (*yiwu xiaci*), and urging him to implement it with due diligence. A similar proposal was submitted by Shanxi Governor Nuo Min, who requested permission to have the full amount of all meltage fees collected within the year remitted directly to the treasury of the financial commissioner of the province. The funds were then to be divided up by the commissioner and used to compensate for deficits for which no official was found who could be held accountable, as well as to provide funds to "nourish the honesty" (*yanglian*) of local officials by providing them additional remuneration to help offset their expenses.[4] Yongzheng readily gave his assent, also approving similar proposals from the governors of Shandong and Zhili, who each recommended that portions of the meltage fees collected be forwarded to the provincial treasury to compensate for outstanding deficits, as well as to offset provincial expenses.[5]

Finally, in July 1724, the emperor pressed Shanxi Governor Nuo Min to openly request approval of his plan of "returning the meltage fees to the public coffers" (*huohao guigong*) from the Grand Secretariat by submitting a routine memorial. The Grand Secretariat firmly disapproved of the measure and remanded a list of objections to the emperor. Yongzheng requested a point-by-point rebuttal from the Shanxi financial commissioner, which was subsequently returned to the Grand Secretariat, the Censorate, and the Council of Princes and Ministers for further deliberation. Once again, the

---

3. The highest rates were reported in the provinces Henan and Shandong. Feng (1985), p. 153.
4. Ibid., pp. 148–49.
5. Zelin (2002), p. 210.

ministers rejected the plan, arguing forcefully that any plan to use meltage fees was a de facto recognition of an illegal arrangement that would serve only to increase the onerous burden already placed on taxpayers. Legalizing the meltage fee was, in their view, tantamount to sanctioning an odious practice long associated with low-level political corruption.

Nonetheless, after considerable discussion, no doubt prompted by the emperor's clear endorsement of the proposal, the court reluctantly approved the plan on an experimental basis to be carried out initially in Shanxi and then only until existing deficits could be cleared. Yongzheng's edict on the matter summarized the benefits of the program for both taxpayers and local magistrates, noting that the regulation of the fee would lower the overall burden on taxpayers, as well as provide a stable and secure source of funding for local yamens. However, given the tenacity of inner-court resistance, the emperor declined to provide a more detailed directive to serve as a guide for the implementation of the new policy and instead allowed the details of its execution to be decided by individual governors and governors-general, providing private guidance by way of memorials.[6]

In addition to the program to "return the meltage fees to the public coffers," which extended and deepened central control over local fiscal practices by placing them under provincial control, Yongzheng pursued a series of measures designed to bring the activities of the yamen's sub-bureaucratic personnel under closer control. In first year of his reign, Yongzheng issued no fewer than eleven edicts in which he addressed the problem of low-level bureaucratic abuses and his commitment to ameliorating administrative problems.[7] Proposals to expand the official boundaries of the state to incorporate the ranks of sub-county functionaries were flatly refused by the court on the grounds that expanding the existing system of formal administration might weaken the power of the state by increasing opportunities for clerical self-engrossment and the subversion of central policies that did not favor powerful local interests. At the same time, the emperor clearly recognized the importance of such actors for the functioning of the state and approved the inclusion of certain sub-county bureaucrats into official ranks on a case-by-case basis.[8] In early 1724, Yongzheng initiated an empire-wide restructuring of local administrations that resulted in the addition of several new sub-county positions and an expanded scope of responsibilities for others.[9]

---

6. Ibid., p. 211; Feng (1985), p. 150.
7. These edicts appear in *Qing Shizong shilu xuanji, juan* 3, Yongzheng *yuannian, zhengyue*.
8. Rowe (2002), pp. 345–46.
9. Antony (2003), pp. 34, 52.

The activities of local gentry proved a more difficult target. The dependence of the deliberately self-limiting Qing state on ambitious local elites lent a rough sort of "illicit legitimacy" to a wide variety of extra-bureaucratic agents as they negotiated between state and society.[10] As one magistrate's handbook observed,

There are many ways of promoting an administration that nourishes the people . . . [that are] recorded in the *Huidian* [Regulations of government]. As for building reservoirs for irrigation, preparing equipment to save people from floods, distributing clothes in cold weather, establishing soup kitchens for the starving, and providing tea for the thirsty, drugs for the ill, coffins and shrouds to bury the dead, and graveyards for burial—these are all activities of government vital for the livelihood of the people. But much of this important work is done by public-spirited gentry (*haoyi shenjin*) and is not recorded in the *Huidian*. Local officials should urgently exhort the gentry to transform the people with their efforts.[11]

Yet the reliance of the late imperial state on the organizing abilities of local elites, as many have demonstrated, proved to be a double-edged sword. The semi-autonomous gentry-led organizations that were so indispensable to the maintenance of social order served equally well to promote the more narrow self-interests of the elites who dominated them, providing local gentry with opportunities for economic gain and decision-making power that sometimes pitted them against the central state. During his reign, Yongzheng repeatedly expressed concern about the relationship between local officials and local elites and expressly forbade any collaboration between the two that could potentially produce conflicts of interest on the part of low-level officials. In one edict addressed to the Grand Secretariat, Yongzheng excoriated in vivid terms those members of the gentry who,

with complete disregard for rules and limits, and paying no heed to reputation and integrity . . . frequent government offices chasing lawsuits, or wander through the countryside wantonly bullying poor people, or evade taxes in contempt for the law of the land, or collect taxes by proxy to engross themselves and their families. It is difficult to enumerate the full range of [their] despicable and foul degradations.[12]

The crisis in local administration triggered by Yongzheng's exhaustive investigation into treasuries and granary stores initially drove some magistrates to seek support from the local elites in their districts to cover the missing resources. In one early edict on the matter of whether willing

---

10. Reed uses the term "illicit legitimacy" in *Talons and Teeth* (2000), p. 12; on the equally fascinating role of litigation masters in the late Qing, see MacAuley (1998).
11. Wu Rongguang, "Yang min" (Nourishing the people), in *Muling shu* (Magistrate's handbook), ed. Xu Dong (1848), as cited by Min Tu-ki (1989), p. 33.
12. *Shangyu Neige* (Edicts to the Grand Secretariat) YZ 4/27/9, as cited by Feng (1985), p. 164.

third parties should be permitted to make up deficits in government accounts, Yongzheng speculated that in cases in which corrupt magistrates had teamed together with errant gentry, wealthy residents might seek to continue their profitable relationship by covering a county's debt, and so he expressly forbade voluntary repayment by third parties. Three years later, in 1727, he promulgated a special edict warning the people of Fujian that a complete reckoning of the province's accounts was already under way, and that it was possible that some corrupt officials may have temporarily "borrowed" the grain of wealthy residents in their districts to stock the granaries in their districts. Any grain "lent" to officials, the emperor cautioned, would become the property of the state and would on no account be returned; officials who had "borrowed" grain would be immediately replaced.[13]

Yongzheng also took measures to limit the traditional tax exemptions granted to degree-holding members of the elite, due in no small measure to the common misuse of such privileges through the practice of proxy remittance. For the purposes of registering households for tax collection, local governments typically designated families with members who were holders of the First Degree (*xiucai*, or *shengyuan*) as "Confucian scholar households" (*ruhu*); families with students of the Imperial Academy (*jiansheng*) were designated as "official households" (*huanhu*). Such households were exempted from regular labor (*ding*) and miscellaneous labor imposts (*chai*); furthermore, they enjoyed special privileges in the payment of regular land taxes not shared by commoner households. Such exemptions commonly provided such households with additional financial benefits: by offering to serve as proxies for their kinsmen or other commoners, "Confucian scholar households" and "official households" could assist others in evading a portion of their tax burden, while pocketing some additional funds for themselves.[14] In the second year of his reign, Yongzheng issued a stern edict resolutely forbidding such practices, and ordered provincial governors and governors-general to abolish these designations. Two years later, the exemptions were further limited to the individual degree-holders themselves, subjecting all other adult male members of "Confucian scholar" and "official" households to the labor imposts.

Yongzheng's attempts to legislate new norms of conduct for members of the gentry both inside and outside officialdom represented an affront to

---

13. As cited by Feng (1985), pp. 143, 146.
14. Ch'ü (1961), pp. 173–90; Hsiao Kung-chuan, *Rural Control in Imperial China* (Seattle: University of Washington Press, 1960), pp. 124–39.

the ideals of liturgical governance propounded by Gu Yanwu and other prominent theorists associated with the *fengjian* tradition, which extolled the virtues of limited political decentralization and advocated an expanded role for lineage and kinship organizations. While proponents of "feudal localism" advocated the strengthening of local social institutions as a way of fostering a social order that would complement, rather than compete with, the structure of the imperial state, local gentry activism was sustained by the very mechanisms Yongzheng sought to curb. The practice of proxy tax remittance that served as a method of self-engrossment at the expense of commoners also protected one's less fortunate kinsmen from the predations of the central state. The filing of petitions and lawsuits could be used to intimidate one's neighbors into compliance, or to protect local interests and resolve potentially destabilizing social conflicts. Thus, many literati saw the state-building measures by which Yongzheng relentlessly pursued political corruption as harbingers of a looming and despotic imperial state. Following in the wake of the Ming collapse, the re-concentration of political power in the center roused the rightful resistance of localist forces, particularly in the Jiangnan region, the ancestral home of several of the academies that promoted increased gentry activism.[15]

CONTESTING CORRUPTION IN JIANGNAN

Yongzheng's intensive investigation of local finances came relatively late to Jiangnan, where memories of his father's early prosecution of gentry tax evasion were still vivid, but revealed arrears on a scale unmatched elsewhere in the empire. In 1725, the third year of Yongzheng's rein, Jiangsu Governor Zhang Kai memorialized that during the period from 1712 through 1723, of all the counties and departments in the province, only 2 had no deficits; 4 had deficits totaling a few hundred taels; and the remaining 47 owed an estimated 7,000,000 or so in unpaid taxes, having paid less than half of the actual taxes due for several years in row. As to how such a large deficit had been allowed to accumulate, Zhang pointed the finger squarely at the obstructionist tactics of local magistrates and their staffs.[16]

As the teams of auditors, many of whom expected to be officials

---

15. See Kai-wing Chow, *The Rise of Confucian Ritualism in Late Imperial China: Ethics, Classics, and Lineage Discourses* (Stanford: Stanford University Press, 1994), particularly chap. 3. On the concept of "rightful resistance," see Kevin J. O'Brien and Li Lianjiang, "Rightful Resistance," *World Politics* 29:1 (1996): 31–55.
16. Dated YZ 3/09/05. Diyi lishi danganguan bian, *Yongzheng chao hanwen zhupi zouzhe huibian* (Chinese vermillion endorsements and edicts of the Yongzheng emperor) (Nanjing: Jiangsu guji chubanshe, 1989), vol. 6.

themselves, pressed on with their investigations, public protests and demonstrations became increasingly common. Zhejiang Governor Fahai suggested that the "evil people" behind such incidents were in fact none other than local degree-holders, many of whom had successfully tested at the provincial level but who had not received their posts. Teaming up with village gentry and local ruffians, these "evil people" incited tax resistance and other unlawful acts. Local magistrates faced with this type of organized opposition tended either to give way to the wishes of the wealthy and powerful, or to excuse arrears and hope to pass the burden of debt on to their successors. Fahai lamented that only a handful of officials, including the Wuxi county Magistrate, Jiang Rirong, managed to rise above such temptations and to attack the problem of deficits in a responsible manner.[17]

Jiang Rirong, a native of Anhui's Jingde county, was recommended as an outstanding and distinctive magistrate at the conclusion of his first personnel review in Hunan's Liuyang county. Two years later, following an imperial audience, Yongzheng commented that he appeared "honest and sincere, sociable (*renwen*), and moreover firm and reliable . . . [but] if he should have hidden talents (*ancai*), that would be very good." As a token of appreciation for his service in Hunan, the emperor awarded him with a commemorative essay in which he elaborated on the virtues of good magistracy. "Magistrates are the parent officials of the people" (*qinmin zhi guan*), wrote Yongzheng, "and their most important [responsibility] lies in serving other people." The emperor warned that in governing the territory and peoples of a county, the local official had to attend to all of the numerous needs and requests pressed on him, as none were without significance. Good officials (*hao guan*) were truly sincere, and moreover they cherished the common people. Upon arrival at a new post, they endeavored to familiarize themselves with the local ways by frequently leaving the yamen to meet their subjects. They were stern and forgiving in appropriate measure and could not be easily hoodwinked by the machinations of those who would importune them for tax forgiveness and special privileges. Finally, upright officials were of sound moral character, with a desire to serve the public good, and did not fall prey to the lure of trickery for purposes of private engrossment.[18] Jiang was subsequently transferred to Wuxi county, in the heart of the Jiangnan region.[19]

---

17. Zelin (1986), p. 229.
18. *Anhui Jingde xianzhi* (Anhui Jingde county gazetteer), (Jiaqing 13) [1808]. Reprinted in 1925, *juan* 10, *zaji puyi lei*, pp. 1456–60.
19. The date given for the imperial audience by Jiang's home county gazetteer is YZ 6/3/9,

The differing accounts in official documents and local historical sources of Jiang's magistracy in Wuxi reflect the fundamental contradictions between the normative agendas of central state-making and local elites. As an agent of imperial authority, Jiang was charged with the duty of making good on the long-standing arrears amassed by the residents of Wuxi county. His effectiveness as a magistrate was measured primarily by his accomplishment of two strategic tasks: the collection of taxes and the maintenance of public order. Neither task could be undertaken without some cooperation from members of the local literati, both those working inside as well as outside the local yamen.

Yinjishan, a Manchu bannerman who was appointed acting governor-general of Jiangsu as the tax-clearance investigation began, memorialized the emperor to express his frustration with the people within his jurisdiction, citing the recent upsets in Wuxi county as one example of the truculent behavior he found typical in the region. Referring to the inhabitants of the entire Jiangnan region as "cunning" and "untrustworthy," Yinjishan complained that despite the fact that tax arrears continued to pile up, the local people preferred to employ various stratagems to avoid paying off the debt. Furthermore,

In the second month of this year [1728], the Jiading county magistrate, Zhu Erjie, initiated an investigation into the long-standing tax deficits [there]. Evil people beat a gong to alert [the inhabitants of one village] and incite them to cut down the suspension bridge [leading to the village]. During the sixth month,[20] the Wuxi county magistrate, Jiang Rirong, punished debtors [by forcing them to] wear the cangue. Evil people caused a commotion in the hall of the yamen, making off with the prisoners. In resisting arrest, they burned [government] boats. I, your loyal minister, have already ordered a serious investigation [of this matter and] the arrest of the chief culprits. These criminals have been captured by the local authorities and I am now awaiting the results of the official inquiry into this matter.[21]

The results of the official inquiry are recorded in the imperial archives, under the confessions of criminals convicted of serious offenses during the Yongzheng period (*zhongqiu zhaoce*).[22] More than a year after the skirmish

---

or April 17, 1728. Ibid., p. 1456. However, his vita, which records Yongzheng's comments, is dated YZ 7. *Diyi lishi dang'anguan, yinjian lülidan*, YZ 7/7.

20. During the sixth year of Yongzheng's reign, 1728, the sixth lunar month began on July 7 and ended on August 5, according to the Western calendar.

21. Dated YZ 6/11/9. Diyi lishi danganguan bian (1989), vol. 13.

22. The original document is no longer available for viewing, but a reprinted excerpt appears in *Kang Yong Qian shiqi chengxiang renmin fankang douzheng ziliao* (The resistance struggles of urban and rural peoples during the Kangxi, Yongzheng, and Qianlong reign periods), ed.

occurred in Wuxi, Jiangnan Board of Punishment investigators assigned final responsibility for the incident to three Wuxi county residents: Yan Bocheng, age 49; Wang Shian, age 44; and Tai Tiansheng, age 36. According to investigating officials, in his effort to collect taxes that year, Magistrate Jiang Rirong subjected to the cangue a handful of local rogues (*diwan*) who were behind in the payment of their taxes. A kinsman of one of those being punished organized a band of villagers to press the magistrate into extending the deadline on the grounds that the method of prompting taxes that Jiang had devised imposed too heavy a burden on local farmers. In particular, local residents claimed that the drought had long since dried up the water in the village's irrigation system, and many farmers had resorted to the time-intensive technique of bucket-baling (*hu shui*) to save their crops, leaving little time for tax-prompting. However, when the supplicating villagers gathered outside the yamen gates, Magistrate Jiang was in the process of adjudicating another complaint, leaving the petitioners, along with those being punished in the cangue, outside the yamen gates. When he failed to emerge, Tai Shenggao, Yan Bocheng, and Wang Shian pried open the cangue, freeing Tai Tiansheng and the others, which created a commotion. All took flight.

Upon hearing of the escape, Magistrate Jiang issued an arrest warrant for those involved, and ordered the constable to apprehend those responsible for the commotion. The constable and his men pursued the crowd, apprehending Tai Shenggao, one of the freed prisoners, and a few others. However, before they could make it back to their waiting boats, Wang Shian attacked the constable with a hoe and wounded him. In the melee, Tai Shenggao and others set fire to the three boats used by the constable and his men. All three were later apprehended and imprisoned. Jiangnan Board of Punishment officials sentenced Yan Bocheng and Wang Shian to be hanged in accordance with imperial law.[23]

Jiang Rirong successfully completed his three-year term of service in Wuxi county and in Yongzheng's ninth year was again commended for his service. The Board of Civil Office submitted his name for an audience with the emperor; his hometown gazetteer notes that he was subsequently promoted to department head (*zhizhou*) and transferred to Taizhou. As a token of gratitude for his continued service to the throne, the emperor bestowed upon him several gifts, including a brush (*sidai*) in

---

Zhongguo renmin daxue Qingshi yanjiusuo (Beijing: Zhonghua shuju, 1979), *shangce*, pp. 321–22.

23. Tai Shenggao, who was again apprehended, died in prison (*binggu*) before he could be sentenced.

acknowledgment of his efforts to "eliminate evil practices and [moreover] promote that which is profitable" to the empire.[24]

However, unofficial historical accounts present a somewhat different account of the events leading up to the burning of the police boats in Wuxi during the summer of 1728. According to one local account, tax-collection efforts in Wuxi had been adversely affected by natural conditions for several years prior to the arrival of Jiang Rirong, which had certainly contributed to the magnitude of the problem. A long-standing drought that began in the sixtieth year of Kangxi's reign afflicted Wuxi county, and lasted through the third year of Yongzheng, driving up the price of rice in the county. Two years later, the price of rice again rose precipitously for two years in a row, prompting the emperor to urge magistrates in the area to take measures to stabilize the price of rice. The speculation caused by rising prices allowed rich households in Wuxi county to increase their normal profits threefold and forced poorer households to stretch out over three days what used to serve as a day's worth of grain. "The rich became richer and the poor, poorer [until] the poor numbered in the hundreds for every one wealthy household."[25]

The strain on the local economy notwithstanding, soon after his arrival, Jiang Rirong attempted to exhort the debtors of Wuxi to make good on their long-standing arrears by employing a "rolling list" (gundan). His method involved compiling lists of households, along with a calculation of their annual tax burden divided into ten installments. The list was issued to the first household, which passed it on to the next on the list after paying its installment. The head of any household who failed to pass the list on to the next household was punished for creating an obstruction in the village tax-collection process.[26]

The "rolling list" was an innovation designed to avoid some of the earlier pitfalls of the old Ming lijia system, which rotated responsibility for local tax collection among adult males recruited from the ten largest households (jia) within a decimal unit (li). However, the lijia system quickly became dominated by "local strongmen and bullies" (haolie qianggun) in some areas; in other regions, eligible males avoided serving as the lizhang at all costs because the post traditionally not only involved prompting others to pay their taxes on time, but the holder of it also assumed responsibility for any unpaid arrears. Although the lijia system was officially used during the early Qing primarily for household registration, by the 1720s, abuses

---

24. Anhui Jingde xianzhi (Jiaqing 13 [1925]), juan 8, chenye lei, p. 1211.
25. Huang Ang, Xijin shi xiaolu (Taibei: Taibei shi Wuxi tongxiang hui, 1972 [1896]) p. 15.
26. Hsiao (1960), p. 96.

of the system had become so widespread that Yongzheng issued an edict to the governor of Jiangxi banning its use in tax collection:

The labor service imposts and land grain taxes are to be paid by the people in person. This is the established practice. We have heard that in Jiangxi province inhabitants of the *li* are required to "prompt" the tax payments. Each of the ten *jia* in the *li* serve by one-year turns. . . . Making petty villagers render this service not only exposes them to the exactions of corrupt yamen clerks but also forces them to neglect their farming, owing to the necessity of running about [in order to carry out the duty thus imposed upon them]. . . . Investigations shall be immediately made and the said practice be generally abolished.[27]

Yet local records noted that Magistrate Jiang Rirong combined the "rolling list" method with the appointment of a *cuitou*, or "prompting chief," who, like the *lizhang*, was held accountable for the tax burden of several households. Although in principle meeting one's household's tax burden was supposed to remove one's name from the list, Magistrate Jiang apparently neglected to see to the removal of names from the list. A few of the designated "prompting chiefs" continued on in their role throughout the summer, threatening punishment for those below them on the list, and engaging in blackmail.

The combined pressures of suffocating heat, the lack of rainfall, and the new oppressive tax-collection method took their toll on the county residents, and "caused their hearts to become restive to the point of rebellion."[28] With frustrations mounting, more than 100 residents of Fuan village gathered outside the county yamen. Bearing sticks of burning incense, they enjoined Magistrate Jiang to offer up prayers for rain in order to break the drought. Jiang, however, failed to emerge from the building, angering the crowd. Breaking open the granary, the residents made off with much of the granary's contents. For good measure, they used a broken stone tablet to block the yamen's middle gate.

Waiting until the commotion subsided, Jiang dispatched his runners to chase down the perpetrators. They managed to catch one or two laggards in the crowd, whom they interrogated in an attempt to discover the identity of the ringleaders of the band. Seizing their unfortunate victims, the guards planned to drag them back to the yamen when the crowd turned to confront them. Some of the villagers began beating a gong to protest the arrest of their fellow townsmen. In the scuffle that ensued, one or more of the runners were wounded; the boats they had boarded to chase down the

---

27. *Shizong shengxun* (Proclamations of the Yongzheng emperor), 15/7a–b. As cited by Hsiao (1960), p. 102.
28. Huang Ang (1972 [1896]), pp. 176–77.

crowd were destroyed and the runners "scurried back [to the yamen] like rats and vermin." In the end, the one or two unfortunate villagers who were captured from the rear of the retreating crowd each received a heavy flogging at the hands of the magistrate, who hastily (caocao) brought the case to a conclusion.[29]

The discrepancies between the two accounts are suggestive not only in their respective attempts to exonerate and blame but also in their divergent evaluations of state power in the local setting. The narrative reconstruction of these events that appears in the Board of Punishment documents specifically interpellates three residents for having "incited a disturbance, engaged in theft, [and] burned boats" in their attempt to evade the authorities, and lists the underlying cause for the disturbance as public resistance to Jiang's rightful use of the cangue to punish tax evaders. From a local perspective, however, Jiang failed to adequately supervise the tax-collection process, allowing unsavory "prompting chiefs" to extort law-abiding taxpayers listed beneath them on the tax rolls. His lack of responsiveness to local needs was further evident in his failure—or refusal— to address the supplicating crowd of villagers who gathered outside the yamen gates, and was suggested as well in his hasty resolution of the case. Significantly, the unofficial version of events in no way contests the right of the state to collect taxes, to make good on past arrears, or to punish tax evaders; rather, the critique focuses on the failure of the magistrate to thwart the predatory activities of a handful of local "prompting chiefs" and to protect honest taxpayers, thereby triggering unrest.

Variations on such themes are repeated time and again in unofficial accounts of local bureaucratic practices during the Yongzheng reign. Magistrates were most frequently lauded for their ability to maintain social order by refracting the moral authority of the imperial center and upholding the spirit, if not always the letter, of the law. Ideally, as non-natives of the areas in which they served and as agents of the central state, they served to mediate and avert potential conflicts at the local level between landlords and tenants, elites and commoners, and wealthy merchants and their customers. Thus, while local elites—wealthy landowners, local degree-holders, and retired officials—are often depicted as serving as brokers between the state apparatus of the early and mid-Qing and local communities, ample evidence suggests that, in fact, social elites looked to the local magistrate to fill this role by suppressing the potential for collective action among the vast and politically powerless peasant majorities, as well as by adjudicating relations between the new aggregations of local interests that were just beginning to

---

29. Ch'ü (1961), pp. 137–38.

appear on the social landscape in large numbers during the early eighteenth century. Localist sources on official conduct during the Yongzheng reign offer an anxiety-ridden discourse that combines flattering self-portraits of local literati serving as traditional moral exemplars in the neo-Confucian vein with expressions of apprehension about the role of new social coalitions ominously forming both inside as well as outside the familiar boundaries of local society. Increasing commercialization, urbanization, and social mobility threatened the dominance of traditional elites, many of whom looked to the state to maintain social stability and enforce common standards of behavior and practice that would serve to protect the established order. In contrast to the portrayal in official sources of the perpetual alliance between corrupt local officials and greedy landowners to defraud an unwitting public and deceive the imperial state, unofficial sources emphasize the crucial role played by magistrates in negotiating a rough balance of power among competing local interests, but furthermore underscore the moral authority of the literati to represent and speak for the greater public good.

BROKERING STANDARDS

The interests of local elites in regulating and maintaining social order coincided with the need of the early-modern state to standardize local practices of various kinds, including the logistics of measurement.[30] The imposition of a unified system of measures—for land, grain, and precious metals—was critical to the early Qing state's project of rendering local practices amenable to central control. The implementation of uniform measures greatly facilitated the management of large-scale commercial transactions and long-distance trade, and while the feudal prerogative of imposing local measures may have benefited established local landowners in remote regions, the rapid pace of economic development during the seventeenth and eighteenth centuries generated support among economic elites for standardizing practices for the collection of rents, levies, and commercial taxes. In addition, the long-term trend toward increased social mobility and the short-term effects of Yongzheng's liberation of the so-called "mean people" produced a growing sense that the common observance of uniform measures would contribute to social stability.

Localist hagiographies during the Yongzheng reign frequently lauded magistrates who either attempted to impose standard measures within

---

30. On the importance to state-building elsewhere in the world of simple and standard measures, see Scott (1998), pp. 25–33.

their jurisdictions, or who scrupulously observed uniform measuring practices in the tax-collection process. For example, during the ninth year of Yongzheng's reign, a group of poor tenant farmers in Guangdong's Qingyuan county led by Zhang Hongsheng applied to the county magistrate for assistance in adjudicating a dispute with a local landlord. Accusing the wealthy landlord of a lust for profit that drove him to perpetrate abuses (*xingli chubi zhi xin*), Zhang Hongsheng and the other tenants reported that the wealthy landlord had been using an inflated and non-standard grain measure (*dou*) in order to collect their rents and taxes, thereby increasing his profits. The magistrate discovered that this was indeed the case, and wrote to the landlord, forbidding him to use the inflated measuring device under threat of criminal charges. Not only did the landlord refuse to heed the magistrate's instructions, he increased the size of his measuring device again, to roughly double that of the standard measure. Zhang Hongsheng and the other tenants responded by contacting the provincial governor to report the abuse. For his part, the governor agreed with the tenants that the measure used for tax and rent collection ought to be of a standard size, but also pointed out that slight variations were not uncommon in the area and could be legitimately employed since the fertility of soil and the price of land in the area were also not uniform. The governor hastened to point out that the rents in Qingyuan county were unusually low and that the landlord was collecting only three-tenths of the total harvest as rent (whereas four-tenths of the harvest was common in other areas). Citing the need to maintain the local established order, the governor-general refused to intervene further; the local magistrate, however, was commended in the Qingyuan county gazetteer for using his own authority to apply for redress in the matter.[31]

Similarly, unofficial narratives frequently lauded local magistrates who were scrupulously honest in observing tax-collection rules. For example, Hao Zhen was appointed magistrate of Jiangsu's Xinghua county in the seventh year of Yongzheng's reign, but served only five months of his term before he was removed on corruption charges. Hao was eulogized in local records for having always made certain to level off the grain-collection boxes during the autumn collection of tribute grain for transport to the capital (*caomi*), thereby ensuring that he took from the peasants only precisely the amount of rice that was required, and no more. The assistant magistrate (*xiancheng*) in the district requested permission to levy an additional tax (*caogui*) to offset the cost of transporting grain to the capital. Magistrate

---

31. *Qingyuan xianzhi* (Qingyuan county gazetteer) (Guangxu reign, date incomplete), *shou juan*, pp. 15-16. Beijing University Library Rare Book Collection.

Hao refused, citing the imperial edict banning the unauthorized collection of wastage allotments. According to the local gazetteer, the assistant magistrate retaliated by filing a complaint against him, asserting that Hao refused to use level measures and had been embezzling the excess grain. According to the gazetteer, the local people were so outraged when they heard about the false accusation that they assembled in the streets, wailing in grief and protest. When Hao Zhen's temporary replacement arrived, the residents refused to allow him to enter the county seat, and used farm implements to jam the city gates shut from the inside, refusing passage to the new magistrate and his retinue. Seeing the commotion, Magistrate Hao purportedly emerged from the yamen and addressed the crowd, saying: "What good have I done for the people here that you are so loyal to me? The new magistrate is a good man; you will not miss me. But if you continue to block the city gate, it is of no use to me, and no good is bound to come of it." Upon hearing this, the crowd removed their tools and opened the gates to the new official. However, the former magistrate was so well loved that the local people built him a small house at their own expense alongside the western wall of the yamen, where he lived during the investigation of his case. While he awaited the final results of the investigation, each day local residents provided him with food at their own expense and attended to his needs. One evening, a rumor spread throughout the city that the former magistrate had left the county, and the local residents streamed out of their houses, pouring into the streets in confusion and dismay. A large group of concerned residents went to Hao Zhen's small home on the west side of the yamen in order to determine if he in fact had left; however, peeking through the windows, they saw that he was still inside, much to their relief. The rumor was thus dispelled, and the crowd quietly dispersed without disturbing the beloved Hao Zhen. In the end, Magistrate Hao was cleared of all charges, reinstated, and transferred to serve as the magistrate of another county. On the day of his departure from Xinghua, it was said that the county residents turned out in great numbers to see him off, and trailed behind his sedan chair, weeping and wailing inconsolably.[32]

The Yongzheng-era magistrate Chen Mengwen of Hunan's Liuyang county found that more than 300 former land-owning families in the county had been forced to sell off their lands to make up past arrears and were laboring as tenant farmers to make good on remaining back taxes. After looking into the county land registers, Chen Mengwen discovered that previous magistrates had failed to use the proper graduated scales in the

---

32. *Xinghua xianzhi* (Xinghua county gazetteer) (Tongzhi reign, date incomplete), 3 *juan*, p. 15. Beijing University Library Rare Book Collection.

assessment of land taxes, which were calibrated to reflect the quality of the land owned by each taxpayer. The oversight resulted in the overpayment of taxes by many county residents for several years, forcing them into abject poverty, while at the same time encouraging land speculation among wealthier members of the community. According to the local gazetteer, Magistrate Chen immediately undertook a complete investigation of all the lands that had been bought and sold in the county for the previous several years, resulting in the return of some lands to their original owners. He furthermore posted public notices around the county notifying taxpayers about the calibrated system of calculating the land tax and was celebrated not only for his enforcement of the graduated scales but also for his redress of past wrongs.[33]

Many unofficial accounts stress the importance of uniform measures and standard tax rates in maintaining social order. For example, one unofficial account records two incidents of collective violence spurred by the collection of inflated meltage fees in Shanxi. During Yongzheng's second year, the magistrate of Wanquan county imposed a meltage fee (huohao) that was considered extremely high and therefore unjust by county residents, who accused him of excessive cruelty. More than 1,000 county residents surrounded the city and then burned down the yamen when he refused to lower the fees; the magistrate and his staff barely escaped with their lives. The outraged residents refused to open the city gates until the prefect (taishou) intervened and was able to arrange a settlement with the community leaders. In another poverty-stricken Shanxi county, the magistrate also attempted to impose an inflated meltage fee on the residents of Jianfen, but met with considerable resistance. When he would not hear the appeals of local taxpayers, they broke down his door and in a frenzy tore off his clothes, as well as the clothing of his family members.[34]

It is perhaps not surprising that many localist narratives attribute the adoption of new standards or the implementation of reforms to magistrates when in fact imperial authorities decreed such changes. Many Yongzheng-era magistrates were acclaimed in local histories for either abolishing "customary fees" (lougui), reducing the meltage fees (haoxian), or abolishing the custom of appropriating the salaries of their underlings (juanfeng) to make up for deficits or to carry out public works projects. The Guangdong Xinghua county gazetteer credits a Yongzheng-era magistrate there for

---

33. *Liuyang xianzhi* (Liuyang county gazetteer) (Jiaqing 23), *juan* 36, *yiwen lei*, pp. 85–86. Beijing University Library Rare Book Collection.

34. Wang Jingqi, *Dushu tang xizheng suibi* (reprint) (Shanghai: Shanghai guji chubanshe, 1995), pp. 38–39.

abolishing the *lijia* system for the purposes of tax collection originally instituted under the Ming.[35] However, in many cases, such accounts also convey anti-bureaucratic sentiments, as when local gazetteers recount how a particular magistrate or prefect put forward a proposed reform for the good of the local people, only to be cashiered and punished for his impudence. When Chen Jirang arrived at his new post in Tongren county in Guizhou, he found that the meltage fees (*huohao*) being charged were excessively high. Hoping to relieve some of the tax burden placed on county residents, Magistrate Chen petitioned his superior for permission to lower the county meltage fees. Not only was he refused permission to make the requested changes, he was relieved of his post as a result of his impudent request.[36] Feng Yong, former magistrate of Dantu county, was remembered in the local gazetteer for having established an orphanage for children in the county following a famine. However, the account notes that apparently he ran afoul of the local gentry as a result of his "public-spiritedness," and they had him transferred to a remote and desolate county in Guizhou populated by a local Miao group that practiced ritual cannibalism. Shortly thereafter, he received notice that he had been cashiered, apparently for having "shifted funds" to cover the costs of building the orphanage. Having sold his family property, Feng returned penniless to Dantu, where a handful of local residents took pity on him and built him a small hut beside the local school. He spent the rest of his days there in abject poverty, composing poetry and leading a solitary life.[37]

The misattribution of particular reforms to local magistrates was not merely an attempt to extol local talent, it also represented an attempt to demonstrate the depth of the commitment of members of the literati to the public good. For example, early in his reign Yongzheng decreed the restriction of gentry exemptions on labor imposts, which was unpopular enough to have triggered an uprising in Henan during which more than 100 degree-holders barricaded themselves in the county seat, and culminated

35. *Xinghua xianzhi* (Xinghua county gazetteer) (no date), 3 *juan*, p. 15. Beijing University Library Rare Book Collection.

36. Chen Jirang was later promoted several times during Qianlong's reign. *Shanyin xianzhi* (Shanyin county gazetteer) (Jiaqing reign, no date), *juan* 15, *xiang chen lei*, p. 32. Beijing University Library Rare Book Collection.

37. *Jinqi xianzhi* (Jinqi county gazetteer) (Daoguang 3), *juan* 14, *wenfan lei*, p. 16. This gazetteer notes that he was in fact cashiered due to the machinations of rich and influential residents of Dantu county (*haoshi wei suozhong ba*). His preface, while specifying the time of his impeachment, does not give the reason. See Feng Yun, *Kaizhou zhi* (Kai department gazetteer) (Yongzheng 5), *xun*, p. 1. The information on the ritual cannibalism practiced by the Miao peoples in Kaizhou County is found in *juan* 4, in an essay penned by Feng Yun, *fengsu lei*, p. 24.

in a boycott of the county exams.[38] Nevertheless, several local gazetteers recount the willingness of local degree-holders during the Yongzheng reign to participate voluntarily in corvée labor projects shoulder-to-shoulder with commoners. Zhu Yuanfeng, from Anhui's Tongxiang county, who expected to be an official, was initially dispatched to Huating county during the audit of the Jiangnan region to help clear accounts there. Shortly before his arrival, a disastrous high tide swept parts of the county, and Zhu is lauded by his home gazetteer for having helped to organize local residents and officials in a joint effort to dig ditches to help drain off the excess seawater, and even donated his salary to the poor families who had lost their homes so that they might rebuild their houses.[39] Shen Jiazheng was acclaimed for participating personally in land-reclamation projects alongside his yamen underlings as magistrate of Shanxi's Leping county. Like Zhu Yuanfeng, Magistrate Shen also donated his salary to the landless residents of Leping county and assisted them in purchasing fields and cows and in building houses, thereby reportedly winning over many who had once been bandits and thieves.[40] In the summer of 1728, when Lu Feixi, the newly appointed magistrate of Anhui's Changshan county, arrived at his post, he found the area deeply afflicted by an over-abundance of rainfall and periodic flooding. The Lu clan genealogy records that Magistrate Lu personally spent all day every day at the banks of the river, making sure the dikes were sound and that no one's fields were threatened by the rising waters.[41] Jiangyin county magistrate Zhang Jin volunteered to stay on at his post while he awaited his transfer promotion to Songjian prefecture. As the magistrate of Jiangyin county, he worked tirelessly to repair the local irrigation system in order to prevent the frequent flooding that plagued the county; on the day before his transfer to Songjian prefecture, the former magistrate bought meat and wine for the local water-control workers and their families, and furthermore donated a portion of his salary to them so that they would be able to complete the irrigation project then under way.[42]

The discursive denial of difference between members of the gentry and the common taxpayers they served in their official posts can be read as

---

38. Feng (1985), pp. 169–71; Zelin (1984), pp. 103–5.
39. *Tongxiang xianzhi* (Tongxiang county gazetteer) (no date). Beijing University Library Rare Book Collection.
40. *Shanyin xianzhi* (Shanyin county gazetteer) (Jiaqing reign, no date), *juan* 15, *xiang chen lei*, p. 32. Beijing University Library Rare Book Collection.
41. *Zhejiang Tongxiang Lushi zongpu* (Zhejiang Tongxiang Lu clan genealogy) (Qianlong 54) *mingchen lei*. Beijing University Library Rare Book Collection.
42. *Shanyin xianzhi, juan* 15, *xiang chen lei*, p. 31.

an attempt, at some level, to build a narrative framework to support a tradition of voluntary gentry activism that transcended the narrower limitations of service to the state. Within the broader historical context, since the late Ming, activist literati had been advocating the establishment of a variety of institutions, including lineage organizations, benevolent societies, and religious associations capable of transcending economic and vocational distinctions that might reduce conflict and contribute to social stability.[43] Models of bureaucratic conduct that evinced a spirit of voluntary cooperation between local communities and officials at the margins of the state contributed to the development of larger frameworks of local identity-formation, including narratives of the local past that presented the locale as a higher source of moral authority than the state, which ultimately relied upon force of law and the threat of coercion.

GRAIN-BASED NARRATIVES OF VIRTUE

Whereas localist genealogies of virtue and venality on the whole tended to complement, rather than contest, the moral authority of the state, when the normally overlapping spheres of shared interests in social and economic stability were threatened by local disasters or other extraordinary events, the competing loyalties of local officials were tested. The stories of local officials who sided with residents of the local communities they served, over and against the explicit orders of central state authorities in Beijing, often appear in local and unofficial historical accounts and are recorded in such a way as to suggest that they constitute a virtually separate genre of hagiographical writing. Collectively, these narratives pit the immediate needs of the local community against the impersonal and unfeeling bureaucratic authority of the central state machinery and depict the moral ambiguity inherent in the role of the local magistrate. As an agent of the central state, the magistrate was responsible for upholding—and following—the law within his district; but as a moral exemplar charged with the traditional Confucian mandate to "educate and nourish" the people within his district, a magistrate was confronted with the moral ambiguity inherent in the structural contradictions of the Qing state. Just as Yongzheng's instrumental use of corruption repositioned various agents and practices on the margins without addressing the structural source of this underlying moral ambiguity, localist genealogies of virtue underscored the bifurcation intrinsic to the state-making process under Yongzheng.

A prime focus of these state-making efforts was the control and

---

43. Chow (1994), pp. 73–80.

management of local grain stores. As noted in the previous chapter, Qing law and administrative codes strictly controlled such supplies, and magistrates who were unable to meet the stringent standards of granary management set by authorities in Beijing were subject both to administrative discipline and criminal penalties. In the case of natural calamity, it was the duty of the local magistrate to investigate the extent of the disaster and to file a preliminary report to his superior immediately; delays of any sort in reporting disasters were severely punished under the code of administrative regulations. Failure to report a disaster in the area under a magistrate's jurisdiction could result in his dismissal. Upon receipt of the local magistrate's preliminary report, his superior organized a team of investigators to visit the disaster site to evaluate the severity of the problem. Within 40 days of the conclusion of the investigation, the magistrate submitted a more detailed report on the nature and extent of the devastation, including estimates of the amounts and types of relief required. Local residents were to be classified into groups based upon their relief needs, and cards were dispensed that indicated the amount of relief from the government for which each household was eligible, depending upon the number of persons in the family. Moreover, the magistrate himself was to oversee the distribution of relief.[44]

The administration of disaster relief under the Qing was at best a laborious and complicated process, designed to be more effective at preventing local abuses than at quickly dispensing assistance to disaster victims. As Huang Liuhong, the author of one magistrate handbook, noted:

The essence of effective relief is that it must be administered at the onset of hard times before people are starving. . . . If the magistrate waits for all the symptoms of famine to develop and for reports of starvation to reach his ears long before he petitions his superiors, it will be too late. It takes a long time for superiors to memorialize the emperor, who refers the matter to the Board of Revenue, which, in turn, will issue a relief order. Official documents travel slowly and by the time the magistrate receives the order, most of the famine victims will have scattered in different directions, and many of them will have died on the roads. If the magistrate does not use the local grain reserves to save the lives of famine victims, he is no different from the person who keeps medicine in stock but refuses to give it to the sick.[45]

This dilemma did not escape the attention of county residents, who paid extraordinary tribute to those local leaders who risked their careers

---

44. Ch'ü (1961), pp. 159–61.
45. Huang Liuhong [Huang Liu-Hung], *A Complete Book Concerning Happiness and Benevolence: A Manual for Local Magistrates in Seventeenth-Century China*, trans. and ed. Djang Chu (Tucson: University of Arizona Press, 1984), p. 558.

and even their lives in order to attend to the needs of starving residents. Local and unofficial histories that record the deeds of such individuals portray the struggle as a moral drama that unfolded simultaneously on several levels: the life-and-death struggle of the local famine victims, the immediacy of local human needs versus the more remote exigencies of the central state bureaucracy, and the moral value of serving the people over that of fulfilling the demands of the central state.

Lu Feixi, former magistrate of Changshan county, arrived at his new post in the summer of 1728, amid heavy rainfall. Eventually, the continual and driving rains that summer led to extensive flooding, which destroyed that year's harvest and ultimately resulted in an area-wide famine. The new magistrate immediately notified his superior and awaited further instructions. However, as the crisis around him deepened, he found his yamen surrounded by silently beseeching hordes of victims. According to the local gazetteer, one day not long after, Magistrate Lu emerged from the yamen and went directly to the county granary, followed by a starving crowd of local residents. As he unlocked the doors of the county granary, a local resident in the crowd stopped him and warned him that if he failed to await the proper notification from his superior, he would place himself in grave danger. Facing the crowd, Magistrate Lu addressed them, saying: "But if [I] await the arrival of the [official] order, the people will already have starved to death long ago." Throwing open the doors to the county granary, he fed the people, who were so moved by his courage and his compassion that they wept openly in the streets. Unfortunately, the local gazetteer records that Lu Feixi was cashiered not long after for his failure to adhere to proper procedures in the management of granary supplies and found himself too poor even to arrange for transportation back to his home county. The local residents, still poverty-stricken themselves, collected enough money to send Lu back home, and he retired from officialdom.[46]

Wang Tingyin, who served as magistrate of Fujian's Xianyou county during the Yongzheng reign, saw his county through a major drought that led to widespread food shortages. When he opened up the ever-normal (*changping*) granary and started selling off the stocks at prices well below the market rate, his superior called him in for questioning. According to local accounts, Magistrate Wang replied that he had sold off the granary stores out of concern for the commoners in his district, who were unable to afford the escalating rice prices in the area. Wang Tingyin purportedly made his case so eloquently and so convincingly that his prefect not only refrained from disciplining him as he had originally

---

46. *Zhejiang Tongxiang Lushi zongpu, mingchen lei.*

intended but even recommended him for special commendation, despite his failure to observe standard procedures. Unlike the unfortunate Lu Feixi, Wang Tingyin was rewarded for his devotion to duty, promoted, and transferred.[47]

In the autumn of 1734, Zhili's Wuchang county magistrate Zhang Jia opened the local granary to feed hungry commoners after a series of floods caused a regional food shortage. According to the local gazetteer, Magistrate Zhang also addressed the hungry crowds, saying: "If [I] wait for orders from above, the people will have already suffered much by the time [the orders] arrive." Opening the granary, he immediately distributed relief grain, and was recorded to have thereby saved more than 10,000 Wuchang residents from imminent starvation. The local gazetteer records that when he took his leave of Wuchang county, so many residents accompanied his sedan chair along the road that led out of the county that the streets were clogged with well-wishers and his retinue was often unable to make forward progress.[48]

When heavy flooding in Rizhao county destroyed the harvest and led to a famine there, Magistrate Chen Yongjian applied to the provincial governor-general for relief funds. According to the local gazetteer, in the interim the magistrate convinced several wealthy families in the county to part with some of their private stores of grain in order to feed those less well off. However, fearing that the disaster victims would be unable to hold out until help arrived, he opened up the tax-storage chests before official permission was granted for him to do so and distributed more than 2,500 taels to starving families for grain purchases, thereby saving hundreds of lives. His biography in the local gazetteer also includes a brief couplet, apparently composed by Chen, entitled "Wangtai Village." In the poem, Chen retells the story of a brief visit he paid to Wangtai village, during which he came across a local woman crying pitifully in the streets because her husband had died and she had been forced to sell off her only child, a daughter. Deeply moved by her plight, Chen Yongjian literally sold the clothes off his own back and re-purchased the widow's daughter from the local family who had bought her. Having reunited the mother and her daughter, Chen himself spent the night in the streets of Wangtai, while "the rich feasted daily on meat and the faint strains of their music could be heard in the streets by the homeless poor." When he took his leave of Rizhao county at the end of his term of service there, the local residents

---

47. Ibid.
48. *Wuchang xianzhi* (Wuchang county gazetteer) (Daoguang 33), *mingchen lei*. Beijing University Library Rare Book Collection.

flocked around him and accompanied him all the way out of the county as a show of their love and respect.[49]

The foregoing narratives are part of a genre within unofficial discourse that represented an opposition that was simultaneously localist and loyalist with respect to the late imperial state. These accounts of Yongzheng-era magistrates who voiced heroic dissent in the face of power were modeled on the celebrated Confucian ideal of the loyal minister who sacrifices himself in order to save the state. At the same time, by relating the flouting of administrative procedure in opening local granaries and distributing their contents to those from whom it was originally collected, such tales pit the more immediate needs of the locale against the extractive machinery of the remote central state. Collectively, these grain-based narratives of virtue expose the same structural contradiction inherent in the early Manchu polity that Yongzheng's strenuous anti-corruption drive attempted to elide. By holding individual magistrates personally accountable for the treasury and granary deficits incurred by the semi-starved county and department yamens, he effectively shifted the normative boundary between the public and private realms in an ambitious expansion of normative, as well as institutional, power. Yet, as these narrative dramatizations suggest, the moral force behind such boundary-drawing exercises could cut both ways: if local magistrates truly were personally accountable for the consequences of the center's unwavering determination to starve the locale, then were they not also morally responsible for those acts of benevolent governance whereby the state was truly capable of fulfilling its mandate to educate and nourish?

TOWARD AN ETHNOGRAPHY OF THE LOCAL QING STATE

While the vigorous efforts of the Yongzheng emperor to reform local finances and granary operations unquestionably marked an important and innovative turn in the development of the modern Chinese state, their impact on the Qing state was a temporary one. The state-making efforts pursued under Yongzheng's leadership that set in place more rationalized, homogenized, and bifurcated modes of governance were abandoned, overturned, or benignly neglected by his son and successor in favor of a return to policies more in keeping with established imperial traditions. Eventually, over time, the program of "returning the meltage fee to the public coffers," which was designed to provide local administrations with

---

49. *Rizhou zhi* (Ri department gazetteer), (Qianlong 18), p. 33. Beijing University Library Rare Book Collection.

an independent source of funds for public works or routine maintenance, was more or less taken over by upper levels as a formal of legal tax, and counties and departments lost control over the resources.[50] The limitations placed on the privileges of local gentry were eventually abandoned, in practice, if not in law: Huang Ang, himself a holder of the first degree (*shengyuan*) and author of the localist account of Jiang Rirong's magistracy, noted that in Wuxi there were thirteen local degree-holders (*shengyuan* and *jiansheng*) during the Shunzhi and early Kangxi periods and seven in the late Kangxi period who "frequented the magistrate's court, controlled the yamen, and treated the common people as if they were [merely] fish and meat [to be consumed]"; nevertheless, throughout Yongzheng's reign, such gentry "did not have a poor reputation in the villages, and caused no mischief." However, by the early part of the Qianlong period, Huang suggests that such activities were once again becoming commonplace.[51]

Yet Yongzheng's robust, albeit short-lived, assertion of central government power to evaluate, control, and normalize the myriad fiscal and bureaucratic practices of local administration served to redefine temporarily the parameters of state control. His bisection of the complex fabric of local power, temporarily shifting the institutional bases that contributed to an alliance between local magistrates and local elites and reorienting the locus of power in favor of the court, certainly reversed the trend of his father's long reign and may have foreshortened what was to become a steady slide into corruption and divisive factionalism during Heshen's domination of the Qianlong court. The Yongzheng interregnum introduced a newly fortified boundary between local state agents and local social forces and managed to shift moral responsibility for transgressing that border to those political agents—magistrates, yamen personnel, local elites, and residents—that he positioned on either side of that divide.

---

50. See Zelin (1984), especially chap. 7; and Rowe (2001).
51. Huang Ang (1972 [1896]), 1.13b–15.

FOUR

Political Corruption and the Nationalist State

If the budget deficits of the early Manchu state provided the Yongzheng emperor with an expedient pretext for pursuing state-making reforms, the Nationalist leadership in 1927 required no such justification. By the beginning of the twentieth century, the combined pressures of rapid commercialization, increasing social mobility, and ballooning demographic growth hastened the erosion of the late imperial state into regional fragmentation and gentry-led militarization. The early promise of Yuan Shikai's constitutional republic quickly evaporated under his swift consolidation of political power and subsequent attempt to revive the monarchy as an instrument of rule. Following in the wake of more than a decade of exacerbating political fragmentation, economic volatility, and social instability under warlord rule, the apparent swift success of the Northern Expedition in reunifying the country generated a new sense of "optimism that verged on jubilation."[1] Buoyed by the rising tide of popular goodwill, the public reception of the Nationalist leadership was arguably the warmest welcome accorded any previous regime in Chinese history. As Lloyd Eastman noted in the opening lines of his classic study of the Nationalists in power, "The people wanted them to succeed."[2]

The flag of the new party-state, with the Nationalist Party symbol of a white sun in a blue field set against a red background, was a symbolic representation of the respective roles that party loyalty and national unity

---

1. C. Martin Wilbur, "The Nationalist Revolution: From Canton to Nanking, 1923–28," in *The Cambridge History of China*, vol. 12, *Republican China, 1912–1949*, pt. I, ed. John K. Fairbank and Denis Twitchett (Cambridge, Eng.: Cambridge University Press, 1983), p. 717.

2. *China Year Book* (1928), as cited by Lloyd Eastman, *The Abortive Revolution: China Under Nationalist Rule, 1927–1937* (Cambridge, MA: Harvard University Council on East Asian Studies, 1974), p. 1.

were intended to play in Nationalist state-building efforts. The late imperial state, with its multiple and discrete "realms within the realm," constituted a ritualized ethno-political order in which the Qing emperor served as the exemplary center of the civilized world. The five-bar standard of the early Republic, like the banner system of the Manchu state, represented a larger collective formed by drawing together ethnically distinct groups under centralized control. The new Nanjing-based regime rejected the early multiracial pennant as a "decrepit bureaucratic flag" in 1925 in favor of one that symbolically suppressed ethnic difference while simultaneously celebrating the victory of the majority Han people under the leadership of the Nationalist Party over the "tyranny of an alien race."[3] In place of the internal divisions of ethnicity represented by the early Republican standard, both the Nationalist and rival Communist parties conceptualized a social realm distinguished by identifiable sectoral interests that could be selectively incorporated into, and subordinated to, the larger interests of the new nation.[4] For the Nationalist Party, socioeconomic classes were social forces that could be mobilized to propagate a "politics of awakening . . . under the supervision of a highly disciplined, pedagogical state" that would bring unity, stability, and economic development to the nation as a whole.[5]

The mobilization and incorporation of these elements was to be overseen by the Nationalist Party through a three-stage process, from military to tutorial to constitutional government. The April 1924 Nation-Building Program of the National Government (*Guomin zhengfu jianguo dagang*) described the goal of the first stage as the "elimination of internal obstacles through the deployment of military force on the one hand, and the opening up of people's minds all over the country by propagation of [party] principles and the promotion of national unification on the other."[6] This first phase of martial law, during which all institutions would be placed under military administration, was to conclude with the cessation of military conflict and the complete pacification of society. During the

---

3. John Fitzgerald, *Awakening China: Politics, Culture, and Class in the Nationalist Revolution* (Stanford: Stanford University Press, 1996), pp. 180–85.
4. On the shifting meanings of "class society" in the Republic, see Michael Tsin, "Imagining 'Society' in Early Twentieth-Century China," in *Imagining the People: Chinese Intellectuals and the Concept of Citizenship, 1890–1920*, ed. Joshua Fogel and Peter Zarrow (New York: M. E. Sharpe, 1997), pp. 212–31.
5. Fitzgerald (1996), p. 3.
6. Zhongguo Guomindang zhongyang weiyuanhui dangshi weiyuanhui (Central Committee of the Nationalist Party's Committee on Party History), ed., *Guofu quanji* (Complete works of our founding father) (Taibei: Committee on Party History, 1973), vol. 1, pp. 751–53.

second phase, that of tutorial government, the party continued its control over the state apparatus in order to effect political, economic, and social reconstruction in preparation for self-government. The Nationalist Party promulgated its Program for Tutorial Government in October 1928, declaring that the third phase, that of constitutional democracy, would begin when all counties in a particular province had attained complete self-rule, a process that was expected to take six years. To facilitate the party's tutelage of both the nation and the state in the practices of constitutional democracy, a parallel system of party and state institutions was established in both the central and local governments, and Nationalist party cells were formed within all state administrative organs. The goal, as stated during the First Nationalist Party Congress in January of 1924, was not merely to "govern the state through the party" (*yi dang zhi guo*) but to "build the state through the party" (*yi dang jian guo*) in accordance with key Nationalist principles.[7]

Theoretically, the Nationalists' reorganization of political and social power was to occur through a simultaneous mobilization at the grassroots level and from the top down, through the creation of formal institutions at the behest of the party center. According to Sun's 1924 draft program, the administrative focus of party tutelage was the county (*xian*). Qualified cadres were to be dispatched to local government units in order to prepare both administrative organs and the general populace for eventual self-rule. The aim was to "train citizens in the exercise (*shiyong*) of their political rights," including the rights of suffrage, recall, initiative, and referendum.[8] Once all counties within a province had attained self-government, the phase of constitutional rule would formally begin; when more than half the nation's provinces were self-governing, the National Assembly was to promulgate a new constitution, the national government would be dissolved, and a new government that was elected by the people would take its place, signaling that the process of national reconstruction was complete.

However, in practice, the Nationalists' ambitious reorganization of local political and social power was exercised almost exclusively from the top down, through honing and elaborating the bureaucratic structure of the apparatus of the party-state. Over time, and under pressure from both

---

7. As cited by Fitzgerald (1996), p. 185.

8. From the preface of the Nationalist Party Central Committee resolution, October 3, 1928, formally establishing the period of tutelage, as reprinted in Zeng Jijun, "Shishi xunzheng yu junzheng jianshe" (The implementation of tutelage and the establishment of military rule), in *Zhonghua Minguo jianguo shi*, vol. 3, *Tongyi yu jianshe* (The history of the founding of the Chinese Republic, vol. 3, Unification and construction), ed. Jiaoyubu zhupian (Ministry of Education) (Taibei: Guoli bianyiguan, 1989), p. 807.

the Japanese and the rival Communist Party, the regime demonstrated a steadily diminishing tolerance for the independent exercise of local political initiative necessary for self-rule. The September 1928 County Organization Law divided local administration into specialized sections (*ke*) under the control of the county manager (*xianzhang*), and specialized county bureaus (*chu*) controlled by analogous bureaus (*ting*) under provincial control. The county manager served as the head of an executive council (*xianzheng huiyi*) consisting of the section and bureau chiefs; the budget and administrative performances of the executive council were to be monitored by an elected local assembly (*xian canyi hui*). All administrative organs below the local assembly were to be elected; however, until a locale had completed its preparation for self-governance, the county manager made appointments to such posts. The law also specified a new unit of bureaucratic control below the level of the county—the ward (*qu*), which could incorporate anywhere from 10 to 50 natural towns or villages and was viewed as a potential site for local self-government in the future, but was also placed under the "tutelage" of the county manager.[9] This distinctly corporatist reorganization of local governance structures, as Fewsmith has pointed out, delimited the realization of self-rule by pre-empting the autonomous formation of interest groups, occupying organizational space, and edging out rival associations, channeling the expression of interests to a narrow range defined by the regime, and compartmentalizing conflict so as to undermine broad class-based coalitions.[10]

While the extension of the formal bureaucracy below the level of the county was intended to consolidate local political power and resources in the hands of the state, in reality it had the opposite effect. County managers theoretically had the power to nominate the directors of specialized county bureaus (*chu*) under provincial control,[11] but in practice the supervisors of the provincial departments to which they reported controlled these appointments. As a result, bureau directors had powers roughly equal to those of the county manager himself, and could issue directives without the approval, or even knowledge, of the county director. Such practices applied even to the crucial county finance bureaus (*caizheng chu*), which,

---

9. Philip Kuhn, "The Development of Local Government," in *The Cambridge History of China*, vol. 13, *Republican China, 1912–1949*, pt. II, ed. John K. Fairbank and Albert Feuerwerker (Cambridge, Eng.: Cambridge University Press, 1986), pp. 344–45.

10. Joseph Fewsmith, *Party, State, and Local Elites in Republican China: Merchant Organizations and Politics in Shanghai, 1890–1930* (Honolulu: University of Hawaii Press, 1985), p. 191.

11. Paul Linebarger, *Government in Republican China* (New York: McGraw-Hill, 1938), p. 179.

over time, tended to serve the interests of the provincial administrations instead of the needs of the counties in which they operated.[12]

Local party branches also contended for power at the county level, pressing for parity in both rank and salary between party and government personnel, as well as preference in the assignment of posts within the bureaucracy. Party officials claimed the power to dispatch agents to conduct special investigations of county and sub-county personnel, tax-collection procedures, and audits of the county budget. In many areas, local party officials exercised de facto control over the state apparatus, issuing orders to their peers in government branches and offices. One Jiangsu resident charged that the personnel in local party branches consistently "act on impulse, raising hell (daodan) with the people, or raising hell with their peers in state offices, or raising hell with their own comrades. . . . They raise hell here, they raise hell there. There is no safe refuge from these conflicts."[13] In 1930, future chairman of the Legislative Yuan Sun Fo complained that local party branches had become "yamenized": acting as "negative, destructive, and secretive 'super-governments' preying on the administration and confusing the people." Party cadres retorted that it was the army and not the party that controlled local administrations, and that local administrations in turn controlled the party branches. Nevertheless, at their Fifth Plenum in June 1931, members of the Nationalist Party's Central Executive Committee proposed to grant district party congresses the rights of initiative and referendum, as well as the authority to select, supervise, warn, and dismiss local state officials as party members saw fit. Although the proposal was not formally adopted, party cadres continued to wield significant political power at the county level, in some areas eclipsing that of the state.[14] On the other hand, under certain circumstances county managers clearly had power sufficient to intimidate county party secretaries: in 1931, Hunan's Anxiang county manager Zhang Longjia was accused of soliciting a bribe from a county party branch official accused in the shooting death of a local resident in exchange for concealing his part

---

12. Philip Kuhn, "Local Taxation and Finance in Republican China," in *Political Leadership and Social Change at the Local Level in China from 1850 to the Present*, ed. Susan Mann Jones (Chicago: University of Chicago Press, 1979), pp. 124–25.

13. "Duiyu yiqian gexian dangwu gongzuo de guannian," *Jiangsu dangwu zhoukan*, no. 34, as cited by Zhong Sheng and Tan Senshu, "Shilun Nanjing zhengfu xunzheng qianqi (1928–1937) de difang dangzheng de jiufen" (On party-state disputes during the Nanjing government's early tutelage period [1928–1937]), *Shixue yuekan* (Historiography monthly), no. 2 (1999): 53.

14. Patrick Cavendish, "The 'New China' of the Kuomintang," in *Modern China's Search for a Political Form*, ed. Jack Gray (London: Oxford University Press, 1969), pp. 158–61.

in the crime.[15] In 1932 in Jiangsu's Ningxiang county, the local militia, operating on the orders of the county manager, arrested the members of the county party committee and searched their offices in a conflict that ultimately required the personal intervention of Jiang Jieshi to resolve.[16] The tensions between local governments and party branches in some areas were so pronounced that they occasionally erupted into armed conflicts for local dominance.[17] Even Jiang Jieshi himself was forced to admit within a few scant years of taking power:

> Party members fail to understand their obligations and are not well versed in their duties, to the extent that the established separation of powers between the party and state has been neutralized, and the scope of their respective functions is muddled. Apparently, the most common relationship between the party branches and the state offices below the provincial level is that the party wants to compete [with the state] by doing what the government is supposed to do, interfering with administrative personnel; and the state refuses to accept the party's supervision, appearing compliant but secretly rejecting [direction], to the extent that the party and state can neither coordinate nor cooperate, and are moreover pitted each against the other, mutually antagonistic.[18]

Whereas county magistrates during the Qing navigated a narrow course between the pursuit of maximalist aims and the practice of minimalist administration in service to the imperial will, local administrations under the Nationalists were challenged in a nearly opposite direction. The strenuous state-building efforts of the Nationalists produced a highly bureaucratized modern party-state ostensibly designed to mobilize social forces for self-rule that proved, in the end, structurally inadequate to the task of ruling itself, let alone to that of transforming the chaotic social environment dominated by local "cultures of violence"[19] into self-governing democratic units. The fragmentation of state power and functions into highly compartmentalized and often redundant administrative organs dispersed scarce bureaucratic and material resources in a manner that consistently served neither local

---

15. Yu Junxian, ed., *Guomin zhengfu jianchayuan shilu* (The veritable records of the Control Yuan) (hereafter, *JCYSL*) (Taibei: Jianchayuan mishu chu, 1981), vol. 2, case #58, pp. 404–11.

16. "Xiao Xuetai an shimo," in *Hunan wenshi ziliao xuanji*, vol. 7, as cited by Zhong and Tan (1999), p. 55.

17. Bradley Kent Geisert, "From Conflict to Quiescence: The Kuomintang, Party Factionalism and Local Elites in Jiangsu, 1927–31," *China Quarterly* 108 (December 1986): 680–703.

18. Jiang Jieshi, "Gaizheng dangwu yu tiaozheng dangzheng guanxi," in *Zongtong Jiang Gong sixiang yanlun zongji*, ed. Qin Xiaoyi (Taibei: Zhongyang weiyuanhui dangshihui yin, 1984), p. 15, as cited by Zhong and Tan (1999), p. 55.

19. Hans J. van de Ven, *War and Nationalism in China, 1925–1945* (New York: Routledge Curzon, 2003).

nor central, party nor state, elite nor mass interests. On a national scale, with a few noteworthy exceptions,[20] the cumulative effect in most locales was a sprawling, maximalist, bureaucratic party-state that proved effective at attaining only relatively modest political goals, and while central officials struggled to impose legal and institutional boundaries to define the scope of state power, they were frequently incapable of maintaining them. Although the failure of the Nationalist regime was due in no small part to the vast internal and external challenges they faced over the course of the Nanjing decade, like those of the Manchus before them, their state-building efforts were shaped by two conflicting, and ultimately contradictory, impulses: a commitment to social mobilization in preparation for self-rule under the principles of tutelary government; and the practical need to mold and channel those institutions produced by local processes of social mobilization. The former accorded varying amounts of political authority, economic power, and social legitimacy to a complex range of local actors with diverse and often conflicting agendas. The latter consumed the administrative and material resources of state agents in their ongoing attempt to monitor, police, and contain such individuals and groups. The net result was an increasingly competitive and chaotic "politics of survival"[21] waged between state and non-state actors at the local level that consistently undermined the capacity of the center to realize even its core tasks of national defense and social stability. The struggle of the Nationalist party-state to interpellate, monitor, and reposition these local agents on either side of the normative boundary projected by the center began with the pacification of social forces during the Northern Expedition, and, over time, consumed increasing levels of administrative and juridical resources following the establishment of the Nanjing-based government.

ADMINISTRATIVE DISCIPLINE AND CONTROL IN THE REPUBLICAN ERA

Three waves of institutional reforms initiated during the late Qing and early Republican era fundamentally altered the manner in which bureaucratic malfeasance was defined and prosecuted by authorities during the Nanjing

---

20. Julia Strauss argues that the Nationalists were surprisingly successful at building effective central government institutions during the 1930s, particularly in light of the challenging context within which state-building took place. Julia C. Strauss, *Strong Institutions in Weak Polities: State Building in Republican China, 1927–1940* (Oxford: Clarendon Press, 1998).

21. Joel Migdal, *Strong Societies and Weak States: State-Society Relations and State Capabilities in the Third World* (Princeton: Princeton University Press, 1988).

decade. In 1902, a court-appointed legal reform bureau (*falüguan*) proposed to eliminate the distinction between "public" and "private" crimes in the Qing legal code, permitting officials to be prosecuted for criminal conduct on par with commoners guilty of roughly equivalent acts. The same bureau also recommended that the system of legal privilege that permitted reductions in penal sentencing for civil and military officials under the "eight categories of persons deserving special consideration" (*bayi*) be repealed on the grounds that all Chinese citizens should be considered equal before the law,[22] and that any constitution should proceed from the "root principle" that public officials should operate within the boundaries of the legal code as opposed to remaining outside or above it.[23] A second set of reforms beginning in the early Republican period involved the adoption of Western and Japanese administrative models in order to control and modernize the Chinese civil service. Finally, the Nationalist government created a new central ministry to monitor, investigate, and discipline civil servants. Collectively, these three sets of reforms redefined the parameters of state control over public administration during the Nanjing decade.

Many of the changes proposed by the legal reform bureau of the late Qing were realized in the series of constitutions promulgated during the early years of the Republic. As early as March 1912, a provisional constitution drafted under the leadership of Yuan Shikai contained a "people's charter" that declared all Chinese citizens equal under the law and guaranteed them "the right to petition parliament or the executive officials, the right to institute judicial proceedings . . . [and] the right to bring actions against members of administration for violations of law."[24] Under the *Laws for Disciplining Public Officials*, promulgated in the third year of the Republic by presidential proclamation, the acceptance of bribes or embezzlement of public funds totaling more than 500 *yuan* were crimes punishable by death; official engrossment totaling more than 1,000 *yuan* that did not involve transgressions of the law was punishable by life imprisonment. Other disciplinary measures included official reprimand, reduction of salary, and reduction in rank.[25] A related 1918 decree added the "recording of misconduct" to the list of disciplinary measures outlined in the original

---

22. Joseph Kai Huan Cheng, "Chinese Law in Transition: The Late Ch'ing Law Reform, 1901–1911," Ph.D. dissertation (Brown University, June 1976); Marinus Johan Meijer, *The Introduction of Modern Criminal Law in China* (Batavia, Indonesia: De Unie, 1950).

23. L. R. O. Bevan, "China's Constitutions: Part I," *Chinese Social and Political Review* 2:4 (December 1917): 108–26. Parts II–IV appear in *Chinese Social and Political Review* 3:2 (June 1918): 153–86; 5:1 (March 1919): 42–82; and 5a:3 (September 1920): 200–24.

24. Bevan (1918), p. 165.

25. Lin Shantian, "Tebie xingfa" (Special penal laws), in *Zhonghua minguoshi falü zhi (chu gao)*

law between "official reprimand" and "reduction of salary," and gave
license to the head of the employing agency to suspend an official under
investigation.[26] These laws were revised again in 1921, mandating prison
sentences for government employees convicted of demanding or receiving
bribes or other usurious (*buzheng liyi*) behavior. Government employees
convicted of illegal and corrupt practices could receive prison terms up
to life imprisonment; court officials faced even more severe penalties, and
those caught absconding with public funds in excess of 5,000 *yuan* faced a
minimum sentence of life imprisonment.[27]

Nationalist Party leaders continued these trends, mandating in 1925 that
all civil servants take an oath prior to the onset of their appointment: those
who subsequently violated the oath faced dismissal, reduction in rank,
reduction in salary, or suspension from office.[28] An April 1928 version of
the order required all civil and military officials to raise their right hands
before the flag, to solemnly swear to devote themselves to public duty, and to
renounce "the pursuit of private gain, corrupt practices, and the acceptance
of bribes."[29] Reversing the imperial-era policy of preferential treatment for
those in office, the Nationalists mandated more severe punishments for
party members who violated the civil service oath, increasing the penalty
for party members by one degree. Party members guilty of counter-
revolutionary and subversive activities, private engrossment, or the
embezzlement of public funds in excess of 1,000 *yuan* were subject to the
death penalty. In addition, party workers who disobeyed party principles
and violated the law were permanently expelled from the party.[30]

In addition to instituting new disciplinary regulations, Republican
activists also sought to update and modernize the processes by which
public administrators were selected and trained. Western-style civil service
examinations were introduced immediately after the founding of the
Republican government in 1911, although the first round of exams was not
offered until five years later. Successful candidates were required to undergo

---

(Legal history of the Republic of China gazette [first draft]), ed. Guoshiguan Zhonghua minguoshi falüzhi bianzhuan weiyuanhui (Xindian, Taibei: Guoshiguan, 1994), p. 502.

26. Franklin W. Houn, *Central Government of China, 1912–1928: An Institutional Study*
(Madison: University of Wisconsin Press, 1950), p. 51.

27. Lin (1994), p. 502.

28. Wang Yongyin, ed., *Zhongguo lianzhengshi* (A history of honest administration in China)
(Zhengzhou: Zhongzhou gujie chubanshe, 1991), p. 269.

29. Guomin zhengfu fazhibu, ed., *Guomin zhengfu xianxing fagui* (Current government laws
and regulations) (Shanghai, 1929), chap. 3, p. 9.

30. Lin (1994), p. 505; Shen Guoqing, ed., *Zhongwai fanfubai shiyong quanshu* (Complete practical manual of Chinese and foreign efforts to fight corruption) (Beijing: Xinhua shuju, 1994),
pp. 301–2.

a period of probationary training, which under Nationalist rule involved both practical study and party indoctrination, followed by a second examination, before being assigned to their posts.[31] Policymakers in the Executive Yuan and the Ministry of the Interior strove to employ Taylorist principles and the tenets of scientific management to "raise administrative efficiency" as part of a larger strategy to "save the nation" (*jiuguo*).[32]

Finally, the Nationalists established a central ministry devoted to the task of administrative control. Sun Yatsen's original Five-Power Constitution envisioned that political power would be apportioned between the citizens of the republic, who were accorded the four rights of suffrage, recall, initiative, and referendum, and the state apparatus, which commanded the five powers of administration, legislation, adjudication, examination, and censorial control. The 1925 charter for the new Five-Power government drafted organizational principles for a Control Yuan (Jiancha yuan), which was charged with the duty of investigating the "behavior of (public) officials, the evaluation of tax collection [methods], and the purposes for which [such moneys] are used."[33] A September 1926 amendment expanded the power of Control Yuan officials to assign disciplinary measures, arrest public officials suspected of criminal offenses, pursue accusations made by private citizens, and prosecute cases against public servants.[34] For the purposes of investigation and surveillance, the country was divided into seventeen districts with a control commissioner assigned to each region. Control commissioners were required to spend at least six months conducting routine inspection tours within their respective jurisdictions and investigating charges and complaints lodged against officials in the region, but could extend the scope of their inquiries at will. The Control Yuan also housed the Ministry of Audit, which established branch offices in most provincial government offices and had broad powers to supervise the general execution of state budgets, as well as to inspect the accounts of operating departments at any time.[35]

However, in practice, the Control Yuan's powers were tightly constrained and depended heavily upon other state agencies over which it had little or no control, delimiting its institutional effectiveness.[36] The

---

31. Ch'ien Tuan-sheng, *The Government and Politics of China* (Cambridge, MA: Harvard University Press, 1950), pp. 235–40.

32. Strauss (1998).

33. Qian Ruisheng, *Minguo zhengzhi shi* (A political history of the Republic) (Shanghai: Shangwu yinshuguan, 1936), *shangce*, p. 223.

34. Shen Guoqing, ed. (1994), pp. 301–2.

35. Ch'ien (1950), pp. 265–76.

36. See, for example, Weng Youwei, "Nanjing zhengfu xingzheng ducha zhuanyuan zhidu

scope of cases that fell within the jurisdiction of the Control Yuan was defined by the *Civil Servants Disciplinary Law*, which also narrowly limited the range of possible penal action against public servants to dishonorable discharge, demotion in rank, reductions in salary, suspension from duty, the assignment of demerits, and the issuance of reprimands. The law furthermore strictly limited allowable penalties: for example, an official found guilty of a crime could have his status reduced only by one rank; salary reductions were limited to an amount between one-tenth and one-third of the official's monthly salary.[37] Recommendations for disciplinary action by the Control Yuan were first remanded to the Central Public Servants Disciplinary Commission (Zhongyang gongwuyuan chengjie weiyuanhui), founded in June 1931 under the auspices of the Judicial Yuan. The Central Disciplinary Commission typically reviewed the case materials prepared by Control Yuan officials but also conducted its own independent investigations before determining if disciplinary action was indeed warranted, as well as whether to heed the punishment guidelines suggested by the Control Yuan. Control Yuan officials could inquire about the status of cases but had no actual power to determine the outcome. Although in theory Control Yuan officials could promptly impeach or suspend public servants of any rank who were guilty of grievous misconduct, in actuality, impeachment orders from the Control Yuan were first handled and processed by the appropriate disciplinary body and then acted upon by an official's superior officer. In some cases, supervisors simply ignored impeachment orders.[38]

The process of routine evaluation was overseen by the Ministry of Personnel (Quanxu bu), which was housed within the Examination Yuan (Kaoshi yuan). The annual evaluation process of each civil servant involved the assignment of an overall grade by his immediate superior. According to the Ministry of Personnel evaluation forms, 50 percent of the assessment was based on work effectiveness, which included competence in "drafting documents," "managing subordinates," "willingness to accept responsibility," and "handling work properly." Administrative expertise accounted for 25 percent of the grade, measured in terms of "special achievements" and "experience"; and the remainder on the basis of deportment, as measured in terms of "diligence," "fairness," and "dependability."[39]

---

de fazhi kaocha" (Legal investigations under the Nanjing Government's system of executive supervisory commissions), *Shixue yuekan* (Historiography monthly) 12 (2004): 48–59.

37. Guomin zhengfu fazhibu, ed. (1929), chap. 3, pp. 1–3.

38. Ch'ien (1950), pp. 259–60, 268–70.

39. Strauss (1998), p. 40.

Despite attempts by the Ministry of Personnel to define national standards, extensive regional and provincial variations were common. County managers and their staffs frequently violated the Ministry of Personnel regulations on hiring and professional qualifications.[40] One 1934 report from the Ministry of Personnel found that in the 92 counties of Shaanxi province, more than 21 county magistrates failed to meet the minimum qualifications for county-level government employees, in large part because provinces observed disparate requirements for civil servants, and the matter of personnel policy was generally left up for individual interpretation by county and provincial governments.[41] Following a February 1931 executive order, in addition to the annual assessment, routine evaluations of county magistrates were to be conducted on a monthly basis. However, only 14 provinces submitted reports to the Ministry of the Interior that year, and only 18 provinces the following year, after which the practice was discontinued.[42] High turnover rates frequently undermined the integrity of the process: posts designated as "temporary" or "acting" (*daili*) assignments were exempt from the normal evaluation procedures, and powerful patrons used series of "temporary" posts to reward their underqualified clients.[43]

The links between the discipline and control mechanisms of the Nanjing-decade state were less directly related to the system of routine personnel evaluation than they had been during the Yongzheng reign. The Personnel Ministry, which oversaw the administration of the civil service, was housed in the Examination Yuan; the tasks of audit and discipline fell to the Control Yuan; and the adjudication of disciplinary measures to the Disciplinary Commission in the Judicial Yuan. The Personnel Ministry had no power to dismiss unqualified public servants, or those whose performance was deficient; neither the Control Yuan nor the Disciplinary Commission had access to routine personnel evaluation files. Thus, while the strenuous state-building efforts of the Nationalists produced impressively elaborate bureaucratic and legal structures to monitor and discipline public servants, the fragmentation and reduplication of relevant administrative offices

---

40. *Hebeisheng duiyu xiuzheng xianzhang renyongfa shishi chengxun* (Hebei province's prefacing remarks regarding the application of the revised personnel laws pertaining to magistrates), archive of the Neizhengbu (Ministry of Personnel archive), dated May 11, 1934. Number Two Historical Archive in Nanjing, PRC (#12–6879).

41. Xingzhengbu report to the National Government dated June 12, 1934. Number Two Historical Archive in Nanjing, PRC (#02–338).

42. Tien Hung-mao, *Government and Politics of Republican China, 1927–1937* (Stanford: Stanford University Press, 1972), p. 131.

43. Strauss (1998), p. 39.

both complicated and slowed its routine operations and provided ample opportunity for a wide variety of agents to obstruct, subvert, or otherwise frustrate the process. Moreover, this pattern of ambitious but ineffectual institution-building was repeated at various levels of the Nationalist party-state, resulting not only in the overcompartmentalization of state power and function in local governments as well as in many central ministries, but also in steeply rising administrative costs. Financing this vast and complex bureaucratic machinery presented a formidable challenge that weighed particularly heavily upon those at the lowest levels of the state, where the process of extracting the resources to fund successive waves of institution-building was a daily struggle.

BUILDING DEMOCRACY FROM ABOVE

The financial burden created by the Nationalists' state-building initiatives fell heavily on local administrations already struggling with substantial debts incurred as a result of heavy military expenditures over previous decades. Both the types and the amounts of taxes and levies collected by local governments rose during the early years of the Republic, but, following the establishment of the Nationalist regime in Nanjing, local tax burdens reached astronomical proportions in many areas. Kathryn Bernhardt's research on Jiangsu demonstrated a dramatic rise in total land taxes after 1927 due to the imposition of additional levies and surcharges (*fujiashui*); similar patterns have been documented in Guangdong.[44] In part to redress this problem, in the summer of 1927 the new Nanjing government passed the Provisional Act to Delimit National and Local Incomes and the National and Local Revenue Demarcation Act, which authorized local administrations to collect revenue from taxes on farmland, deed and mortgage taxes, commercial taxes, livestock, slaughtering and fisheries taxes, transportation fees, and levies on an additional six or seven types of transactions. However, provincial administrations retained the right to negotiate revenue-sharing agreements with lower-level administrations, and the provincial governments naturally claimed the lion's share of these funds. As a result, rising administrative expenses at the county and sub-county levels were generally funded by miscellaneous surcharges to the

---

44. Kathryn Bernhardt, *Rents, Taxes, and Peasant Resistance: The Lower Yangzi Region, 1840–1950* (Stanford: Stanford University Press, 1992), pp. 208–9; Chen Hansheng and Feng Fengyi, eds., *Jiefang qian de dizhu yu nongmin: Huanan nongcun weiji yanjiu* (Landlords and tenants before Liberation: research into the crisis in Huanan's rural villages) (Beijing: Xinhua shuju, 1984), p. 89.

land tax, acreage levies (*mujuan*), and provisional imposts (*tankuan* or *tanpai*), which began to multiply shortly thereafter.[45]

The Finance Bureau (Caizheng bu) responded by mandating that total surcharges on the land tax could not exceed the annual base tax, and that the combined total could not exceed one percent of the market value of the farmland taxed. However, no date was set for the implementation of this rule, and provincial administrations in any case had no way to ensure county compliance, and so surcharges continued to climb.[46] By 1934, only eight provinces officially collected fewer than 10 surcharges on the land tax; the Jiangsu provincial government, at the other end of the scale, collected 147 such surcharges.[47] The total revenues represented by these surtaxes ranged from just over twice those collected as base land tax in Henan, to 30 times the base tax in Hunan.[48] In addition, most counties, wards, and some villages levied separate surcharges, as well as assorted fees (*fei*), levies (*juan*), and provisional imposts (*linshi tanpai*) designed not only to fund specific development projects, but to cover routine administrative expenses as well.[49] In the districts surrounding Shaanxi's Wei county, the salaries of all public servants below the county level were funded either through provisional apportionments (*linshi tanpai*), land-tax surcharges, or surtaxes on the sale of specific items. In Wei county itself, such levies supported a staff of seven ward leaders (*quzhang*), the decimal unit leaders (*lizhang*) beneath them, and at the bottom tier, a layer of village headmen (*cunzhang*) or hamlet leaders (*zhuangtou*), who were in charge of tax and levy collection, each of whom claimed a cut of the revenue collected.[50] In one county in Jiangsu, a reform-minded local administrator complained that prior to his arrival, no fewer than 3,000 officials were supported by the proceeds of land-tax collection alone.[51]

---

45. He Taoyuan, "Lun tianfu fujia" (A discussion of land-tax surcharges), *Duli pinglun* (Independent commentator) 89 (February 25, 1934): 6; cf. Peng Yuxin, pp. 2–3.

46. Sun Xiaocun, "Kejuan zashui baogao" (Report on extortive levies and miscellaneous taxes), *Nongcun fuxing weiyuanhui huibao* (Rural Village Revitalization Committee bulletin) 12 (May 1934): 5–6.

47. Zou Fang, "Zhongguo tianfu fujia de zhonglei" (Types of surcharges on China's land tax), *Dongfang zazhi* (Eastern miscellany) 31:14 (July 1934): 312.

48. Zhu Qihan, *Zhongguo nongcun jingjide xiushi* (Perspectives on China's rural economy) (Shanghai: Zhongguo yanjiu shudian, 1936), pp. 226–27; Dong Ruzhou, "Zhongguo nongcun bengkui ji qi jiuji fangfa" (The collapse of China's countryside and some methods of economic recovery), *Jianguo yuekan* (Nation-building monthly) 8:4 (April 1933): 6.

49. Shen Lansheng, *Jiangnan caizheng luncong* (Collected essays on Jiangnan's fiscal administration) (Shanghai: Jinglun chubanshe, 1943), p. 40.

50. Xingzhengyuan nongcun fuxing weiyuanhui, ed., *Shaanxi sheng nongcun diaocha* (Investigation of rural Shaanxi) (Shanghai: Shangwu yinshuguan, 1934), pp. 145–46.

51. C. M. Chang, "A New Government for Rural China: The Political Aspect of Rural Reconstruction," *Nankai Social and Economic Quarterly* 6 (1936): 262

Not surprisingly, this swift and dramatic increase in the overall tax burden in turn led to mounting social unrest: most scholars of the Republican era concur that incidents of tax and rent resistance, protests, and acts of banditry rose steadily through the mid-1930s. Bernhardt's research indicates that incidents of collective action in Jiangsu more than doubled during the 1927–31 period compared to similar incidents from the previous four-year period; from 1932 to 1936, they nearly doubled again.[52] In addition to the escalating incidence of anti-fiscal agitation, conflicts between tenants and landlords escalated, and protests against involuntary conscription, looting, and rioting were also widespread.[53]

Caught in the vise created by increasing taxes and rising social unrest were the county managers (*xianzhang*), whose administrative performance was judged, as it had been in the imperial period, primarily upon their ability to collect tax revenues and to maintain social order. Their key role in ensuring the success of the Nationalists' state-building efforts was acknowledged by President Jiang in a 1932 address to local officials organized by the Central Bandit-Extermination Bureau in Hankou, who admitted that "the most important priorities rest on the shoulders [*shenshang*] of county managers":

We in the Nationalist Party, under the direction of Sun Yatsen, have taken the county as the unit of self-government, [and] under this provision, we have taken the position of our magistrates and raised it even higher [in importance]. The county is the basic foundation of our polity, and the manager is a basic cadre of our revolutionary government.

Hailing them as the "fundamental political force" (*zhengzhi de jiben liliang*) of the Nationalist government, Jiang enjoined county managers to preserve law and order, take preventive measures against flood and drought, and build public health programs to improve the quality of life for residents in their respective jurisdictions.[54] Yet the nature of the state-building efforts undertaken by the Nationalists had already significantly eroded the power of county governments by multiplying the numbers and functions of political organizations competing for power within a particular jurisdiction. With the intermittent introduction of ad hoc groups and commissions and the

---

52. Bernhardt (1992), pp. 216–17.
53. Lucien Bianco, "Peasant movements," in Fairbank and Feuerwerker, eds. (1986), pp. 270–73.
54. "Xianzhang shi zhengzhi de jiben liliang" (The magistrate is the fundamental political force), reprinted in Jiang zongtong yanlun yanbian bianji weiyuanhui, ed., *Jiang zongtong yanlun yanbian* (*yanjiang*): *tongyi shiqi* (*yi*) (President Jiang's [Jiang Jieshi] collected speeches and writings [addresses]: the period of unity [pt. I]) (Taibei: Zhengzhong shuju, 1956), pp. 114–20.

development of local party cells and affiliated organizations, the pattern of feverish institution-building continued to undermine the authority of local state managers over the course the decade, even as the central leadership redoubled its efforts to mobilize residents for the purposes of national reconstruction.

CULTIVATING NEW BOUNDARIES

The long-term goal of preparing citizens for eventual self-rule increasingly gave way to a more corporatist and militaristic model of governance in which mass mobilization was encouraged only for specific ends, and was tightly controlled by central authorities. In one February 1934 address, President Jiang invoked three terms—"training" (*jiao*), "cultivation" (*yang*), and "protection" (*wei*)—to represent the three cardinal principles underlying Nationalist rule. In order to achieve the first goal, that of training or tutelage, Jiang urged officials to expound the four ancient virtues of regulated demeanor (*li*), proper or just conduct (*yi*), integrity (*lian*), and conscience (*chi*) to the masses within the context of the party-led movement. "Cultivation" was to be realized in the clean, simple, and orderly manner in which one conducted one's daily life. "Protection" referred not only to the development of a community's ability to protect itself, but also to the larger sphere of militarization and martial values associated with self-defense: discipline, obedience, union, and solidarity. Returning to these themes two years later at a conference of higher-level administrative officers in Nanjing, Jiang added a fourth principle for administrative reform: control (*guan*). Without strong and decisive administrative control over the land, labor, productivity of the populace, and facilities of communication and transportation in a given area, the effective realization of the other Nationalist Party goals would be impossible. The fulfillment of his plan to revitalize the nation morally and to instill new life in the party hinged on centralization of political authority and the continued "pacification" of social forces across the nation.[55] Speaking before one audience of district-level officials about his plans to reinvigorate the country, Jiang acknowledged:

Perhaps everyone thinks that our personnel and resources cannot easily be moved [in these directions]; [but] if we administrators now wish to undertake [such projects], how can they be accomplished? . . . Everyone knows that if we wish to pacify our society, [good] governance is easy to promote, in accordance with

---

55. Ray Chang, "Trends in Chinese Public Administration," *Information Bulletin of the Council of International Affairs* 3:5 (Nanjing, 1937), pp. 100–101.

all that I have just delineated, as long as we ourselves first do not twist the law in order to obtain bribes (*tanzang wanfa*), do not listlessly engage in corruption (*weini fubai*), [but instead] create an incorrupt government that will again by way of personal character, spirit, and attitude transform the common practices [of our] people.[56]

The Nationalists' re-orientation of the goals of tutelage was reflected not only in newly framed normative expectations for local public servants but also in the disciplinary regime of the Control Yuan. In a 1931 speech commemorating the founding of the republic, Control Yuan President Yu Youren noted that whereas the local magistrate had long been hailed as "the parent-official of the people" (*qinmin zhi guan*), his Nanjing-decade counterpart, the county manager, should thenceforth also be known as the "the building-the-foundations-of-party-rule official" (*jianzhu dangzhi zhi guan*). A county manager demonstrated his competence by enthusiastically complying with the directives issued by the party-state, even if they contravened the more immediate dangers threatening the community over which he presided, including poverty, drought, and famine. By way of example, President Yu cited the case of a particular Shaanxi Shen county manager described by local residents as an ideal county official, "diligent, always working for the common interest, and close to the people." When pressed by his superiors in the provincial capital to raise additional revenues to fund military expeditions, he forcefully solicited the requested contributions even as the people in his county were faced with both severe drought and looming food shortages. The president of the Control Yuan lavishly praised the Shen county magistrate for his foresight in placing the long-term needs of the central government over the immediate needs of the people of his district and held him up as an exemplar to which all local Nationalist leaders should aspire.[57]

CORRUPTION CONTROL UNDER THE NATIONALISTS

The most common charges for which early Yongzheng-era magistrates were disciplined—tax and granary deficits (*kuikong*) and "shifting" public funds between accounts (*nuoyong*)—are notably absent in Nanjing-decade corruption cases. Instead, the majority of district officials named in the cases handled by the Control Yuan and Disciplinary Commission under

---

56. Jiang Jieshi, "Xingzheng renyuan zhuanjing ganbu zhi diwei yu zeren" (The position and responsibilities of administrative personnel, special police forces, and cadres), September 7, 1935, in Jiang zongtong yanlun yanbian bianji weiyuanhui, ed. (1956), p. 232.

57. See Yu Youren, "Xianchang yu zhuyi" (Magistrates and doctrine), in *JCYSL*, vol. 1, pp. 71–72.

Nationalist rule were charged with "twisting" or "violating" the law (*wanfa* or *weifa*), "delinquency" (*shizhi*), or "malfeasance" (*duzhi*). Republican law defined administrative crimes of "delinquency" (*shizhi*) as "acts that violate the rules and regulations governing the terms of service, or [other] improper measures," whereas "malfeasance" involved deliberate violations of criminal law.[58] In practice, because the penalties for the former were generally less severe, deliberate but relatively harmless violations of administrative procedures were generally treated as cases of misfeasance, whereas charges of malfeasance were reserved for serious and intentional violations of law. Crimes of malfeasance included demanding and/or receiving bribes, abusing one's authority to arrest or detain private citizens, the use of coercion in extracting a confession, the intentional arrest and/or punishment of an innocent person for a crime that he or she did not commit, mistreatment of prisoners, levying unauthorized taxes and fines, withholding revenue or goods from the central government, negligence, obstructing an official investigation, disclosing state secrets or information pertaining to national defense, or the abuse of office to allow, aid, or abet in criminal activities.[59]

The charge of corruption (*tanwu*, *tanlan*, or *tanmo*) represented a particular type of malfeasance in office. Corrupt and avaricious behavior referred to the siphoning off (*guaqu*) of public funds, extortion attempts against private citizens (*lesuo*), or the illegal appropriation (*qintun*) of public or government goods. The charge of corruption (*tanwu*) was frequently leveled in cases that involved the abuse of office for private ends, generally involving the use of unsanctioned violence against members of the public to extract money or goods or to coerce their compliance for non-state-related goals. When the pursuit of such aims endangered the welfare of private citizens, officials were charged with "transgressing the law and bringing disaster upon the people" (*weifa yangmin*), "dereliction of duty and harming the public" (*duzhi haimin*), "gouging and harassing the people" (*kejuan raomin*), or "corruption and tyrannizing the public" (*tanwu nüemin*). By and large, such cases stemmed from accusations that the officials in question levied excessive or illegal taxes or fees, and then resorted to force or the threat of force in order to ensure payment. Alternatively, officials were accused of "tyrannizing" or "bringing injury to" the public (*nüemin* or *haimin*) when they repeatedly mishandled criminal

---

58. Zheng Jingyi, *Falü daci shu (zengding zhongyin)* (Dictionary of law [enlarged and reprinted]) (Taibei: Shangwu yinshuguan, 1972), *shangce*, pp. 204, 2151.

59. Zhao Chen, ed., *Xingfa fenze shiyong* (Applied penal statutes), Zhongyang zhengzhi xue-xiao jiaofaguan xunlianban falü yeshu (Chongqing: Dadong shuju, 1946), *diyi fence*, chap. 4, "Duzhi zui," pp. 38–105.

investigations, murder cases in particular. In one such case, in 1933 Hubei's Yichang county manager Xiao Tiegong was charged with "transgressing the law and bringing disaster upon the people" (*weifa yangmin*) by both angry local residents and members of the local party branch when he illegally jailed and cruelly punished the county business association's chairman, a local court recorder, and the manager of the local financial newspaper, all for supposed minor infractions of the law. In addition, investigators noted that the manager's wife, "due to her wild and outlandish style of dress, attracted undue attention throughout the city," frequently drawing throngs of curious onlookers. On one occasion, two Yichang county youths who once engaged her in a ribald exchange (*tiaoxi*) were immediately arrested by the county manager, who had them both thrown into prison and beaten until one died from his injuries, and the other was permanently crippled. The Control Yuan official who forwarded the case asserted that Manager Xiao's actions involved "savage oppression [of the people] and excessive cruelty" (*baoli canku*) that not only represented a "blemish on the exemplary conduct of all officials but moreover violated criminal statutes." The Disciplinary Commission concurred: Manager Xiao was immediately discharged by order of the Hubei provincial government, and his case was transferred to a military tribunal for criminal prosecution.[60]

The charge of "bringing disaster on the people" (*yangmin*) in particular was associated with the mishandling of public security and criminal matters, but did not always result in administrative dismissal: in 1938 Anhui's Yingshang county manager Zhong Tingjia, three of his ward leaders (*quzhang*), and one political security officer were investigated on charges of engaging in drug trafficking, mishandling public "contributions" to the county's coffers, and hiring a known local bandit to serve as county constable. Although investigating Control Yuan officials determined that none of the three accusations could be proven conclusively, it was found that one local bandit on the county payroll as an informant had indeed falsely accused several innocent citizens of crimes for which they were punished. Manager Zhang was fined one-tenth of his monthly salary for a period of four months for his part in "bringing disaster upon the people" by virtue of his failure to investigate properly the accusations leveled by the bandit-turned-informant.[61]

Disciplinary action was sometimes recommended on the grounds that public servants showed "no respect for human life," or that they "treated human life as grass" (*caojian renming*). In one 1935 Disciplinary

---

60. *JCYSL*, vol. 2, case #109, pp. 159–62.

61. Jiancha yuan dang'an (Control Yuan archive), (hereafter, *JCYDA*), Number Two Historical Archive (Nanjing, PRC). Case file #08-0906, dated February 14, 1938.

Commission case, Hunan's Suining county manager Yu Ruyu was said to have had one of his ward heads (*quzhang*) repeatedly punished and rewarded according to his whims (*shanzuo weifu*) and not as a result of his administrative performance. Furthermore, on one of his circuits through the county, Manager Yu seized a poor unfortunate named Huang Ying, a local country bumpkin (*xiangyu*), after his name came up in the context of a criminal investigation. Apparently in the course of the interrogation of Huang and the village blacksmith, Magistrate Yu was overcome with rage and beat both to death with his bare fists. As it turned out, neither man had anything to do with the crime in question. The Disciplinary Commission moved to transfer the case of Manager Yu to a military tribunal for criminal prosecution.[62]

However, the charge of demonstrating "no respect for human life" did not always indicate cruelty or violence on the part of a public servant. Occasionally the charge suggested complicity in a particularly heinous event or official apathy with respect to the same. In 1934, a female resident of Henan's Fangcheng county filed charges against Manager Sun Jingting on grounds that he showed "no respect for human life" (*caojian renming*). According to the investigative report, in the autumn of 1928 the complainant's husband, He Wancheng, and his colleague, Yu Lugan, were accused of brigandage in the area of Fangcheng county. The Lu Village People's Militia captured both He and Yu and transported them to the village's detention area to await prosecution, but a member of the militia instead killed He, confiscated the property in his possession, and proceeded to dash to death (*shuaisi*) He's four-year-old daughter and nine-month-old son. The members of the militia, however, falsely reported that that their prisoner had committed suicide in the village militia's holding area and did not report the deaths of the two children to the county manager, who declined to investigate. The widow of the alleged bandit immediately filed three murder charges against the members of the Lu village militia. Manager Sun never visited Lu village to investigate, nor did he examine the corpses of the victims; instead, he concluded on the basis of oral testimony provided by two local residents that the militia members were innocent of all charges and dismissed the case. The widow then took her case to the Henan provincial courts, which turned it over to the Control Yuan and the Disciplinary Commission in the spring of 1933. After reviewing the details of the case, the Disciplinary Commission found Manager Sun guilty of "negligence" (*shizhi*) for his failure to investigate the crime, and fined him one-tenth of his monthly

---

62. *JCYSL*, vol. 6, case #433, pp. 34–35.

salary for three months; a county legal clerk who signed the report finding the village militia members innocent of all charges was also assigned a demerit for his part in the affair.[63]

PROSECUTING STATE FAILURE UNDER NATIONALIST RULE

The foregoing case of Henan's Fancheng county manager Sun Jingting exemplifies two noteworthy trends in the formal disciplinary charges leveled against local officials during the Nanjing decade: a considerable increase in charges of misfeasance or delinquency (*shizhi*) over those lodged during the Yongzheng reign, and the proliferation of charges stemming from the inappropriate use of force or coercion against private citizens, either by county managers alone or in concert with local militias, public security organs, or other armed groups. While neither type of case was unheard of during the mid-Qing, such accusations appear as frequently in Control Yuan and Disciplinary Commission documents as charges of "shifting funds" (*nuoyong*) and "deficits" (*kuikong*) did during the Yongzheng reign and reflect the different character and institutional legacies of the state-making process under Nationalist rule. The records of disciplinary proceedings overseen by the Control Yuan and Disciplinary Commission reflect the persistent and widespread problem of local state capture by armed forces during the Nanjing decade, while discursively shifting moral responsibility away from the central leadership toward the outer margins of state control. By framing the regime's failure to disarm, disband, or otherwise control armed militias and to quell both episodic and routine explosions of violence as a form of nonfeasance of duty on the part of individual county managers, central leaders and disciplinary officials discursively elided the deeper imbrication of the Nationalist state with the exercise of coercive might that brought the regime to power and the bloody suppression of its former allies in the years immediately following its assumption of power.

The instability introduced into the realm of local politics during the warlord era was only partially quelled by the apparent victory of the Nationalists nearly a decade later. Prior to the Northern Expedition, some regional military commanders had imposed de facto martial law in the areas under their control, violently suppressing any expression of popular protest or resistance; in other areas, regional powerholders ceded the task of maintaining public security and basic defense to local organizations, provided that such units did not obstruct the flow of tax

---

63. *JCYSL*, vol. 5, case #311, pp. 78–81.

revenues to provincial coffers.[64] The county and sub-county officials who served under warlord rule were detained in large numbers by the National Revolutionary Army (NRA) as they advanced. In practice, once they had taken control of a particular area, NRA leaders laid claim to all existing local government offices and ordered the resignation of the county's public servants. Military officers occupied government buildings and immediately transferred all funds and offices to the Political Department of the NRA, which appointed provisional administrations to oversee the establishment of new local governments.[65] In areas of Hubei, Hunan, and Jiangxi where Communist activists were relatively influential, the Northern Expedition wrought two transfers of power to local governments: with the support of Communist organizers, local peasant associations initially supplanted the local militias and crop protection societies organized by landlords and other elites, confiscated their weapons, and reorganized themselves as armed peasant self-defense forces. However, following Jiang's purge of the Communists in 1927, these forces were brutally suppressed by anti-communist militias loyal to the Nationalists, a tactical decision that tended to shore up the power of local elites at the expense of both the peasant masses and the Nationalist regime.[66] Thus, even as Jiang declared victory and brought the Northern Expedition to a formal close in the summer of 1928, the cycles of local violence set in motion before, during, and after the Northern Expedition continued to spiral ominously throughout the period of nominal demilitarization and pacification that followed. With the outbreak of civil war between the Nationalists and their erstwhile warlord allies in 1929, the local militias, self-defense forces, and crop protection societies that had dominated the rural social landscape for the better part of the decade were once again pressed into service in areas in which violence had become endemic.

Not surprisingly, the relationship between these new county administrators and local armed organizations was often tenuous. Although the 1928 County Reorganization Law created public security bureaus (*gongan ju*) under the supervision of the county manager, in practice, preexisting militias, self-defense forces, and local protection societies continued

---

64. Hans J. van de Ven, "Public Finance and the Rise of Warlordism," *Modern Asian Studies* 30:4 (October 1996): 829–68.

65. Donald A. Jordan, *The Northern Expedition: China's National Revolution of 1926–1928* (Honolulu: University of Hawaii Press, 1986), p. 249.

66. William Wei, *Counter-revolution in China: The Nationalists in Jiangxi During the Soviet Period* (Ann Arbor: University of Michigan Press, 1985); Xin Zhang, *Social Transformation in Modern China: The State and Local Elites in Henan, 1900–1937* (Cambridge, Eng.: Cambridge University Press, 2000).

much as they had before the transfer of power, sometimes joining with the new county bureaus to create hybrid police forces (*jingchadui*).[67] One study of public security organizations in Hebei's Jinghai county from 1928 to 1933 found that police and local militia appropriations accounted for more than half of the annual county budget expenses, yet due to poor training and chronic shortages of basic equipment, they still failed to provide even minimal security for county residents.[68] These logistical shortcomings were compounded by the widespread administrative failures of county government personnel. Some county managers exercised little if any control over the various armed groups operating within their jurisdictions and appeared reluctant to intervene even when such organizations were involved in egregious violations of law. In other cases, county managers cooperated with armed groups, either overtly or covertly, to pursue objectives ranging from the maintenance of basic public order to the routine intimidation and extortion of resources from local residents.

In an attempt to redress such inadequacies, in 1930 the Nationalists ordered county public security bureaus to take control over all local militia forces and to combine them into a single, unified official militia (*baoweituan*) overseen by county managers, beholden to the regulation of provincial civil affairs departments. All local able-bodied men between the ages of 20 and 40 (and, later, between the ages of 18 and 45) were conscripted and placed under the command of a leader and assistant leader selected by the county magistrate at the neighborhood, village, district, and county levels, where they were responsible for basic law-enforcement duties. Conscripts received military training from county-appointed instructors, participated in periodic training exercises, and received basic political education with respect to Nationalist Party principles.[69] In July 1936, new police regulations established county police bureaus (*ju*) independent of the county government and the *baoweituan*, which were nominally under the jurisdiction of provincial governments, but which were in practice frequently controlled by county managers with the assistance of a local police force commander (*jingzuo*).[70]

Despite such policy changes, in practice the records of the Control Yuan

---

67. William Wei, "Law and Order: The Role of Guomindang Security Forces in the Suppression of the Communist Bases During the Soviet Period," in *Single Sparks: China's Rural Revolutions*, ed. Kathleen Hartford and Steven M. Goldstein (New York: M. E. Sharpe, 1989), pp. 40–43.

68. Chang (1936), pp. 279–80.

69. Wei (1989), pp. 44–45.

70. Frederic Wakeman, Jr., *Policing Shanghai, 1927–1937* (Berkeley: University of California Press, 1995), p. 246.

and Disciplinary Commission reveal that the inability or unwillingness of state agents to exercise control over local armed groups was by no means uncommon. The collective failure of local officials to effectively manage public security is clearly manifest in the explosion of delinquency or dereliction of duty (*shizhi*) charges lodged against county managers during this period. The range of mobilized groups implicated in such cases runs the gamut from roaming bandit gangs and secret societies to military police units and special forces traveling through various districts on their way to and from battle sites. By failing to fully subdue and disarm such regional forces, either during the Northern Expedition or soon after, the Nationalist regime effectively relegated the task of pacification to fledgling county administrations that held little sway over well-armed local strongmen. The equivocal relationship between local state agents and armed groups is amply recorded in the archives of the Control Yuan and Disciplinary Commission: charges stemming from the mismanagement of local public security figure in nearly three-quarters of the cases handled by these two bodies.

In some cases, troops associated with either the central government or regional military commanders wreaked havoc in rural communities in which resources were already in short supply, and local officials declined to intervene. For example, in 1931, Anhui's Guichi county manager Yuan Jin was accused of permitting a special-forces military unit (*tejundui*) to run amok in a local hamlet, brandishing their weapons and terrorizing residents. In the deposition against Yuan Jin, one member of a local militia who testified that Manager Yuan ordered local security forces not to engage the outside troops, also acknowledged that they normally solicited various "contributions" from local residents. In urban areas, the "contributions" often took the form of "cash donations" of approximately 30 to 40 *yuan* per resident per month, while in rural areas, the militias freely "solicited" rice, firewood, ducks, and chickens from local residents. When the disciplinary commission investigator proposed that such practices were a form of banditry that the local militia was pledged to prevent, the militia members defended the practice by arguing that, "in actuality, bandits take even more than this." However, further inquiries revealed that the special-forces unit in question made even more extortive demands on residents than did the local militia, confiscating large amounts of food, clothing, and cash at gunpoint before retiring to the county seat for a brief respite. Furious residents chased the unit down in the county seat and marched on their encampment, capturing the platoon leader and dragging him off to the county government offices. After turning him over to the county manager for punishment, the villagers dispersed; however, the local shopkeepers staged an apparent sympathy strike in support of the village residents, and closed their shops—ostensibly in protest, but perhaps also partly because of fear of the itinerant troops. Manager Yuan Jin quietly released the platoon leader two days later without reprisals and sent him on his way, infuriating both the harassed villagers and local shopkeepers, who proceeded to press provincial authorities for redress. Control Yuan investigators recommended that Yuan Jin be discharged for dereliction of duty for failing to exercise supervisory control over the troops during their passage through the county.[71]

In some cases, county authorities cooperated with such marauding groups, either permitting or even participating in raids on local stockpiles of resources. Gansu Huining county manager Guo Chenxu not only allowed the commander of a local military base (*fangjun bingzhan zhanzhang*) to organize a raid against a local walled village for funds and grain but also dispatched a few dozen men from the county forces to assist in the effort. In a surprise attack in July 1932, the joint forces set fire to the village gate and lobbed explosive devices over the walls, destroying several houses in the process. The men made off with several piculs of beans, millet, and some "solicited contributions" in cash under the pretense of amassing military rations; several residents were permanently crippled as a result of the attack, and at least one elderly clan leader suffered a stroke and subsequently died. The Disciplinary Commission concurred with the assessments of Control Yuan and Gansu provincial government investigators that Guo Chenshu was "not worthy of his post" (*youtian zhishou*) and reduced him in rank by one degree for dereliction of duty.[72] In a similar April 1931 case, Zhejiang Dongyang county manager Chen Shilin descended on a local village with 30 armed military police (*junjing*) because he suspected a newly opened shop there was selling meat without proper authorization. Finding a cowhide and a few catties of beef drying in the sun nearby, Chen ordered his men to shut down the establishment by nailing the front door closed. He dispatched a member of his entourage to procure some nails from a nearby dry-goods store while he waited at the corner. However, when the elderly shopkeeper was either unable to make change or was unwilling to cut the price of the nails by ten dollars, the military policeman shot her in the head; he then shot another elderly resident who emerged from the barbershop next door as a result of the commotion. Upon hearing the gunshots, County Manager Chen Shilin fled, but later sent a state employee to dissuade the family members involved

---

71. *JCYSL*, vol. 2, case #32, pp. 244–48.
72. *JCYSL*, vol. 3, case #113, pp. 173–79.

from filing a complaint against the county. The Control Commissioner who investigated the case noted that while County Manager Chen's "complicity was not intentional, his lax control over the soldiers and the inescapable fact of his indolent and neglectful supervision made him an accessory to the deaths of two people," and recommended that he be dismissed for dereliction of duty.[73]

Likewise, in 1933 Yang Weixiong, the leader of Baoshan county's third ward, was accused by an assemblage of local villagers of having wielded his power in an abusive manner by openly collaborating with local bullies (*tulie*) to tyrannize ward residents by "subverting the people's will" (*fan minyi*), repeatedly refusing the advice of village elders, "squeezing" (*guaqu*) money out of innocent local residents, and then, finally, flooding more than 400 *mou* of prime farmland and inundating more than 100 family homes in one hamlet by deliberately destroying a series of protective dikes in an act of retribution against village residents who questioned his authority. Despite repeated pleas for help from the residents of the third ward, the county manager did nothing to intervene, and he was disciplined for nonfeasance of duty.[74]

In some regions of the country, the lucrative opium trade facilitated the formation of illegal cartels between local officials and local strongmen who cooperated not only in drug smuggling schemes but also sometimes in coercing poor farmers to plant and grow opium. In other areas, the prohibition against opium possession fueled cooperation between local officials and armed groups under the pretense of stamping out drug use within local communities. For example, in 1938 five local ward leaders in Yunnan's Tatiao county, along with sixteen police officers (*jingzhengyuan*) and the county prison warden, descended upon one rural village, brandishing guns, axes, and farm tools. Claiming that the county manager suspected a local family of running an opium den, they ordered the residents from their homes and marched them to a nearby walled compound. The residents were forced into a tiny room three or four feet deep with large holes in the walls, and were detained there for two days while their homes were searched by the armed posse. The money and valuables of the residents were confiscated as possible evidence, and, although no criminal charges were ever filed against the village residents, the confiscated property was never returned. The five ward leaders were cashiered as a result of the incident, and charges of delinquency were

---

73. *JCYSL*, vol. 2, case #67, pp. 464–70.
74. Administrative Yuan (Xingzheng yuan) archives, case #02-414, dated November 1933, Number Two Historical Archive (Nanjing, PRC).

sought against the county manager who failed to restrain or discipline the ward heads.[75] Drug addicts were particularly vulnerable to extortion by official and unofficial public security forces. In 1938, Hebei Yanshan county manager He Xiaoyi was charged with "transgressing the law and negligence" (*weifa nizhi*) for colluding with the chief of the county's public security force (*gongandui duizhang*) to extort money from five known opium addicts residing in the county seat. Beginning in 1935, the two regularly received amounts ranging from 50 to 830 *yuan* from each of the five addicts for agreeing to keep them out of jail. In his defense, Manager He argued that both practices had been carried out by previous Yanshan county administrations, so he assumed that such activities were legal. He was ultimately punished for misfeasance of duty, in light of his apparent ignorance of the law.[76]

POLICING THE NATIONALIST STATE

The efforts of central officials to square such conduct with the evolving legal and administrative codes of the new republic as recorded in Control Yuan and Disciplinary Commission documents reflect the problematic nature of the state-making efforts of the Nationalists: the process of social mobilization in preparation for self-rule empowered and granted a degree of legitimacy to a broad range of local actors with varying degrees of commitment to the regime, while the ongoing struggle to monitor and control such groups challenged the limited capacities of new administrations already compromised by the dearth of material and political resources at their disposal. The waves of ambitious institution-building that followed the Nationalists' initial consolidation of power resulted in a proliferation of party and state organizations with sometimes multiple and overlapping jurisdictions at the county level and below and placed enormous pressures on those living in their collective shadow. Over time, the competition for both power and resources generated an increasingly unstable politics of survival that pitted local agents of the state against party activists and other mobilized groups seeking to defend, pursue, or expand their interests, which slowly attenuated the power and authority of the regime.

These challenges proved insurmountable for many local officials and served to destabilize the Nationalist regime in power. Nationalist Party

---

75. Internal Administration Department (Neizhengbu) archives, case #12-8560 (dated May 3, 1938), Number Two Historical Archive (Nanjing, PRC).

76. *JCYDA*, case file #08-843, dated February 5, 1938.

Central Executive Committee member Chen Lifu noted that in the aftermath of the Northern Expedition and party purge, the leadership strove to fill the numerous posts vacated by deposed county officials with loyal party members. However, these positions, highly coveted during the Qing, found few enthusiastic applicants in the late 1920s: most Nationalist Party members adamantly refused, despite pressure from high-level party officials.[77] Many who were dispatched either failed to report for duty at their new posts or did not complete their term of service. Each month, the bulletin of the Administrative Yuan published lists of magistrates who had simply deserted their posts, leaving what appears to have been dozens of rural counties unattended at any given time. Data gathered by the Ministry of the Interior for the year 1932 demonstrated that in Hubei, 86.8 percent of the 68 counties there experienced at least one turnover in the position of district magistrate during the year; in Henan, where 84.7 percent of the positions changed that year, 38.7 percent of the counties experienced two turnovers, and 13.5 percent experienced three changes in leadership. One unfortunate county in Henan saw no fewer than four new magistrates arrive and then leave within the space of the year.[78]

In theory, the Nationalists continued to pursue social mobilization in preparation for the eventuality of self-rule. Yet in practice, the regime exercised little effective control over the actual dynamics of mobilization, and while Nationalist policymakers assiduously crafted a wealth of legislation designed to redress the regime's shortcomings in this regard, the state as a whole fundamentally lacked the administrative and material resources to maintain order at the local level. The framing of the persistent failures of the state to disarm, disband, or pacify local cultures of violence spawned during the Nationalists' consolidation of power as a form of delinquency or dereliction of duty (*shizhi*) on the part of local authorities reveals how lightly the mantle of legal authority rested on the often chaotic and bloody realm of local politics during the Nanjing decade. The legal and bureaucratic formalism of the Control Yuan and Disciplinary Commission served to elide the deeper involvement of the Nationalist state with the visceral processes that brought it to power by discursively shifting moral responsibility for widespread social and political violence outside the imagined boundaries of the party-state. Yet even as the feverish pace of

---

77. Sidney H. Chang and Ramon H. Myers, eds., *The Storm Clouds Clear over China: The Memoir of Ch'en Li-fu, 1900–1993* (Stanford: Hoover Institution Press, 1994), p. 93.
78. C. M. Chang, "A New Government for Rural China: The Political Aspect of Rural Reconstruction," *Nankai Social and Economic Quarterly* 9:2 (July 1936): 243–44.

institution-building continued, the failure to quell recursive violence at the margins of the state continued to attenuate both the authority and capacity of the center to rule. As the impetus toward local self-government eventually gave way to the coercive imposition of corporatist structures, the Nationalists sought new ways to reconfigure the form of local governance that would promote the interests of the Nanjing-based regime.

FIVE

Localist Communities and Political Corruption During the Nanjing Decade

Despite the ambitious attempts of the Nationalist leadership to expand control over local political administration, effective and efficient supervision of actual county government operations eluded central authorities for the better part of the Nanjing decade. This failure was due in no small part to their persistent ambivalence regarding the issue of social mobilization. The goal of the Northern Expedition was to sweep away regional contenders for power, along with their myriad collaborators at the local level, and to restore the authority of the central state under the tutelage of the Nationalist Party. With the cessation of military conflict, the new party-state ostensibly committed its resources and personnel to the mobilization of society for the purposes of national reconstruction and, eventually, for full participation in a constitutional democratic republic. However, as van de Ven argues, the visceral realities of the Nationalist state-making process incited or aggravated local cultures of violence, first against regional warlords and their collaborators, followed by the purge of the Communists and their sympathizers, and then, in some areas, through a succession of civil wars waged by the former military commanders who participated in the Northern Expedition as the erstwhile allies of the Nationalists. Thus, neither the elimination of internal political rivals nor the pacification of local communities was successfully completed on a national scale when the new central government was established in Nanjing in October 1928, and the subsequent building of local state administrations necessarily took place in concert with bandit suppression, social pacification, and remilitarization under the direction of the party. The apparent victory of the Northern Expedition in reunifying the country was a partial one at best; at worst, it represented little more than a tenuous façade of national political unity that was more reflective of popular aspirations than of the underlying political realities that threatened to undermine the authority of the new regime at every step.

Directly beneath the façade of national unity and social stability lay myriad overlapping webs of power and influence connecting a broad range of state and non-state agents jockeying for local and regional dominance in the aftermath of the Northern Expedition. As early as 1925, the Nationalists supported and participated in a broad-based social movement designed to eliminate "local bullies and evil gentry" (*tuhao lieshen*). "Local bullies" were individuals who openly defied the law in collaboration with "local ruffians" (*dipi*), "hoodlums" (*liumang*), and "local bandits" (*tufei*), and who therefore challenged the authority of the regime; "evil gentry," on the other hand, insinuated themselves into existing power structures and used them to serve their own private interests. "Local bullies" were the enemies of national revolution; "evil gentry" opposed progress toward social revolutionary goals. However, following the 1927 break with the Communists, the Nationalists' campaign against "local bullies and evil gentry" quickly shed its association with the larger goal of social transformation in favor of a more immediate, instrumental aim: the suppression of local opposition to the Nationalist consolidation of power.

This early tactical shift, and the politics of accommodation that it produced, reflected a broader tendency on the part of the Nationalist leadership to substitute instrumentalist tactics designed to handle short-term needs for more far-reaching and ideologically motivated policies aimed at long-term transformation. The triumph of political instrumentalism over ideology contributed heavily to the steady erosion of central state authority within local communities over time and ultimately facilitated the demise of the regime. The strongmen who dominated county and sub-county politics during the 1930s—frequently engaging in tax-farming schemes with the tacit approval of state agents or dominating local politics extra-legally by way of banditry, extortion, and other explicitly criminal activities—circumvented and undercut central authorities, not only by selectively implementing national policies but also by sowing popular mistrust and cynicism that attenuated popular support for Nationalist leaders. Subsequent efforts at social mobilization—including the movement to implement self-government and the much-vaunted New Life Movement (*Xinshenghuo yundong*)—met similar fates, as the principles of popular suffrage, democratic representation, and cultural revival were traded away in favor of the more immediate objectives of social pacification and increased control.

In consolidating political power, Nanjing-based central leaders intermittently targeted a succession of parties, groups, and agents at the local level for surveillance and prosecution. However, the frequency with which such campaigns were subverted by policy shifts, produced cases that languished in courts without resolution, or resulted in judgments that were subsequently overturned served to undermine the effectiveness of these efforts. In addition, the institutional weaknesses of the disciplinary and judicial systems sowed widespread disillusionment with the process of administrative control, which gradually deepened into a broader public cynicism with respect to the Nationalist regime as a whole. Many who lamented the widening gulf between the moralistic rhetoric of the Nationalists and the bureaucratic reality over which they presided heartily concurred with Lin Yutang when he observed in 1935,

> What China needs . . . is not more morals but more prisons for politicians. It is futile to talk of establishing a clean and irreproachable government when unclean and reproachable officials can safely book a first-class berth for Yokohama or Seattle. What China needs is neither benevolence, nor righteousness, nor honor, but simple justice, or the courage to shoot those officials who are neither benevolent, nor righteous, nor honorable. The only way to keep the officials clean is to threaten to shoot them when they are caught.[1]

The vexing contradictions that shaped Nationalist state-building—the concomitant efforts to mobilize specific social actors for particular tasks, and to surveil, control, and contain such groups—produced a sprawling bureaucratic machinery that steadily lost the ability to discipline itself effectively with respect to both material and administrative resources. The ponderous increases that funded the new militias, new schools, and new public facilities proposed by modernizing state-makers in Nanjing all too frequently translated into dramatic increases in taxpayer burdens without commensurate improvements in the quality of life for the majority of residents, particularly in the countryside. The continuing expansion of often overlapping state and party agencies was funded by increases in miscellaneous fees and levies, which in turn required an increasing number of tax collectors and state agents to calculate, levy, and administer them.[2] Nor did the expansion of the party-state increase the effectiveness of the Nationalist regime: the combined fragmentation of party and

---

1. Lin Yutang, *My Country and My People* (New York: Reynal and Hitchcock, 1935), pp. 212–13.
2. For some examples, see Patricia M. Thornton, "Beneath the Banyan Tree: Bottom-up Views of Local Taxation and the State During the Republican and Reform Eras," *Twentieth Century China* 15:1 (November 1999): 1–42.

state branches and the stunning variety of quasi-official and civic groups operating at the local level frequently generated internecine conflicts that destabilized local communities. As a result, as Bianco notes, rural residents increasingly viewed the state as both parasitic and alien to the social body of the communities in which they resided.[3]

Such sentiments are reflected in unofficial historical narratives of the Nanjing decade, in which local-level politics is frequently portrayed as an arena dominated by a rapacious and predatory pseudo-bureaucratic apparatus composed of local notables, low-level officials, and outlaws, all seeking to engross themselves at the expense of the common people. Yet, by the same token, there is scant evidence of a "localist" genre of Nanjing-decade historical writings comparable to that of the mid-Qing. Unofficial and popular historical accounts of the Republican era abound, but they are far more diverse in terms of their authorship, narrative conventions, and perspectives than even the rich corpus of "wild histories" that circulated at the height of the Qing. The localist genealogies of virtue and vice produced during the late imperial period were the product of a stable social order that supported a scholar-gentry elite whose interests were closely tied to those of the court; the models of bureaucratic conduct offered in such sources suggested various arrangements that enhanced the prestige and power of the local literati within the social order maintained by the regime.

By contrast, the shift in elite strategies in favor of increased involvement in military mobilization over the course of the nineteenth century, as well as the end of the imperial examination system, served to reconfigure the role of the gentry during the Republican era.[4] The resulting decline in resident proprietorship of land in the countryside, and concomitant rise in the urbanization and diversification of elite interests during the early twentieth century, greatly reduced the numbers of traditional literati with enduring ties to the rural counties for which they had previously served as informal representatives and, not infrequently, ardent advocates. Instead, an estimated 50 to 90 percent of the traditional landed gentry had become, by the Nanjing decade, absentee landlords who delegated the task of rent collection to bursaries and other third-party agents that worked closely with state "prompting" agencies and local armed forces.[5] The local notables who remained in the countryside and rose to prominence after

---

3. Bianco (1986), p. 305.

4. Philip Kuhn, *Rebellion and Its Enemies in Late Imperial China: Militarization and Social Structure, 1796–1864* (Cambridge, MA: Harvard University Press, 1980); Frederic Wakeman, Jr., "Rebellion and Revolution: The Study of Popular Movements in Chinese History," *Journal of Asian Studies* 36:2 (February 1977): 201–37.

5. See, for example, Bernhardt (1992), pp. 163–72.

1927 not only hailed from more diverse socioeconomic backgrounds than had their predecessors but also tended to seek power and influence for different reasons: more often than not, as Duara points out, the rural leaders of the Nanjing decade were motivated by the desire for personal gain at the expense of the community.[6] Nor were these elites as closely bound by the traditional Confucian conventions that motivated their mid-Qing counterparts to emphasize the moral authority that legitimated their social prominence. Rather, in the more heterogeneous climate of the 1930s, Nanjing-decade elites sought social influence and power from a broader diversity of sources than did their late imperial counterparts and by no means eschewed military might in favor of literary skill.

This change is reflected in both the form and the content of local and unofficial historical narratives of the period, which frequently portray local-level politics as an arena dominated by a rapacious and predatory pseudo-bureaucratic apparatus composed of local notables, low-level officials, and outlaws, all seeking to engross themselves at the expense of the common people. As Alitto notes, the ambiguous nature of local state agents, their motives, and practices all gave rise to a peculiar political rhetoric linking delegitimizing prefixes—such as "bandit" (*fei*)—to legitimate official titles, producing a plethora of unique hybrid terms such as "bandit officials" (*feiguan*), "bandit soldiers" (*feibing*), and "bandit style" (*tufei shi*).[7] Personal memoirs, private accounts, and letters of petition penned by local citizens and citizens' representatives during the Republican era are replete with such appellations, and are suggestive of a widespread popular belief that the Nationalists exercised political power at the local level alongside—and frequently at the behest of—criminals, outlaws, and local ruffians. Thus, despite the frequent and vigorous attempts of Nationalist leaders to assert normative control over bureaucratic practices at the margins of the state and to project the moral authority of the regime over the chaotic and often violent realm of local politics, local and unofficial historical accounts underscore the insufficiency of the Nationalist agenda and the larger failure of the regime to fulfill its mandate to rule.

SHIFTING ENEMIES OF THE STATE

The initial stance of the Nationalists toward those local elites who came to dominate the ranks of sub-county self-government personnel in the chaotic

---

6. Duara (1988), especially chap. 6.
7. Guy Alitto, "Rural Elites in Transition: China's Cultural Crisis and the Problem of Legitimacy," *Select Papers from the Center for Chinese Studies* (Chicago: University of Chicago Press, 1979), p. 227.

years of warlord rule was markedly hostile. During the early phase of the Northern Expedition, the combined Nationalist and Communist forces labeled local notables who opposed the advancing NRA troops as "local bullies" (*tuhao*), "evil gentry" (*lieshen*), or "counter-revolutionaries" (*fan geming fenzi*) and accused them of acts detrimental to the nation (*wuguo*) and injurious to the people (*haimin*). Those who held official or quasi-official positions in county or sub-county administration were often charged with the unlawful occupation of government offices and improper use of state property, or with various forms of political corruption. Their cases were handled by military officials in special tribunals designed to prosecute such crimes: in a few cases, justice was swift and harsh, but in others, the accused languished in prison for months and even years before being released.[8] Following the purge of the Communists in 1927, the Nationalists backed away from their earlier condemnation of these power-holders in favor of more neutral, and finally, even friendly policies toward such individuals and groups. In many instances, earlier convictions were overturned, and, after a brief interregnum, those once accused were eventually returned to positions of considerable influence a few years later at the behest of the Nanjing leadership.[9]

Local party branches subsequently took up the significant work of investigating the cases of those detained and accused during the Northern Expedition, as well as documenting the ideological pedigree of those who remained in positions of power in a nationwide effort to "cleanse the party ranks" (*qingdang*). In May 1927, Nationalist Party branches at the county level were ordered to eliminate all "Communists, local bullies, and evil gentry (*tuhao lieshen*), corrupt officials and [their] venal underlings (*tanguan wuli*), and [all] reactionary, opportunistic, corrupt, and evil elements" from their ranks.[10] On August 18, 1927, the Nationalists amended the penal code by mandating the punishment of "local bullies and evil gentry" in order to "develop the spirit of party rule and safeguard the public interest." The regulations specified eleven types of behavior punishable under the new law: deceiving and oppressing the common people, to the point of death, debilitation, disability, or injury; using violence or intimidation against

---

8. Leonore Barkan, "Patterns of Power: Forty Years of Elite Politics in a Chinese County," in *Chinese Local Elites and Patterns of Dominance*, ed. Joseph W. Esherick and Mary Backus Rankin (Berkeley: University of California Press, 1990), p. 211.

9. Ibid., pp. 209–11; Geisert (1986), p. 689; Fitzgerald (1990), pp. 332–37.

10. Zhongguo Guomindang qingdang tiaoli (Regulations on Nationalist Party purification) (May 21, 1927), in *Zhongguo Guomindang xuanyanji* (Declarations of the Nationalist Party), ed. Zhongguo Guomindang dangshi weiyuanhui (Taibei: Jingxiaochu Zhongyang wenwu gongyingshe, 1976), vol. 69, pp. 182–83.

the weak or orphaned in order to force them into marriage; depriving another of personal freedom in order to confiscate his property; charging usurious interest; abetting in the unauthorized use of opium; instigating litigation by manufacturing criminal accusations in an attempt to strip another of his property; attempting to coerce government officials in their handling of criminal cases; stirring up trouble and assembling mobs for purposes detrimental to the public good or national reconstruction; fabricating evidence or allegations, or inciting hoodlums to plot against innocent citizens; excessively relying on one's influence in order to engage in the usurious purchase or sale of real estate or personal goods; and, lastly, the unauthorized occupation of public facilities, encroachment on public property, or the misuse of an official title in order to collect public moneys or property in order to enrich oneself.[11]

The March 30, 1927, promulgation of the Regulations concerning Counter-revolutionary Crimes (*Fangeming zui tiaoli*), signaled the shifting focus of the campaign away from the perceived enemies of social revolution. Within a few months, these Regulations were replaced by the Temporary Law Against Counter-Revolutionary Crimes (*Zhanxing fangeming zhizuifa*), which mandated a death sentence or life imprisonment for any activity "designed to subvert the Nationalist Party or government or destroy the Three People's Principles and incite violence." If such crimes also involved collaboration with foreign imperialists, those found guilty automatically incurred the death penalty. The revised "Provisional Articles for the Punishment of Counter-Revolutionaries" ordered prison terms for those "propagandizing ideologies not consistent with the Three People's Principles and not beneficial to the national revolution."[12] An October 1928 proclamation offered reduced sentences to members of the Communist Party who willingly surrendered themselves; if they agreed to name fellow Communist Party members, they could avoid punishment altogether.[13] In 1931 an additional amendment was made to the penal code outlawing disruptions of the public order and the distribution of anti-government propaganda, as well as the incitement of members of the military to violate the terms of their service, to abandon their posts, or to collaborate with insurgent forces.[14] In 1934, the Nationalists mandated that

---

11. Guomin Zhengfu fazhibu, ed., *Guomin zhengfu xianxing fagui* (Current government laws and regulations) (Shanghai, 1929), chap. 9, pp. 42–43.

12. Lin (1994), pp. 505–6; Guomin Zhengfu fazhibu, ed. (1929), chap. 9, pp. 41–42. The latter contains only the draft of the regulations as issued by the Nanjing-based regime.

13. Lin (1994), p. 508.

14. See the description of the "Extraordinary Criminal Laws for the Protection of the Republic," in ibid., p. 509.

complaints leveled against suspected Communists were to be heard first by juries organized by local party officials before being transferred to local criminal courts for sentencing.[15]

Additional legislation was passed that applied to specific regions and that reflected the wide variation in local conditions under Nationalist rule: for example, the Central Political Council in 1928 considered a draft calling for the punishment of village bandits in the greater Shanghai municipal area. These regulations not only mandated the death penalty for all forms of banditry and brigandage in the Shanghai area, but also promised that collaborators, conspirators, and those who failed to report their knowledge of bandit activities to local authorities would all receive the same punishment as the bandits themselves once they were apprehended.[16] In early 1927, the Wuhan regime instituted judicial reforms that required basic-level people's courts to establish auxiliary judicial organs to assist in handling the burgeoning numbers of cases that surfaced in the wake of the NRA sweep. These people's "councilliary" bodies and county and municipal juries were to be staffed by panels of jurists, consisting of four members from each of the following local organizations: the party bureau, the peasants' association, labor union, chamber of commerce, and women's bureau.[17] Before the purge of the Communists in Luoyang, a special "Luoyang County Committee to adjudicate 'local bullies/evil gentry'" was established by the county party branch and people's revolutionary organizations (labor, peasant, and women's unions).[18] After the purge, Nationalist Party leaders evinced concern that such attacks could turn into a mass campaign and hastily established a system of local "special courts" (*tebie xingshi difang linshi fating*, or *tezhong xingshi fating*) in August 1927 to adjudicate Communist cases and thereby to limit the numbers of spontaneous attacks on enemies

---

15. Lin Houqi, "Guomindang tongzhi shiqi de sifa gaishu" (An account of the judiciary during the period of unity under the Guomindang), in Zhongguo renmin zhengzhi banshang huiyi Fujiansheng weiyuanhui, *Facao neiwai* (The ins and outs of legal cases) (Fuzhou: Wenshi ziliao yanjiu weiyuanhui, 1989), pp. 33–34, 42.

16. *Zhongguo Guomindang Zhongyang zhixing weiyuanhui zhengzhi weiyuanhui* (The Central Executive Council of the Political Council of the Chinese Nationalist Party), document dated October 26, 1928. Archives of Central Political Council (*Zhongyang zhengzhihui*), the Nationalist Party History Committee (*Dangshihui*), Yangmingshan, Taiwan (hereafter, ZYZZH). File #011-62.

17. Shen (1994), p. 302. Geisert dates the establishment of the "special courts" (*tezhong xingshi fating*) to a directive from the party center in August 1927. Geisert (1986), p. 684.

18. Qiu Shi, "Jiu Luoyang xian jindai zhengquan zuzhi" (Old Luoyang county's modern political organization), in *Luoyang wenshi ziliao*, ed. Luoyang qu weiyuanhui wenshi ziliao yanjiu weiyuanhui (Anyang: Henan renmin chubanshe, 1988), vol. 2, p. 105.

of the state.[19] In 1928, the special criminal tribunal for Fujian province was established for the express purpose of handling cases against suspected Communist agitators as well as accused "local bullies and evil gentry"; the chief justice of the Fujian Provincial Supreme Court concurrently served as the chief justice of the tribunal, presiding over a panel selected by either the chair of the provincial party bureau, or from the pool of provincial Supreme Court jurists.[20]

The campaign against "local bullies and evil gentry" was not without its opponents within the Nationalist power structure. Right-wing Nationalist Party ideologue Dai Jitao argued that the party's call to overthrow "local bullies and evil gentry" was a dangerous one, insofar as the party's success in local communities would necessarily involve some degree of cooperation from the landed gentry who largely controlled such areas:

> For several thousand years the country's political foundation has been preserved through a form of gentry politics. Today, to issue a call out of the blue to overthrow "local bullies and evil gentry" before a new base had been solidly established would inevitably shake [the country's] social, economic, and political foundations, and topple [the gentry] to a position from which they will never recover.[21]

Fellow party activist Wu Zhihui countered that the Nationalists had no grudge against the "landed" (*tu*) and the "gentry" (*shen*), but only against the "landed bullies and evil gentry" (*tuhao lieshen*),[22] which was a political and sociological category rather than a reference to a particular socioeconomic class. Debate erupted within the Central Political Council regarding the merits of legislation targeting "local bullies and evil gentry," given the inherent conceptual difficulties in defining such a category and the possibility that it would lead to frivolous charges and local political witch-hunts, destabilizing the already fragile state of most county government operations. One high-ranking justice petitioned the Central Political Council in October 1928 to repeal the law on the grounds that in

---

19. Geisert (1986), p. 684; of the provisional court system, Kuhn notes that the local judiciary "handled communist cases as well as *tuhao lieshen*" (local bully and evil gentry) cases. Kuhn (1975), p. 294.

20. Lin Houqi (1989), p. 42.

21. Huang Jilu, "Dai Jitao xiansheng yu zaoqi fangong yundong" (Dai Jitao and the early anti-communist movement), in *Dai Jitao xiansheng shishi shizhounian jinian tekan* (Special issue commemorating the tenth anniversary of the death of Dai Jitao) (Taibei: 1959), p. 12; as cited by Fitzgerald (1990), p. 336.

22. Wu Zhihui, "'Quanmin geming yu guomin geming' de shangguo" (A discussion of "all people's revolution and national revolution"), in *Quanmin geming yu guomin geming* (All people's revolution and national revolution), ed. Tao Qiqing (Shanghai: Guangming shuju, 1939), p. 8.

practice, local notables of questionable moral stature were making frequent use of the law to level spurious accusations against their competitors and opponents. The justice argued that county officials could easily make use of pre-existing criminal statutes, including the laws against corruption and bribery, abuse of administrative authority, self-engrossment and malpractice in office, and conspiring with bandits and bandit gangs, to handle such cases. A law against "local bullies and evil gentry" was not only superfluous, the justice argued, but dangerous as well, and furthermore not in accordance with the spirit of tutelage.[23] The Central Political Council declined to repeal the law, but instead in March 1928 promised a new round of punishments for those who loosely applied the terms "counter-revolutionary," "local bully," or "evil gentry" in filing criminal complaints. Additional administrative regulations were added to prevent the hasty processing of such cases, and public officials were warned to evaluate such allegations carefully to ascertain that the complaints were indeed valid and not motivated by personal gain.[24]

Such concerns were well founded. As Kuhn notes, in Qing times a "local bully" (*tuhao*) tended to be "a man of wealth, usually landed wealth, generally but not necessarily literate, but with no formal degree status, whose community power was exercised in coercive and illegal ways"; the term "evil gentry" (*lieshen*), on the other hand, "was a local degree-holder who broke the law so flagrantly and consistently that he could not cover it up." By late 1920s, however, both terms were frequently used to describe members of the rural elite involved in sub-county administration: a "local bully" tended to be involved in outright armed political resistance or violent criminal behavior, whereas "evil gentry" were more frequently involved in "usury, pettifogging (*baosong*), and engrossment of taxes (*baocao* or *baolan*)." When employed in tandem in Republican-era political discourse, the terms were "neither a formal status designation nor a rigorously defined category of social analysis, but a popular term of opprobrium which hardened into a political slogan . . . in a generalized attack on holders of power and wealth in the rural scene."[25]

The Communist-controlled *Hunan minbao*, which reported on many such cases prior to 1927, identified "local bullies" as those who openly defied the law, often in collaboration with regional or local non-state

23. *Zhongguo Guomindang Zhongyang zhixing weiyuanhui Zhengzhi weiyuanhui* (The Central Executive Council of the Political Council of the Chinese Nationalist Party), document dated July 17, 1928. ZYZZH, file #011-61.

24. See "Zhanxing tezhong xingshi wugao zhizui fa" (Provisional punishments for libelous accusations), in Guomin Zhengfu fazhibu, ed. (1929), chap. 9, pp. 43-44.

25. Kuhn (1979), pp. 287-88, 292.

forces—in many cases, working in concert with "local ruffians" (*dipi*), "hoodlums" (*liumang*), and "local bandits" (*tufei*)—and who thereby undermined the political authority of the central state. "Evil gentry," on the other hand, insinuated themselves into the existing local power structures and manipulated them to serve their own private interests. "Local bullies" were accused of being enemies of the state revolution; "evil gentry" were portrayed as the opponents of social revolutionary goals. For example, on February 16, 1927, the *Hunan minbao* reported on the arrest of "local bullies" Hu Elou and his son in Ningxiang. The two purportedly had "flaunted their money and influence, treating the common people as if they were [merely] meat and fish [to be consumed]" (*zicheng caishi, yurou xiangyu*). Their crimes included an unprovoked attack upon and murder of two members of the local militia during the Dragon Boat Festival who were preparing to slaughter a pig to serve to the conscripts in their unit, as well as the forcible extortion of 1,000 *yuan* from an elderly local resident on the slim pretext of collecting some sort of miscellaneous excise tax.[26] In one exposé, which ran for several days and which focused on the activities of Gengyang's "great local bully" (*da tuhao*), Li Quanzi, the *Hunan minbao* published the following list of his purported crimes: (1) during one province-level constitutional convention, Li purchased for himself the position of delegation chairperson for the hefty sum of 1,000 *yuan*, "forcefully contravening the will of the people and committing numerous evil acts"; (2) he joined forces with Zhao Hengti, the warlord who took control of large parts of Hunan in the mid-1920s, and his collaborators, "making common cause with evildoers" (*weihu zuo chang*) and making use of the provisional county government established during that time to "cheat and oppress the common people"; (3) he embezzled public funds intended for the use of the Beita village school, surtaxes he himself had collected, which, over a ten-year period, amounted to at least 5,000–6,000 piculs of grain; (4) he opened a private press to promulgate wild rumors and false reports in an attempt to undermine the peasant movement in Hunan; (5) he illegally levied excessive surcharges on the residents of Beita village for the ostensible purpose of funding a village education project, but in actuality he used the money to fund his own lavish lifestyle, "extravagantly feasting on cock's blood wine"; and (6) he brutally beat to death a local activist involved in organizing the peasants in the county. When the local peasants' association convened a meeting to review Li's handling of local educational affairs, he amassed a group of his relatives and clansmen to wait outside the west gate of the school in which the meeting was being held,

---

26. *Hunan minbao*, February 26, 1927, p. 8.

and a melee ensued in which four members of the peasants' association were seriously injured.[27]

By contrast, "evil gentry" tended to work through local bureaucratic offices to defraud the public, either by embezzling government funds or property, or by tax engrossment.[28] Occasionally such men served as county managers, but they were frequently to be found in the position of director of one of the county bureaus or departments. For example, on November 3, 1926, the *Hunan minbao* reported the arrest of the "counter-revolutionary evil gentry" Liu Youlou of Shanba, who had reigned as the district manager of Hengshan county under the auspices of the warlord government of Zhao Hengti. During his tenure in Hengshan, Liu purportedly made use of his power and influence to "stir up trouble and impede the progress of the revolution . . . terrorizing [local residents] with his words" by falsely underreporting to the citizens of Hengshan the progress of the NRA during its Northern Expedition, as well by employing various ruses to undermine the local peasant association (*nongmin xiehui*), including accusing the chair of its central committee of being a bandit.[29]

The conflation of the two terms in popular and unofficial rhetoric during the Nanjing decade suggests that the primary focus of popular concern was not the socioeconomic background of such individuals but, rather, their efforts to wrest control over the local party-state and wield it as an instrument of private gain. In petitions to disciplinary officials composed by private individuals, local groups, or people's representatives, the appellations appear most frequently as a popular indictment of state capture by local strongmen, and frequently preface collective appeals for higher authorities to intervene to protect the public interest. For example, one petition submitted to disciplinary officials in 1932 by a group of Anhui Su county residents named a group of at least four people, collectively referred to as *tulie*, involved in extracting enormous sums of money in the guise of a "special" opium tax on local poppy farmers. One of the named collaborators, Liu Yihua, was accused of abusing his authority as director of the county finance bureau (*caizhengju juzhang*) by imposing unbearable taxes upon the people of the county (*hengzheng baolian*); other collaborators, including the head of the local militia (*baoweituan tuanzong*) Ma Xingwu, were accused of having abused their authority by enacting unduly harsh criminal penalties and by wrongfully causing the deaths of certain local residents. According to the letter of petition, in the year before County

---

27. Ibid., March 20, 1927, p. 8; March 22, 1927, p. 8; March 28, 1927, p. 8.
28. See "Lieshen wuli" (Evil gentry and venal clerks), in *Hunan minbao*, March 12, 1927, p. 8.
29. *Hunan minbao*, November 3, 1926, p. 8.

Manager Chen Jiting arrived at his post, the provincial tax bureau imposed a fixed tax on the county as a whole. However, the newly arrived Manager Chen raised special surcharges within the county to a level six times the previous rate and then dispatched a squad of tax collectors to pressure local growers into paying the new surcharges in full as soon as possible. Chen and his six collaborators were furthermore accused of manufacturing heroin to peddle on the black market in Shanghai.[30] Accused "local bullies" did not hesitate to hurl counter-accusations: as Lucien Bianco noted, when Su county manager Cheng Jiting's extortion scam provoked a massive revolt involving poppy farmers in Su county, he attempted to crush the resistance with military force on the grounds that the protesters were "Communist bandits."[31]

In October of the same year, Gansu Ningyang county manager Zhang Wenquan and two county department heads (*kezhang*) were found guilty of collaborating with a local "evil gentry" (*lieshen, huaishen*) in the attempt to extort money from rural taxpayers. The local newspaper reported that when one of the four encountered a gambling addict in one village who refused to hand over the requisite sum, the "evil gentry" had him strung up and beaten to death. Manager Zhang subsequently dispatched one of his own relatives to "investigate" the death. The gambler's death was subsequently ruled an accident, and the family of the victim was offered a mere ten *yuan* toward burial costs.[32] The 1936 investigation of a Shaanxi Chenggu county manager revealed evidence that one of his underlings, a department head, had accepted a bribe offered by an "evil gentry" surnamed Wang, who raped another man's wife and then accused an innocent man of the crime.[33]

Petitioners often appealed to central authorities for help in unseating predacious local notables who held semi-official posts and were therefore not formally classified as "public servants," but who nonetheless had access to government or public funds and were therefore capable of exacting a negative toll on local government operations. For example, in 1934, the Henan Provincial Bureau of Finance (Caizheng ting) received a petition from the Shenxu Business Association to investigate the activities of an

---

30. Case #142 in *JCYSL*, vol. 3, pp. 310–14. The Anhui provincial government's investigative report into the case is reproduced in the *Jiancha yuan gongbao*, vol. 6 (November 1932–January 1933), as reprinted under the same title by Nanjing: Dier lishi dang'an guan, 1989, pp. 42–49.

31. See Lucien Bianco, "Peasant Uprisings Against Poppy Tax Collection in Suxian and Lingbi (Anhui) in 1932," *Republican China* 21:1 (November 1995): 105.

32. *JCYSL*, vol. 3, case #143, p. 316.

33. *JCYSL*, vol. 7, case #745, p. 723.

accused "evil gentry," Li Zefen in Yancheng county. The chairman of the association, Song Cuiwen, attested that Li, trading solely on the power and influence of his connections, closed down the county cooperative society (*hezuoshe*) and in its place opened up a county "progressive association" (*gaijin hui*). Declaring himself president of the new association, Li began levying special fees against local businesses and ultimately collected more than 10,000 *yuan*, which he promptly pocketed. Li's "progressive association" apparently performed no services for the community in return.[34] Similarly, in a case brought before the Control Yuan, one Henan county manager was disciplined in 1936 when it was discovered that he was secretly harboring "evil gentry," He Shichang. Although He Shichang was a known opium addict, he nonetheless served as the head of a village protection squad, which assisted him in "forcibly extorting money from the people, swindling them out of their property, and pursuing private ends in the name of public duty" (*jiagong jisi*).[35] In such cases, the legal boundary between criminal activity and political corruption was frequently a matter of debate, and, while such cases languished for months or years while administrative and judicial officials wrangled over questions of legal jurisdiction, the larger issue of disciplining local state agents and subverting state capture frequently went unresolved, much to the chagrin of the public.

Attempts to enforce the spirit, rather than the letter, of the law were also punished: in March 1931, a year before the statute against "local bullies and evil gentry" was finally repealed, an Anhui Tongcheng county party branch official was disciplined for "meddling" in one such case that had apparently languished in the local court system for several years. A group of Tongcheng county residents, allegedly under the influence of accused "local bully" Ye Fen, usurped control over the local militia, extorting funds and resources from county residents at will. Once apprehended, Ye's band was found to have embezzled and extorted sums totaling more than 32,500 *yuan*. In early 1929, the local tribunal pronounced Ye and two others guilty of violating the "local bully and evil gentry" statutes and sentenced them to prison for three years. Ye was ordered to return to its original owners all stolen property still in his possession and was fined 1,000 *yuan*. However, a zealous local party official demanded that the cases be reheard on the grounds that the sentence imposed failed to reflect the seriousness of the gang's crimes. In the end, the higher court not only upheld the

---

34. Petition of Tahe village Shenxu Business Association (Shengxu tongye hui) to Henan Provincial Bureau of Finance, dated September 21, 1934, in the archives of the Yu-E-Wan san-sheng jiaofei zong siling bu (Henan-Hubei-Anhui Provincial Central Bandit Extermination Headquarters), Number Two Historical Archive (Nanjing, PRC), case #795-222.
35. *JCYSL*, vol. 7, case #642, pp. 275–81.

original sentence, but also punished the local party worker for attempting to manipulate the judicial process. In commenting on the case in March 1931, central disciplinary officials sternly warned all local party and state agents against interference of any sort in such cases, which "by order of Party Central possessed extraordinary and revolutionary significance," and were therefore not to be manipulated to serve local ends.[36]

The inauguration of the period of tutelage government and the abolition of the special tribunals in January 1929 marked the unofficial end to both the period of martial law and the campaign against evil bullies and local gentry, although the criminal statute was not formally repealed until April 15, 1932.[37] Although in some areas the backlog of cases went untried and the charges were dismissed,[38] in some locales the tribunals continued to operate for several more years, hearing cases against suspected Communist Party members and other "counter-revolutionaries" before Jiang Jieshi himself finally ordered them to be abolished in 1936.[39]

The inadequate capacity of the Nanjing-decade state to project and maintain a clear normative boundary demarcating it from illegitimate local strongmen was reflected in popular rhetoric, not merely in the common usage of hybrid appellations like "bandit officials" (*feiguan*), as noted by Alitto, but also in public accusations that local party and state officials were incapable of "discerning the public from the private" (*gongsi bufen*), either in their own affairs or in the affairs of their underlings.[40] The dramatic transformation of a campaign originally designed to realize social revolutionary goals into a rough tool with which to effect anti-communist suppression and political consolidation was not only ineffective at building popular support for the regime, but furthermore propped open the door to a long-term politics of compromise with local power-holders and the armed groups that supported them. As one provincial official in Jiangsu acknowledged, despite the early efforts to wipe out the "local bullies and evil gentry" in the wake of the Northern Expedition, within only a few years in the countryside there arose "a fearful new force: new local bullies and evil gentry" who sought to collaborate with unscrupulous local officials

---

36. *JCYSL*, vol. 1, case # 5, pp. 55–63.

37. Lin (1994), p. 507.

38. Kuhn (1975), p. 294. Some cases, however, were apparently handled through the county court system, with appeals processed by the highest tier of the provincial court system. See Barkan (1983), p. 208; vol. 1, pp. 55–63.

39. Hu Ji, "Jiu sifa zhidu de yixie huiyi" (A few recollections of the old judicial system), in *Facao neiwai*, ed. Fujiansheng weiyuanhui wenshi xiliao yanjiu weiyuanhui (Fuzhou: Fujian renmin chubanshe, 1989), p. 158.

40. For example, see the case of Anhui Su county manager Qu Shuwun, *JCYDA*, case file #08-903, dated December 8, 1936.

and their subordinates in the sub-county bureaucracies and were all too often indistinguishable from these low-level civil servants.[41]

Control Yuan President Yu Youren noted in his 1931 inaugural address the persistent presence of these designated "enemies of the people" and their continuing influence on local state and party branches. Two years after the special tribunals had been abolished, Yu reported that "local bullies and evil gentry" continued to be one of the primary sources of political corruption among local civil servants under Nationalist rule, because they had encouraged the collaboration of officials with local militarists to defraud the people and fragment the nation. In an open acknowledgment of the Nationalists' failure to fully eradicate the warlord forces that had previously "brought calamity down upon the nation and disasters upon the people," Yu warned that if the military efforts of the Nationalist troops were not followed up by "political methods" to "sweep out" the "filth" caused by "corrupt officials and their rapacious underlings," then all of the military sacrifices of the previous year would have been in vain.[42]

POPULAR VIEWS OF POLITICAL CORRUPTION

Frequently at issue in unofficial historical narratives during the Nanjing decade is the increasing difficulty of local residents who sought to distinguish between legitimate and illegitimate claims to political authority, particularly with respect to revenue collection. While the provisions that permitted county governments to levy their own special surcharges and miscellaneous taxes during the Nanjing decade were originally designed to provide a stronger and more independent financial base for local governments, the system of taxation became a focal point for popular dissatisfaction for those who came to view the party-state and its agents as predators. In the accounts of local residents during this period, popular objection to this system of taxation revolved not merely around the issue of the total tax burden placed upon the community as a whole, but also stemmed from the sheer number of sources to which such taxes needed to be paid. The decentralization of the revenue-collection process was itself a source of great confusion and unhappiness for many communities. As one resident of a rural village in Henan during the Nanjing decade opined:

the types of taxes and levies were numerous, too many to count. From the counties down to the villages and hamlets, from the top on down each level raising the

---

41. As cited by Kuhn (1979), p. 293.
42. "Yu Yuanzhang xuanshi jiuren ci" (The inaugural address of Control Yuan President Yu), dated February 2, 1931, in *JCYSL*, vol. 1, p. 69.

quota, from the top on down each level shaving off the hard-earned property of the people, plundering at their own discretion, the [common] people spending their entire lives not daring to open their mouths [in protest].[43]

Frequently, the deployment of local militias, public security units, or other armed groups to intimidate and coerce reluctant taxpayers further blurred the perceived boundaries between legitimate and illegitimate uses of state power, as well as between state officials and local agents operating with the tacit approval of the state. As one Henan Yancheng county resident pointed out in a letter to the Control Yuan with respect to County Manager Liu Junma,

Those who serve as county managers, with regard to the entirety of the peasant burden, should use whatever powers [they possess] to remedy and lighten it, and to ease the people's hardships; shockingly, Junma, on the other hand, collected a four *fen* acreage levy without any authorization, and when handling the matter of tax collection, routinely sent the army. These soldiers were frequently dispatched in flagrant violation of the orders of [the Control Yuan], and moreover in the aftermath of our recent floods, did not show the slightest humanity, most certainly adding unendurably to the people's burden. Who would ever have expected [Manager] Junma to send out soldiers on his authority on the slightest pretext, abuse his authority, and to line his own pockets? Now that's a list [of charges] that can be investigated and proven![44]

In the 1932 case of Manager Chen Jiting of Anhui's Su county, astronomical increases in the "special" taxes levied against opium-growers incited a revolt against the county government in which no fewer than 10,000 to 20,000 rural residents actively participated, and lasted over a month. In this case, when a poor harvest and a precipitous drop in the market price of opium-producing poppies coincided with the illegal increases in taxes, local poppy farmers found themselves hard-pressed to meet the tax burden. Aware that one method long utilized by local farmers to evade the full brunt of the tax burden was to underreport land under cultivation, Manager Chen sent out special commissars to survey the poppy fields. These commissars, moreover, themselves charged the farmers for having to survey their lands. Once the survey had concluded, the manager recalculated the amount of tax due for each poppy farmer and sent out dunning heads to collect the revised amounts. The unscrupulous band of tax collectors (*pai wei zuocui*) dispatched by Chen, "as urgent as

---

43. Yuan Shuhe, "Liutan Guomindang zhenfu shi kejuan zaxue" (Remarks on the miscellaneous taxes and levies of the Guomindang government) in *Guangze wenshi ziliao*, ed. Fujiansheng Guangze weiyuanhui wenshi ziliao weiyuanhui (Fuzhou: Fujian renmin chuban she, 1990), vol. 3, p. 68.

44. Letter of petition dated November 13, 1931, in *JCYSL*, vol. 2, case #64, p. 436.

shooting stars, without the slightest delay" (*jiru xinghuo, shaowei chiyan*), immediately began pressing the taxpayers.[45] When such measures proved unsuccessful, the tax collectors stooped to confiscating farm animals from peasants who could not pay, and, finally, to arresting members of peasant households themselves. When the farmers began fleeing into the hills in order to escape arrest as tax evaders, the collectors resorted to beating and abusing the women and children left behind. In one village, a band of several hundred women whose farmer husbands had fled armed themselves with various weapons and struck back at the tax collectors, seriously wounding and killing a number of them.[46] Finally, when the Su county residents turned to open revolt, Manager Chen notified his superiors in the provincial government that Communist insurgents had incited a local rebellion, and military forces were dispatched. Two of the units sent to Su county refused to attack the rioting poppy farmers, presumably after they had surveyed the situation and investigated its causes; as a result of the report of the battalion commander of one of these units, a recommendation that Chen be relieved of his post was forwarded to the provincial government.[47]

Petitions and appeals submitted to disciplinary and judicial authorities during the Nanjing decade frequently stressed the contrast between the predatory behavior of local state and party officials and the passive and compliant conduct of local residents. For example, in the 1938 case of Yunnan Tatiao county manager Zhu Chang and other members of his administration, who illegally detained and imprisoned the entire population of Xici village for three days while local constables ransacked their homes, the residents' petition to central government authorities described themselves simply as "the plaintiffs, all of us leading frugal and diligent lives, with few luxuries in food or clothing" (*yisheng qinjian, yiliang xiaoyu*), preyed upon by the unscrupulous Manager Zhu, whose "mind was beclouded by greed" (*liyu xunxin*).[48] Likewise, a petition submitted by Anhui Guichi county residents in 1931 accused County Manager Yuan Jin of having

risen on the coattails of another, by luck or by chance, and in a single great leap [he is] now serving as manager, a blind man leading a blind horse. Having already

---

45. Anhuisheng zhengfu cheng fuwen (Investigation report of the Anhui provincial government), dated August 13, 1932, *JCYSL*, vol. 3, case #142, p. 310.
46. *JCYSL*, vol. 3, case #142, pp. 310–14; and Bianco (1995), pp. 93, 104.
47. Bianco (1995), p. 105.
48. Public petition from "residents and farmers of Xici village, Third ward, Tatiao county," in Internal Administration Department (Neizhengbu) archives, case #12-8560 (dated May 3, 1938), Number Two Historical Archive (Nanjing, PRC).

succumbed to various excesses, [he has turned to] extorting the hard-won fruits of the people's labor, pocketing all the profits with nothing off limits. Furthermore, he installed his relatives in official posts, erasing the fears of all [government] employees against committing prohibited acts . . . failing to distinguish between his relatives and his employees, to the extent that there was no difference between his family and the county administration. He pounced upon and snapped at good people (*boshi liangmin*). How can this be tolerated?[49]

Yet frequently the bureaucratic practices that occasioned public petitions during the Nanjing decade were not violations of administrative or criminal law, nor were they contraventions of government regulations per se. Rather, in some cases, even the intendance of routine duties provoked indignation on the part of taxpayers, who had clearly come to view even the quotidian operations of the local party-state with suspicion, resentment, and outright hostility. For example, in 1937 a group of enterprising residents of Guangdong's Taishan county mass-produced neatly printed handbills in order "to make known the corruption" of their county manager, "to propagate his stench both near and far . . . and to reveal the charges against him and to employ as a weapon this diatribe," listing the 22 "great crimes" of Tan Yuanzhao, including his "ruthless oppression of [county] fishmongers" and "excessive deployment of [county] personnel."[50] However, the disciplinary officials who investigated the case found little evidence that County Manager Tan had violated any laws or regulations. His alleged unfair treatment of local fishmongers, for example, involved his scrupulous observation of existing regulations concerning taxation and commercial licensing requirements; the "excessive deployment of personnel" appears to be a reference to the squads of tax collectors Manager Tan dispatched to investigate tax evaders.

County self-government organizations were another source of common concern in popular petitions submitted to Nationalist authorities. In 1928, with the campaign against "local bullies and evil gentry" still well under way in many areas, the new regime promulgated the County Organization Law, the Implementation of Township and Village Self-Government Law, and the Election and Recall of Township-Village-Lane Officials Law, all of which ostensibly asserted the commitment of the new party-state to self-governance. At the First National Administrative Conference, party leaders furthermore directed all counties and municipalities to prepare to

---

49. Public petition from "Anhui Guichi county citizen XXX and others," in *JCYSL*, vol. 2, case #32, pp. 244–45.
50. Poster entitled "Qing kan Tan Yuanzhao sanshi er dazui" (Please read the twenty-two great crimes of Tan Yuanzhao), in Internal Administration Department (Neizhengbu) archives, case #12-8538 (dated December 25, 1937), Number Two Historical Archive (Nanjing, PRC).

carry out elections for sub-county posts at the township, neighborhood, and lane levels, and to set up village and township people's committees. Yet even as the preparations for self-government were undertaken, as one Jiangsu provincial official noted, in the countryside there arose "a fearful new force: new local bullies and evil gentry"[51] who sought to dominate these new institutions by conniving to have the county manager appoint them as local representatives. As Chen Boxin noted a few years later,

The result of the government's haste to meet its deadline for carrying out self-government was a conveniently opened door for the despotic gentry class [haoshen jieji]. For the most part, the nominal self-government organizations at all levels became hives [chaoxue] of "local bully and evil gentry" activity from which the common people not only failed to benefit, but furthermore suffered increased political oppression. Previously, "local bullies and evil gentry" were quite powerful in rural society, but their position was not founded on law. Now, by linking up with the local administration under the rubric of self-government organizations, they assist officials in implementing the law, collecting taxes, and investigating wrongdoing. On the one hand, it is as if they are now helping the people to petition the government, perhaps working on behalf of local public interest. But in reality, they frequently oppress the people in the name of the government, or coerce the government in the name of the people, never acting on their own behalf, but have nonetheless emerged as a privileged class.[52]

The ambiguous nature of the self-government organizations established under Nationalist rule proved problematic not only for the central government, which subsequently found that in some areas, self-government organizations contravened directives and/or selectively implemented the orders of superior officials,[53] but also for the mass of local residents whose interests they ostensibly represented. For example, one 1931 petition submitted by "the representative of the six hundred families of Yanhai village" began:

We report that local bullies and evil gentry have illegally assembled; judges have committed malfeasance in office; the manager continues to procrastinate; and the local residents have been exploited. Earnestly entreating, we submit this report for your consideration, that we may guard against corruption and moreover bring to light the situation of our self-government organizations. We have steadfastly [pursued] the road to self-government and carried out the exhortations of the late father of our country: the people of our village stress that this has been the

---

51. As cited by Kuhn (1979), p. 293.

52. Chen Boxin, *Zhongguo de difang zizhi ji qi gaige* (Reforming the foundations of China's system of local government) (Nanning: Guangxi jianshe yanjiu hui, 1939), p. 235.

53. See Xin Zhang, *Social Transformation in Modern China: The State and Local Elites in Henan, 1900–1937* (Cambridge, Eng.: Cambridge University Press, 2000), especially chap. 6.

source and foundation of all of our actions. Our founding father, in harmony with Heaven and the revolution (*yingtian xun geming*), brought to light the rights of the people to directly select and recall government officials. During the current period of tutelage government, under the principles which serve as the foundation of constitutional government . . . we villagers have participated in the process of establishing our [self-] government [organizations]; however, there are those [in the county] who would absolutely not act in accordance with these principles would frustrate [our attempts].

The petition subsequently recounts the events of the spring of 1930, when "local bully evil gentry" Li Jinglian "singularly possessed by wild ambitions launched a surprise movement to have himself put in office. Once so installed, before anyone even knew [precisely] what his position was, he began to make use of it to commit evil" against the innocent and patriotic citizens of Yanhai village.[54]

The 1931 letter of one citizen of Zhengding county in Hebei accused the manager of collaborating with local bullies and evil gentry, and furthermore

committing malpractices to engross himself, embezzling tax moneys and public funds, cheating the people out of their property, stealing and then illegally selling government property, falsely incriminating members of the gentry and village elders (*shenqi*), using government offices to solicit bribes; there is no evil that he will not commit, his wickedness is extreme, he oppresses those below while hiding the truth from those above. The indignation of the people is seething, with each person fearing for himself.

In the climate of paranoia that resulted from the manager's preferential treatment of the wealthy and powerful, the author of the petition recounted how numerous county residents had also turned against a local "citizen's representative" who had previously submitted their plaint to provincial authorities two years earlier to no avail; suspecting him of collusion with the manager, a group of residents themselves jointly sent four letters directly to the governor of Hebei province, which also went unanswered.[55]

The contradictory response of the Nanjing leadership to the development of representative self-government, much like its earlier commitment to the campaign targeting local bullies and evil gentry, was the result of substituting instrumentalist policies aimed at consolidating political power for long-

---

54. Letter of accusation and request for investigation from "the representative of the six hundred families of Zhenhai county, Lingyan township, Yanhai village," dated April 16, 1931, in *JCYSL*, vol. 2, case #20, pp. 153–54.
55. Letter submitted to Control Yuan officials from Zhengding county citizen XXX and others, dated March 29, 1931, in *JCYSL*, vol. 2, case #11, p. 99.

term political change. Over the course of the Nanjing decade, preparations for self-government were gradually abandoned and local state governments were ordered to reinstitute the traditional *baojia* system as part of the larger program of bandit "encirclement and suppression" efforts. In Qing times, the *baojia* system of hierarchically arranged, decimally based units of population pledged mutual cooperation and mutual responsibility for the maintenance of local order, the apprehension of criminals, and the oversight of local household registration. However, in 1932 under Nationalist rule a revised set of regulations postponed preparations for self-government indefinitely in so-called "bandit suppression" zones, and effectively abolished self-government organizations below the level of the ward or township nationwide and replaced them with *baojia* units for the purposes of self-protection.[56] In 1934 under a further set of revisions, popular elections for village and town mayors (*xiangzhang* and *zhenzhang*) were postponed indefinitely; however, according to Liang Hancao, the secretary-general of the Legislative Yuan, the overriding hope of the administration at the time was to "integrate (*dacheng yipian*) self-government and self-defense, incorporating both *baojia* and self-defense units" under the same auspices.[57] By 1939, Nationalist leaders proposed yet another set of administrative revisions, placing the *baojia*, village (*xiang*), and township (*zhen*) under the direct control of the county, as grassroots organizations within the formal apparatus of the state.[58] Thus, as Fei Xiaotong observed nearly a decade later, the gradual incorporation of the traditional *baojia* system into the administrative hierarchy of the local state under Nationalist rule further curtailed its use as an instrument for local self-governance. While in imperial times, *baojia* leaders had some power to mediate between state and society and thereby to shield local interests from the harmful intrusions of central authorities, under Nationalist leadership "the local community has become a dead end in the political system," with even less autonomy than it had under imperial rule.[59]

56. "Jiang Jieshi zai quanguo di'er ci neizheng huiyi shangde jianghua," *Zhongyang ribao* (December 17, 1932).
57. "Lifa Yuan mishuzhang Liang Hancao dui jizhe tanhua," *Da gong bao* (August 1, 1936).
58. Qin Tan, "Difang zhengzhi," *Guomindang zhongyang zhengzhi xuexiao*, p. 24, as cited by Zhang Hao, "Minguo shiqi xiangcun zizhi tuixing zhi qianyin houguo—cong *Minguo xiang-cun zizhi wenti yanjiu* tanqi," (The ins and outs of implementing rural self-government during the Republican period—a discussion of *Research into the Problems of Rural Self-Government During the Republic*), *Shixue yuakan* (Historiography monthly) 5 (2003): 77.
59. Fei Xiaotong, "Basic Power Structure in Rural China," reprinted in *China's Gentry: Essays on Rural-Urban Relations*, ed. Margaret Park Redfield (Chicago: University of Chicago Press, 1953), p. 89.

VIRTUOUS OFFICIALS OF THE REPUBLICAN ERA

Although the citizens of the 1930s most often sought out central government authorities to shield them from the abuses of unscrupulous local administrators, residents were also occasionally moved to write letters to central authorities in which they commended local leaders for their efforts on behalf of the local community they served. In such cases, local authorities were evaluated both on their ability and willingness to respond to the economic needs of the communities over which they served, as well as their degree of responsiveness to local social norms and obligations. Managers who had significantly contributed to projects that were designed to improve the welfare of the community were most often the subjects of such letters, as they were in Qing times. County managers who built and established schools, refurbished parks and public buildings, repaired dikes and waterways, and replenished local granaries were all praised by rural residents for their efforts on behalf of the counties they served. The 1940 letter of "local gentry" (*shishen*) Zeng Xiuze of Jiangxi's Yugan county is typical. Zeng and a group of 40 other Yugan county residents extolled their manager, Hu Quan, for his efforts on behalf of the local community in five key areas. First, Manager Hu had reportedly emphasized the central importance of local self-government institutions in Yugan county by making certain that every town and hamlet had well-established *baojia* organizations for protection and self-defense. Although these organizations certainly predated the manager's arrival, according to the authors of the letter, they had fallen prey to various abuses by those who sought to control them for their own purposes. Manager Hu conducted a thorough investigation of all such units, and made certain that all representatives serving in self-government offices were popularly elected on a regular basis, and cleared the ranks of all members of warring factions. Second, Manager Hu had sought to promote education within the county, both by renovating existing schools and by creating new training programs for all public servants, militia members, and *baojia* organization leaders. Third, the manager had actively pursued policies that protected the productivity of local enterprises, from organizing workers to dredge the county dikes in the spring and to dig new irrigation canals, to reclaiming new arable lands from the banks of local waterways. Fourth, Manager Hu had applied himself to carefully administering the existing corvée labor projects in the county, making certain that such projects were completed according to schedule, and that all available conscripts actively serving in local militias participated. Furthermore, the manager had furthermore undertaken revisions to the county gazetteer, a project that had not been attempted since the Tongzhi reign (1862–74). Finally, the residents praised Manager Hu for his prompt and careful collection of taxes, his moral instruction of the residents of his district, and his efforts to raise the general agricultural productivity of the district.[60]

As under the Qing, managers were of course often praised for their careful management of county finances, for reducing the tax burden, or for simplifying the tax-collection process in their jurisdictions. For example, the Fujian Le county manager Yu Wuwei was recommended for special commendation to state authorities in Nanjing by the residents of his district for having renovated the offices of the county government "without charging local residents a cent" (*bu fei difang fenwen*) and for having "used public moneys sparingly." Apparently without turning to the much reviled system of "solicited contributions" or imposing any additional surtaxes on the county residents, Manager Yu was able not only to refurbish the county offices but also to make repairs to a public hall and to renovate a public park.[61] As had been their predecessors in the early eighteenth century, many Republican-era managers were much admired for taking an active and personal role in the process of overseeing the financial affairs of the county and the process of tax collection. For example, when his extensive audit of Ci county finances revealed that one office staff of the county government had behaved in a fiscally irresponsible manner, Manager Chen Zhongyue was lauded in the county gazetteer for having eliminated the department in question by assigning its budget and duties to another county office, thereby saving the taxpayers more than 360 *yuan* a month.[62] Hunan Yongxun county manager Teng Yichan was praised in part for having substantially revised the county fiscal system by directly handing over the land-tax rolls to the *baojia* personnel and permitting the unit members to police themselves; for making ample allotments in the county budget for local militia provisions and supplies; and for strictly overseeing the process by which taxes were collected by the various branches of county government by appointing special personnel to actually go out into the villages (*chuxiang*) and interview taxpayers.[63]

---

60. Letter submitted by local gentry Zeng Xiuzhi and others, to the Internal Administration Department, Internal Administration Department (Neizhengbu) archives (hereafter, NZBA), case #12-7426 (dated March 15, 1941), Number Two Historical Archive (Nanjing, PRC).

61. Letter submitted by Lecheng resident Yuan Shilian to the Fujian provincial government, NZBA, case #12-7399 (dated September 15, 1929), Number Two Historical Archive (Nanjing, PRC).

62. *Cixian xianzhi* (Ci county gazetteer) (Taibei: Chengwen chubanshe, 1968), *chenji lei*, p. 297.

63. Letter submitted by Yongxun citizen representative Wu Jie, NZBA, case #12-7366 (dated April 13, 1938), Number Two Historical Archive (Nanjing, PRC).

However, while such hagiographical accounts of the careers of local officials sometimes resemble those written in late imperial times, important differences exist. Rural villages during the Nanjing decade faced numerous challenges that were comparatively rare during the mid-Qing, ranging from regional disintegration and the perpetual threat of marauding bandits to severe, long-term economic dislocation and foreign encroachment. Thus, during the Nanjing decade, official and unofficial discourses faulted bandit gangs, regional power-holders, and the threat of foreign invaders for the range of social ills they faced, and praised local leaders who tried to protect and shelter their jurisdictions from predation. One telling feature of these narratives is the manner in which the detached language of modern bureaucratic formalism overlays the visceral and bloody realities of local politics under Nationalist rule. The case of Shao Hongji, a former county executive of Henan's Gong county who ultimately served as a regional commissioner for the Control Yuan and who compiled and authored many of the official depositions and reports discussed in the previous chapter, illustrates how deeply enmeshed Nationalist authorities were with the local cultures of violence that shaped the Nanjing decade, as well as the complicity of the regime in inciting, and then often failing to contain, episodic political turmoil. As a district official, Shao organized a local militia and led several raids on the nearby bandit lair of Nanshan, and always insisted on returning with live captives whom he personally decapitated with a large knife back in the public square of the county seat. He festooned the town's east gate with the bloody heads of his former captives "until those who passed the gate covered their eyes and did not dare look."[64] Nonetheless, Shao was fondly remembered by several local residents for having organized a stealth attack on the ill-reputed Second Route Army, part of the NRA forces, when they were forced to beat a hasty retreat in 1925 that took them through a narrow gorge in the county. Upon hearing of the approach of the troops, Shao grabbed a rifle and assembled 30 or so men to hide along the top ravine where they opened fire on the troops, slaughtered the survivors, and then confiscated their weapons. When a local Red Spears leader learned of the attack and the cache of weapons Shao had amassed, he laid siege to the town and kidnapped Shao, who was released only after an extensive round of negotiations conducted by a group of local notables.[65] Not long after his assault on the Second Route Army, Shao was summoned to Nanjing

---

64. Sun Yimin, "Ershi niandai houqi hi sanshi niandai chu gong xian de san ren xianzhang (zhai chao)" *Gongxian wenshi ziliao,* no. 3 (Anyang: Henan renmin chubanshe, 1983), pp. 32–33.

65. Liu Chuangshao, "Gongxian zhishi Shao Hongji" (Gongxian Magistrate Shao Hongji), *Henan wenshi ziliao* no. 24 (Anyang: Henan renmin chubanshe, 1984), p. 161.

by Control Yuan President Yu Youren who, coincidentally, was one of the original organizers of the Second Route Army against which Shao had organized his guerrilla attack. Upon his arrival in Nanjing, Shao was invited to serve as a high-ranking commissioner of the Control Yuan on the basis of his reputation among the residents of Gong county.[66] The archives of the Control Yuan and Disciplinary Commission amply attest that Shao pursued bureaucratic malfeasance with the same degree of ruthlessness that he applied to persecuting bandits.

Yet not all localist narratives of the period celebrated the visceral contests that formed the core of the Nationalist state-making process. Many accounts reflect a profound sense of war-weariness and a concomitant yearning for peaceful stability and social order. Local and unofficial historical sources of the period frequently eulogized not only county managers who demonstrated a strong personal commitment to the public welfare of the district they served, but also those who undertook the mending of social and political divisions within the community. Thus, for example, in a letter submitted to national government authorities by the county representative of Zhennan county in Yunnan, local residents commended their manager of the previous four years, Zhao Zhengyue, for the

earnest and inspirational manner in which he led all of the people of our district, gentry and commoners (*shenmin*) alike, with the spirit that if something needed to be done, it could be accomplished (*ruo ganshi ganzi jingsheng*); and in the midst of insoluble dilemmas, he always thought of a solution. In just a few months [after his arrival in the summer of 1936], all of the aspects of the society that had been broken and destroyed were completely recovered, and the people of our district again resided in peace, the officials and the gentry (*guanshen*) joined together in working for the common good once again, with all in power acting in accord with established regulations.[67]

Likewise, in 1939, residents of Hunan's Nan county commended their manager, Bin Huzhao, for his efforts to promote the overall unity of the community by earnestly encouraging them to engage collectively in mutual assistance projects, and in so doing to eliminate the numerous divisions that had previously divided the people of the county. Creating

---

66. Yan Jinan and Bai Wenmei, "Shao Hongji er san shi" (Two or three things about Shao Hongji), *Gongxian wenshi ziliao* no. 3 (Anyang: Henan renmin chubanshe, 1983), pp. 35–36.
67. Petition from the "all citizens' representative" of Zhennan county (*Zhennan xian quanxian minzhong daibiao*) to the Internal Administration Department, NZBA, case #12-7418 (dated September 13, 1940), Number Two Historical Archive (Nanjing, PRC). Zhennan county in Yunnan is alternatively listed as either a county (*xian*) or department (*zhou*) on Republican-era maps that I have seen. The author of the petition identifies it as a county that was formerly a department.

an umbrella organization staffed by members of the local gentry (*difang shishen*) to oversee the activities of other semi-official associations in the county, Manager Bin

patiently demonstrated that, by actively and sincerely uniting forces, ever attentive to the severity of national problems, and by avoiding [the tendency] to divide into factions, together we could succeed. In the several months since that time, representatives (*renshi*) from the party, state, military, academic, and business communities have been united from top to bottom, as one in their hearts.[68]

READING THE REPUBLICAN STATE

The popular desire for both stability and unity emerges as a common theme among the widely diverse unofficial and local historical accounts of bureaucratic conduct during the Nanjing decade. Tragically, the imposing edifice of the bureaucratized party-state constructed by Nationalist leaders proved inadequate to the task of disciplining itself and therefore was largely incapable of transforming the myriad local cultures of violence—spawned at least in part by the Nationalist consolidation of power—into efficient and stable self-governing communities. As was also the case during the Yongzheng reign, the state-building efforts that characterized the Nanjing decade were driven by paradoxical impulses: an ideological, or at least rhetorical, commitment to democratic mobilization that steadily waned in the face of mounting internal and external challenges on the one hand; and the more urgent and therefore instrumental need to co-opt and control the mobilized local groups that resulted from this process on the other. The Nationalists' efforts in this respect empowered a range of actors at the local level whose goals and activities frequently challenged, subverted, or diluted central control, and the subsequent attempts to monitor, police, and contain such middlemen consumed significant administrative and material resources from the central party-state. While in theory the Nationalists continued to support self-rule as a desired end, in practice the regime's corporatist reorganization of local communities proved ineffective over the long term at building popular support for the regime, and ultimately at overcoming the internal and external challenges that brought about the regime's demise.

---

68. Letter of petition from Hunan Nan county resident associations to Internal Administration Department, NZBA, case #12-7393 (dated February 1939), Number Two Historical Archive (Nanjing, PRC).

SIX

Political Corruption and the Maoist State

If the treasury shortfall vexing the Qing throne was framed as a crisis by the Yongzheng emperor to pave the way for ambitious state-making reforms, and the violent turmoil of the 1920s a crisis that was inherited and then unfortunately exacerbated by the Nationalist Party, then the human catastrophe of the Great Leap Forward was a crisis of almost inconceivable proportions generated by the Maoist regime itself. In retrospect, the cataclysmic failure of the Great Leap can be seen as an institutional by-product of the marriage between a utopian "high-modernist" vision of socioeconomic transformation and the precision machinery of a Leninist party-state.[1] The arduous, two-decade-long struggle that brought the Communists to power produced a highly disciplined party organization staffed by a core of seasoned veterans. It also solidified the prestige and authority of Mao Zedong as the charismatic leader at the helm of the revolutionary core, granting him wide latitude to shape party and state norms. During the initial consolidation of power, the utopian idealism characteristic of the Yenan period[2] generally yielded, on a day-to-day basis, to the political realism and orderly administrative development of the bureaucratized party-state guided by collective decision-making at the upper echelons; however, the stability of standard organizational routines was intermittently interrupted by extraordinary pressures and policy shifts due to Mao's interference or to the periodic oscillations of political campaigns that unleashed frenzied activity on

---

1. The "high-modernist" impulse is described by Scott (1998); for an analysis of the institutional roots of Great Leap policies, see David Bachman, *Bureaucracy, Economy, and Leadership in China: The Institutional Origins of the Great Leap Forward* (New York: Cambridge University Press, 1991).
2. Mark Selden, *The Yenan Way in Revolutionary China* (Cambridge, MA: Harvard University Press, 1971).

the part of local party organizations in pursuit of specific goals.[3] Of the numerous mass campaigns waged during the first decade of Communist rule, the Great Leap Forward remains unparalleled in human history, not merely in terms of the scale and scope of the undertaking, but also for its cataclysmic consequences for the Chinese polity.

The disjunction wrought by the Great Leap in the larger history of Chinese state-making began with Mao's startling January 1958 announcement that the pragmatic restraint that characterized economic planning in 1956–57 under the policy of "opposing rash advance" represented an error of "political line" abetted by "rightists." This unanticipated announcement sent shockwaves through the leadership and signaled a sea change in the evolution of the Maoist party-state. In violation of the established preference for frank and collective discussions among the veteran core of the party elite on matters of policy, Mao openly criticized both Chen Yun and Zhou Enlai for exercising undue moderation in setting production targets. As a result of the blistering attack, Zhou lost his "right to speak" on economic matters, prompting him to offer his resignation two months later; a subsequent reshuffling of the economic decision-making apparatus also shifted Chen to the margins.[4] With Mao exerting direct managerial control over economic planning, ad hoc conferences involving provincial party cadres eclipsed in many respects the hierarchical policy process represented by the state planning ministries. Ambitious local cadres fed Mao's vast appetite for revolutionary enthusiasm and optimism;[5] Mao, in turn, fostered a competitive atmosphere among the discussion participants, rewarding with favor and praise the more radical elements of the planning process. The state's capacity for economic coordination was quickly overwhelmed by the centripetal dynamics of collective utopianism. Yet the Leninist party discipline that had proved so indispensable at forging unity during the Yenan period, both within the ranks of the cadres and between the cadres and the masses, virtually ensured that the disastrous policy decisions and unrealistic production targets produced by

---

3. Frederick C. Teiwes, "The Establishment and Consolidation of the New Regime, 1949–57," in *The Politics of China: The Eras of Mao and Deng*, ed. Roderick MacFarquhar, 2nd ed. (New York: Cambridge University Press, 1997).

4. Frederick C. Teiwes with Warren Sun, *China's Road to Disaster: Mao, Central Politicians, and Provincial Leaders in the Unfolding of the Great Leap Forward, 1955–1959* (New York: M. E. Sharpe, 1999).

5. See, for example, Yang Dali's discussion of provincial responses to central directives in his *Calamity and Reform in China: State, Rural Society, and Institutional Change Since the Great Leap Famine* (Stanford: Stanford University Press, 1996), especially chap. 2.

ad hoc planning were imposed on those below, with an application of coercive force when necessary.[6]

Light industrial output dropped into a three-year slump. Colossal shifts in labor allocations from the countryside to the cities and urban industrial centers, harsh weather conditions, and a shortage of draft animals set in motion a disastrous chain of events that the agricultural sector could not easily absorb. Famine conditions prevailed in the winter of 1959, and continued unabated in most rural areas through 1961. Workers laboring in a semi-starved state found it difficult to complete their assigned shifts, and moved to shorter work periods out of dire necessity. Labor productivity declined. Angry PLA soldiers in 1960 complained: "At present what the peasants eat in the villages is even worse than what dogs ate in the past. At that time dogs ate chaff and grain. Now the people are too hungry to work and the pigs are too hungry to stand up. Commune members ask; 'Is Chairman Mao going to allow us to starve to death?' "[7] Indeed, millions perished during the campaign: statistics show that the national mortality rate doubled between 1957 and 1960, with conservative estimates suggesting that between 16.4 to 29.5 million people died during the Great Leap Forward who would have otherwise survived.[8]

Public morale plummeted. One November 1960 People's Liberation Army (PLA) Organization Department report noted an alarming increase in cases of sabotage, assassination, plunder, and theft: "Since the beginning of this year, there has been a marked increase in the activities of counter-revolutionaries and bad elements. There is also a steady increase in cases of counter-revolutionary slogans, anonymous letters, anti-revolutionary blocs, defection, and murder."[9] Reports surfaced that incidents of rural collective action in resistance to state authority were on the rise as well.[10] According to Li Ruojian, a comparison of public records before 1957 to those during the Great Leap period reflects rising levels of popular unrest in a variety of forms. These ranged from incidents of sustained armed insurrection in Tibet, Qinghai, and Xinjiang's Yili district, to "counterrev-

---

6. Teiwes with Sun (1999).

7. MacFarquhar (1983), p. 329.

8. Nicholas Lardy, "The Chinese Economy Under Stress, 1958–1965," in *The Cambridge History of China: The People's Republic, Part 1*, ed. Denis Twitchett and John King Fairbank (Cambridge, Eng.: Cambridge University Press, 1987), pp. 360–91.

9. PLA General Political Department's *Work Correspondence*, Issue 1 (1960), as cited by Li Tienmin, *Crisis of the Chinese Communist Regime—As Seen from the Lianjiang Documents* (Taibei: Asian People's Anti-Communist League, 1964), p. 30.

10. Elizabeth J. Perry, "Rural Violence in China, 1880–1980," *Theory and Society* 13 (May 1984): 447–48.

olutionary armed rebellion" in at least four Gansu counties between 1958 and 1963, insurrection in Sichuan's Aba district from 1956 through 1961, and an armed rebellion in nearby Kai county in 1960. Several counties in Yunnan were plagued by rampant bandit activity throughout most of 1958, while others witnessed sporadic violent uprisings by ethnic minorities during the Great Leap period, resulting in the displacement of some 80,000 local residents. In Yunnan's Muding county, a crowd of residents unhappy with the implementation of Great Leap policies attacked and killed local public security forces and then laid siege to the district office. Numerous counties in Guizhou, Guangdong, Anhui, and Hubei recorded similar incidents of rioting and unrest from 1958 to 1962. Dramatic increases in crime, particularly in cases involving the theft of grain and other foodstuffs, were recorded as well: in Anhui province, incidents of theft, pillage, and plunder (*qiangjie*) rose an astronomical 310 percent during the Great Leap over that of the previous three-year period.[11]

The painful recovery process that followed was itself riddled with contradictions. As Shih Chih-yu observed, because in the Great Leap "the Chinese moral regime reached its climax," its catastrophic failure signaled nothing less than the demise of the CCP party-state as a moral agent, seriously hampering subsequent efforts to restore and extend central control over the economy and society. The widespread corruption and moral alienation that began during the years of famine persisted through the subsequent period of recovery and beyond.[12] The sheer magnitude of the disaster initially precluded the formation of a systematic strategy to redress food shortages and economic woes on a national scale. State-making efforts in the aftermath of the Leap involved restoring centralized state control over the provinces through the reestablishment of regional bureaus. Bureaucratic regularity returned to state offices, particularly in industrial sectors of the economy, and the various ministries circumvented by Mao's ad hoc planning process resumed their oversight of the economy. Financial control was recentralized in Beijing, and the principles of vertical leadership, uniform planning, and supervision by upper echelons were reaffirmed in accounting and finance. Most important of all, de facto control of agricultural production and labor was entrusted by the communes and brigades down to the team,

---

11. Li Ruojian, "Da yuejin yu kunnan shiqi de shehui dongdang yu shehui kongzhi" (Social instability and social control during the Great Leap Forward and period of difficulty), *Ershiyi shiji* (Twenty-first century), no. 60 (October 1990): 37–46.

12. Shih Chih-yu, "The Decline of a Moral Regime: China's Great Leap Forward in Retrospect," *Comparative Political Studies* 27:2 (July 1994): 272–301.

and private plots, family sideline occupations, and free markets were restored.[13]

The task of restoring the moral agency of the regime was more complex. As Gao Hua notes, the rectification campaign known as the Socialist Education Movement was a direct response to the Great Leap, rooted in Mao's determination that the rural food shortages were caused by the continuing destructive activities of hidden class enemies. In early 1960, with reports of "excessive mortality" (*feizhengchang siwang*) trickling in from several provinces, central authorities in Beijing sent word to local cadres that such deaths were no doubt caused by the incomplete nature of the democratic revolution in those areas, "the deviant nature of the local party roots, and serious impurities in the local party organizations." One frantic March 1960 cadre report detailing mass starvations in three Gansu counties earned the following assessment from the party center: "From the county down to the grassroots, all have been infiltrated by counter-revolutionary and bad elements; a major cause of the problems that have occurred is impurity in the cadres' ranks." In June 1960 Mao began advancing his theory that "five winds" (over-egalitarianism, exaggeration, commandism, blindly leading production, and bureaucratic elitism) among local cadres were to blame for continuing problems in the countryside. The November 1960 party directive on rural work commonly known as the Twelve Articles set in place emergency measures reversing some earlier measures, but also reaffirmed Mao's analysis that "rightist mistakes" were at fault, and ordered rectification. In 1961, Mao called for a series of careful investigations into local conditions in rural areas, paving the way for further policy readjustments, but also seeking to hold cadres accountable for any errors committed in the implementation of Great Leap policies. Mao found evidence in many of these early investigations to confirm his suspicions that political factors were to blame in the hardest-hit locales, even as others in the leadership circle sought to postpone policies aimed at sharpening class struggle until the economy had stabilized.[14]

At the Tenth Plenum of the Central Committee in 1962, two contradictory trends in post-Leap state-making reforms were already well in evidence: the party, and particularly the People's Liberation Army under the control of Lin Biao, reaffirmed its commitment to the radical ideological tenets of Mao's vision, whereas the state moved to consolidate a pragmatic

13. Byung-joon Ahn, *Chinese Politics and the Cultural Revolution: Dynamics of Policy Processes* (Seattle: University of Washington Press, 1976), pp. 46–59.
14. Gao Hua, "Da jihuang yu siqing yundong de qiyuan" (The great famine and the origin of the Four Cleans Movement), *Ershiyi shiji* (Twenty-first century), no. 60 (October 1990): 56–68.

series of policy readjustments under the stewardship of then-president Liu Shaoqi designed to promote economic recovery and stabilization. The growing divergence between ideological revitalization on the one hand, and actual bureaucratic practices on the other, set the stage for the "Four Cleans" rectification of local cadres and the Socialist Education Movement that swept the country beginning in 1962. These early efforts were originally conceived not only as an important corrective to the standard system of bureaucratic discipline and control enacted by the formal apparatus of the state but also as an attempt to shift moral responsibility for the Great Leap disaster away from the center of power. The failure of these measures to mend the growing cleavage between the party's ideological center and the bureaucratic practices embraced by the state contributed to the subsequent upheaval of the Cultural Revolution.

Whereas Nationalist state-makers increasingly found themselves embroiled in an instrumentalist "politics of accommodation" that undermined the regime's capacity to achieve its more ideologically oriented aims over the long term, Mao-era state-makers in the aftermath of the Great Leap manifestly committed themselves to reproducing the dialectics of ongoing class struggle, even as the party's ideological constructs grew increasingly divorced from actual economic conditions. The success of the earlier land-reform campaign and collectivization of agriculture destroyed the material foundation of the rural elite under the old regime, theoretically rendering obsolete the initial system of social stratification based on class status (*jieji chengfen*) put in place at the time of land reform. Yet, paradoxically, Mao's September 1962 exhortation to "Never forget class struggle" resurrected and reframed the pivotal importance of socioeconomic classes in revolutionary China. No longer solely a reflection of an individual's relationship to the means of production, class status came to refer also to a particular attitude toward the regime as manifested in personal behavior. Individuals belonging to either the "five red classes" (workers, poor and middle peasants, cadres, family members of revolutionary martyrs, and designated revolutionary intellectuals) or the "five bad categories" (landlords, rich peasants, counter-revolutionaries, "bad elements," and rightists) could be "recruited" to the opposing camp by a simple shift in perspective. Once untethered from its basis in objective material conditions, preserving or improving one's revolutionary class status over time required regular, even daily, public demonstration or expression of support for the party line.

The rebuilding of both state and society in the aftermath of the Great Leap was thus increasingly shaped by an opposing set of norms: one supporting a notion of class status based on distinctions made at the time of land reform, the other a countervailing claim that anchored social status to political subjectivity and behavior in the present. The established political elite, whose revolutionary credentials had been honed through political struggles waged over the preceding decades, generally supported the former view. The latter interpretation was favored by marginal and dispossessed groups, including the families of former social elites and intellectuals, who sought recognition on the basis of their professional qualifications or loyalty to the regime.[15]

In practice, at the local level the tension between these two views of class status created a widening gulf between the actual lived experience of rural residents and the officially sanctioned discourse on the meaning of class struggle. As Huang recently argued, the model of rural class relations imposed across the board during the land-reform campaign often did not accord with the social and economic realities of village life. Designated "struggle objects" were frequently selected by work teams not on the basis of objective criteria defined by the Land Reform Law, but instead upon political or even social considerations, creating a category of "class enemies" that was both internally heterogeneous and politically nebulous. This disjunction between representational and objective reality, moreover, not only did not abate but intensified over time.[16] Mao's 1962 clarion call to return to this initial discontinuity under the rubric of the Socialist Education Movement opened the door to the re-examination of class status across the board, by both work-team members and ordinary commune residents, in an attempt to determine whether the words and deeds of local cadres accorded with their true class status. This redrawing of the boundary between the moral agency asserted by the party-state and those suspected of having been secretly recruited by the "enemy camp" resulted in a massive reshuffling, not only among local agents of the party-state but also between village residents on both sides of that imprecise and shifting line.

State-Making and Local Government in the PRC

The Maoist era was punctuated by recurrent attempts to systematically purge the state apparatus of undesirable elements and suspected hidden enemies of the regime, a legacy that is partially rooted in the manner in which the CCP took control over local governments. In the transitional phase of CCP rule, local administrations represented an eclectic hybrid of

---

15. Jean-François Billeter, "The System of 'Class-Status,'" in *The Scope of State Power in China*, ed. Stuart Schram (New York: St. Martin's Press, 1985), p. 149; see also pp. 133–35.
16. Philip Huang, "Class Struggle in Rural China: Representational and Objective Realities from the Land Reform to the Cultural Revolution," *Modern China* 21:1 (January 1995): 105–43.

military, "old" and "new" bureaucratic personnel, and officials who owed their positions primarily to either ideological or technocratic credentials. Even as the new regime undertook ambitious state-building measures to increase the reach of the government, concerns about the purity and efficacy of lower-level units plagued central administrators, and increasingly convulsive measures were undertaken during the Maoist era to purge the ranks and assert the moral authority of the center.

In 1953, in preparation for the campaign to form lower-stage cooperatives, an attempt was made to establish party branch committees below the county level, at the level of the town (*xiang*). From 1953 to 1954, work-team members sent down from the county party branches, where they had received training, joined these town committees. Many such team members had previously played significant roles in the land-reform effort. Under the supervision of the county agricultural work departments, these teams initially did little more than provide advice to town residents on how to form lower-stage agricultural cooperatives, consisting of approximately 3–5 production teams, each of which represented 10–20 households. However, by the fall of 1954, increasing pressure was placed on households to join the cooperatives through the manipulation of taxes and state procurement quotas under the "unified buying and selling" *(tonggou tongxiao)* program, and by early 1955 the vast majority of households were indeed participating in the lower-stage cooperatives. Not long after, there was a move to incorporate the leaders of these cooperatives, who were generally younger farmers who had taken the initiative to cooperatize, into the town party branch structure. By the end of 1954, most town committees included at least four main administrative positions: the town manager (*xiangzhang*), the chief of the People's militia, a security cadre (who was also generally in charge of the *zhian baowei wei-yuanhui*, or peace preservation committee), and the chair of the agriculture committee; most of these administrators, along with many of the leaders of the cooperatives, were also party members. In 1956, with the drive under way to establish higher-stage cooperatives, each cooperative incorporated nearly all the households within a town; two years later, in most regions each of the former villages became a "production brigade" (*shengchan dadui*) and the former administrative districts or wards (*qu*) within a county were converted into communes (*gongshe*), although in some counties communes were formed out of one or several former administrative towns.[17]

With the disastrous failures of the Great Leap Forward, central state-makers moved to restructure the commune system beginning in 1959. The

---

17. A. Doak Barnett, *Cadres, Bureaucracy, and Political Power in Communist China* (New York: Columbia University Press, 1967), p. 121.

communes themselves were initially subdivided into two or three units, and the labor management and basic accounting unit was moved down from the commune to the production brigade, which averaged approximately 100 to 350 households. After a time, the basic accounting unit shifted finally to the production-team level, which represented approximately 20 to 40 households on average. The early version of the work-point system, which remunerated commune members on the basis of labor contributed to the team, was reinstituted. Small private plots and free local markets were again restored, and peasants were once again permitted to keep the harvests grown on reclaimed land. Individual households once again were permitted to keep domestic animals, to maintain their own farming tools, and to plant fruit trees near their homes.[18]

Yet despite the fact that these measures appeared to signal the decentralization of state control over agricultural production and therefore to represent a retreat from the overtly ambitious state-making policies of the Great Leap Forward, central authorities in the retrenchment period simultaneously moved to strengthen state control over all phases of the production and distribution processes, and actually increased state control over the activities of the lowest administrative unit. In ensuring the achievement of the goals of the new party-state with respect to production and taxation, CCP leaders in the early 1960s sought to mobilize mid-range agencies outside the commune's administrative hierarchy in order to ensure the compliance of local production teams with central state goals. In managing the levels of production and procurement for the teams, the Beijing leadership set specific targets that were allocated directly to the provinces, and that were then distributed to regional, county, commune, and brigade authorities. Team progress toward the fulfillment of these goals was strictly monitored in the retrenchment of the early 1960s by the imposition of various controls and the intensification of routine scheduling, reporting, and investigative measures. The return to limited private production and the reinstatement of free local markets took place under the watchful eye of state-managed supply and marketing cooperatives, which established contracts with teams and even individuals to procure certain commodities at state prices. Finally, the use of work and inspection teams dispatched or "sent down" by central authorities to monitor political and economic activities within rural communities rose dramatically in the post–Great Leap period: Bo Yibo estimates that at the height of the Four Cleans Movement, nearly 10,000 cadres, youths, and teachers were mobilized within each county to

---

18. William L. Parish and Martin King Whyte, *Village and Family Life in Contemporary China* (Chicago: University of Chicago Press, 1978), p. 34.

eat, live, and work with the commune members in the effort to mobilize class struggle.[19] Thus, whereas the economic retrenchment policies of the early to mid-1960s have often been viewed as measures that decentralized state administration and accordingly increased the autonomy of local team units,[20] in fact during this period, local communities experienced fewer opportunities for autonomous decision-making than ever before, and were instead subjected to steady rises in the scope and intensity of state intervention in local affairs.[21] Local cadres at the county level and below, as well as the ordinary commune members they supervised, were scrutinized and tightly controlled not only through their vertical links to provincial offices and central ministries in Beijing but even more directly by the extended visits of work teams dispatched to investigate and mobilize local communities.

ADMINISTRATIVE DISCIPLINE AND CONTROL

Just as the transfer of political power to the Nationalists at the end of the Qing had serious ramifications for the manner in which civil servants were scrutinized and evaluated, the establishment of the People's Republic fundamentally altered the ways in which bureaucratic malfeasance was defined and prosecuted. Anxious to distinguish itself from what it considered to be the endemic corruption of the previous regime, the Central Committee of the CCP announced that "the work of the people's judiciary should not be based on the Nationalist Party's Six Codes, but should be based on new people's laws," and denounced the previous system of reactionary laws as having been "designed to preserve the domination of the feudal landlords, compradors, and bureaucratic bourgeoisie and to suppress the resistance of the broad masses of the people" in the judicial process.[22] Under the Common Program, "people's governments" from the county (*xian*) level upward were instructed to establish supervisory organs to evaluate the performance of state officials and public functionaries of all types (*renhe gongwu renyuan*) and to administer disciplinary action to

---

19. Bo Yibo, *Ruogan zhongda juece yu shijian de huigui* (Recollections of some important policies and events) (Beijing: Zhonggong Zhongyang dangjiao chubanshe, 1993), *xiajuan*, pp. 1119–20, 1135–36.

20. For example, see the discussion of economic retrenchment policies in Bill Brugger, *China: Liberation and Transformation, 1942–1962* (Totowa, NJ: Barnes and Noble, 1981), pp. 230–37.

21. Birrell (1969).

22. North China People's Government 1, *Faling huibian* (Collection of laws and directives) (Beijing, 1949), as cited by Alice Tay, "Law in Communist China: Part One," *Sydney Law Review* 6:2 (1968): 171.

punish either illegal acts (*wanfa*) or negligence (*shizhi*) on the part of civil servants.[23] Article 18 of the Common Program stated: "All state organs of the People's Republic of China must enforce a revolutionary work-style (*zuofeng*), embodying honesty, simplicity, and service to the people: they must severely punish corruption (*tanwu*), forbid extravagance, and oppose the bureaucratic work-style, which alienates the masses of the people."[24] While many of the Nationalists' judicial and law-enforcement organs were retained with few changes in the years immediately following the revolution,[25] often, criminal and corruption cases were handled by a loosely and hastily organized network of "people's tribunals" and procuracies that tried, sentenced, and executed alleged criminals and other political enemies on an ad hoc basis. For example, one Tianjin newspaper reported in 1951:

The Beijing Municipal People's Government held a huge public meeting for the accusation of counterrevolutionaries on May 20, 1951. Speaking before the aroused crowd, Lou Ruiqing, Minister of Public Security, "suggested" that some 220 criminals be sentenced to death. He was followed by Mayor Peng Zhen, who wound up the drama by saying: "What shall we do with such a group of beasts as these vicious despots, bandits, traitors, and special agents?" "Shoot them!" the audience shouted. "Right, they should be shot," the mayor replied. "Following this meeting we shall hand over the cases to the military court of the Municipal Military Control Commission for conviction. Tomorrow, conviction; the next day, execution." The crowd responded with wild applause and loud cheers.[26]

Such rallies were condoned by early Communist leaders under the auspices of "revolutionary justice"; the Organic Regulations of the People's Tribunals, promulgated on July 20, 1950, allowed such tribunals to be organized on an ad hoc basis "in response to practical needs" and granted them the power to arrest, detain, try, sentence, and impose on the spot criminal penalties up to and including the death sentence.[27]

The 1954 Constitution provided for the establishment of a formalized judicial system under the direction of the Supreme People's Procuracy

---

23. Shen (1994), p. 6.

24. *Zhongguo renmin zhengzhi xieshang huiyi gongtong gangling (jielu)* (September 29, 1949), *di shiba tiao*, reprinted in *Jianguo yilai fanfubai huilu fagui ziliao xuanbian* (Anthology of anti-corruption and bribery laws and regulations since the founding of the People's Republic), ed. Zuigao renmin jianchayuan (Supreme People's Procuracy) (Beijing: Zhongguo xiancha chubanshe, 1991), p. 1.

25. Victor Li, "The Role of Law in Communist China," *China Quarterly* 44 (October–December 1977): 77.

26. *Da gong bao* (Tianjin) May 23, 1951; article cited by Jerome A. Cohen, "The Chinese Communist Party and Judicial Independence," *Harvard Law Review* 82:5 (1969): 977.

27. Alice Tay, "Law in Communist China: Part Two," *Sydney Law Review* 6:3 (1970): 350.

(Zuigao renmin jianchayuan). "Local people's courts" were organized in a three-level hierarchy from "basic" to "higher" people's courts and entrusted with "ordinary civil and unimportant criminal cases" arising from "contradictions among the people";[28] however, all courts as "organs of state," from the Supreme People's Procuracy down to the special people's tribunals that handled routine matters, were expected to follow the party's leadership in their rulings as well as to "rely on the masses of the people, constantly maintain close contact with them, heed their opinions, and accept their supervision."[29] In practice, particularly at the lower levels of the judicial system, this involved court officials working in close consultation with the local party branch secretary in order both to assess guilt and to mete out the appropriate punishment to those convicted of illegalities. In addition, trial judges were subject to popular opinion as well, since in all cases except for the most mundane and routine ones, each judge was required to hear the case alongside two "people's assessors," who could outvote him or her if necessary. During the Anti-Rightist Movement of 1957–58, even this limited form of judicial autonomy was sharply curtailed. The party conducted a broad-scale purge of cadres serving in the judiciary and moved to exclude all non-party members from serving as judges in the future; public-security offices were again permitted to directly impose sanctions against those accused of crimes without having to go through the formality of holding a trial. Finally, central authorities notified local cadres serving within the judiciary that if they failed to obey the express orders of the local party committee, they would be guilty of contravening the party constitution and undermining party unity and would be disciplined accordingly.[30]

This intermingling of the party and the state judicial organs meant that in practice the prevailing party policy at any given time, commonly referred to as the "party line," could carry the same political weight and legal force as the formal laws established by the state. At various periods following the establishment of the People's Republic, public servants (*gongwuyuan*), party members (*dangyuan*), and ordinary residents were all prosecuted under prevailing state laws that stipulated punishment both for specific crimes and for violations of party directives on matters of general public policy. For example, during the "Three Antis, Five Antis" movement of 1951–52, individuals were prosecuted for having violated the spirit of policies set forth by the secretary of the Central Committee to Investigate and Practice Economy (Zhongyang jieyue jiancha weiyuanhui) established under the

28. Ibid., p. 360.
29. *Zhonghua renmin gongheguo xianfa (jie lu)*, September 20, 1954, *di shiqi tiao*, as reprinted in Zuigao renmin jianchayuan (Supreme People's Procuracy), ed. (1991), p. 2.
30. Cohen (1969), pp. 984–90.

direction of the party's Central Committee; the state anti-corruption laws were not promulgated until several weeks later. The first set of guidelines, created by the aforementioned committee and issued by the Government Ministry of Personnel (Zhengwu yuan) on March 8, 1952, were collectively known as "Certain Regulations on the Punishment of Corruption, Waste, and Overcoming the Error of Bureaucratism" ("Guanyu chuli tanwu, lang-fei ji kefu guanliao zhuyi de ruogan guiding");[31] the state anti-corruption laws, promulgated on April 21, 1952, were referred to as the "People's Republic of China Statute Punishing Corruption" ("Zhonghua renmin gongheguo chengzhi tanwu tiaoli"). The former document outlined broad policy goals framed in a discussion of particular "problems" (*wenti*); the latter statute stipulated in formal legal language that "all employees of state organs, enterprises, schools, and auxiliary organs" who committed "embezzlement, theft, fraud, misappropriation (*taoqu*) of state property, confiscation (*qiangsu*) of another's property, receiving bribes, and other illegal practices to engross oneself at the expense of the public" were guilty of the crime of corruption. The actual text of the statute specifies eleven crimes, in addition to monetary graft and embezzlement, punishable under the terms of that ordinance: the endangering of public safety in state-owned or socialized enterprises; selling confidential information about the state economy or secretly working to collect the same; graft; extortion; forming "corrupt" (*tanwu*) organizations; repeat offenses by those who have not reformed themselves; crimes by unrepentant criminals or by those who confess only their own part in larger crimes; destruction of public property by those attempting to conceal their crimes; attempts to conceal crimes by shifting the blame onto another; failure to provide thorough confessions or later discovery of even more serious offenses that the crimi-nal failed to confess initially; criminal behavior evincing particularly evil (*elie*) designs.[32]

However, in practice, criminal charges raised against individuals dur-ing the "Three Antis, Five Antis" political campaign included a wide range of activities, many of which were not specifically addressed in either document. For example, in 1952 in Gansu's Lanzhou municipality, more than 600 workers were investigated during the "Five Antis" movement for "doing shoddy work with inferior materials" or "jerry-building" (*tou-*

---

31. The text of this set of regulations appears in Zuigao renmin jianchayuan (Supreme People's Procuracy), ed. (1991), pp. 307–13. However, in the discussion of the adjudication of "*sanfan*" cases in Shaanxi province, the provincial gazetteer dates the release of this document as March 8, 1952. See Jiao Langting, ed., *Shaanxi shengzhi* (Xian: Shaanxi renmin chubanshe, 1994), p. 399.

32. Zuigao renmin jianchayuan (Supreme People's Procuracy), ed. (1991), pp. 78–81.

gong jianliao): while it was determined that more than 400 of those investigated were either "law-abiding" (*shoufa hu*) or "basically law-abiding" (*jiben shoufa hu*), the remainder were found guilty of having engaged in "jerry-building" for illegal purposes. Also in conjunction with the campaign, nearly 8,500 workers were found guilty of evading taxes, although only 1,553 were found to have done so illegally.[33] In Shaanxi province, cases of officials accused during the campaign were heard by special "Three Antis People's Tribunals," staffed by the county manager (*xianzhang*), the county legal department assistant manager, the assistant prosecutor of the Public Security Bureau, Supervisory Council, the Procuracy, and those holding posts in various mass organizations. At the provincial level, two "people's courts" were established, one to handle "Three Antis" cases that were fiscal or monetary (*caizheng*) in nature, and the other to handle "educational" or "cultural" (*jiaowen*) violations. Four hundred and sixty-seven "tigers" (*laohu*) were found guilty of crimes of corruption by the provincial courts and received punishments ranging from demotion in rank to transfer to a post in another county. Some 255 of these "tigers" who were accused of less serious crimes of corruption had their cases heard instead by people's tribunals; 36 (29 percent) of these individuals were found guilty, but the majority (87 individuals, or 71 percent of the total) went unpunished.[34]

This merging of state law and party policy statements was again in evidence in the early 1960s. For example, in one case prosecuted during the Socialist Education Campaign in 1963, the Materials Department manager of the Shaanxi Xi'an Municipality Metallurgical Machine Building and Repair Factory, Li Yinggui, was tried for the crimes of "corruption, larceny, and plotting to betray the nation" (*tanwu daoqie panguo*); he was accordingly sentenced by the Xi'an Municipal Intermediate People's Court "in accordance with the statute (*tiaoli*) of the People's Republic of China punishing corruption, the [state] statute (*tiaoli*) punishing counter-revolutionaries, and other related [party] regulations (*guiding*)." For his crimes, Li Yinggui and his accomplices were instructed to return all the property they had illegally pilfered from their respective work units (*danwei*), after which they would be put to death. The Supreme People's Court of Shaanxi

---

33. Hu Fusheng, ed., *Gansu shengzhi* (Gansu province gazetteer) (Langzhou: Gansu renmin chubanshe, 1991), pp. 144–45. Those investigated for such crimes were classified into five categories: "law-abiding," "basically law-abiding," "seriously criminal" (*yanzhong weifa hu*), "completely criminal" (*wanquan weifa hu*), and one intermediate category that suggested elements of both law-abiding and criminal behavior (*liang ban hu*).

34. Jiao (1994), pp. 399–400.

Province heard the appeal but upheld the ruling of the lower court, and Li Yinggui was executed.[35]

Thus under the new regime both administrators and ordinary citizens were subject both to the laws and statutes promulgated by the state, and to the often far more ambiguous policy directives of the Communist Party. While the Nationalist regime had also made judicious use of politically motivated legislation in pursuit of particular aims, under the Communist Party the amalgamation of formal law and "policy winds" was even more complete. Furthermore, the sanctioning apparatus of the new regime included representative elements of all sectors of society—state administrators, party cadres, and ordinary citizens—in a comprehensive system of social and political control that did not necessarily rely upon judicial and law enforcement organs to carry out directives. Instead, both the citizens and the cadres of the new regime were simultaneously subject to sanctions from a wide variety of sources, including central state authorities, members of work teams, representatives of mass organizations, and higher-ranking authorities of local political organizations, all of which employed a variety of means, from "criticism" and "re-education" to the death penalty, in their attempts to ensure compliance and mete out "revolutionary justice." The pursuit of discipline and control under the new regime, while by no means uniformly successful, was totalizing both in scope and method, and represented a radical break with the past.

ROUTINE EVALUATION AND DISCIPLINARY CONTROL IN THE PRC

For cadres working below the level of the county, discipline was exercised in a sporadic manner in the immediate aftermath of the Communist victory, but gradually grew more stringent during the mid-1950s. There was widespread variation in the implementation of party policies at the lowest tier of administration: for example, after the establishment of low-level cooperatives, a general lack of clarity as to precisely how the resources of the cooperative ought to be distributed led to burgeoning numbers of graft and misappropriation cases among town and village personnel. The rise in such incidents was so marked, in fact, that in 1955 central authorities launched a cooperative rectification campaign (*zhengshe yundong*) to eliminate abuses; the campaign was repeated annually through at least 1964, taking place at the level of the commune instead of that of the cooperative after 1958. Pressure to ensure proper compliance with party directives at

---

35. Ibid., pp. 405–6.

the sub-county level intensified considerably after 1954 or so, and in 1960 the annual commune rectification campaign in one county revealed that as many as 40 percent of the work-point recorders had committed some kind of error and many of these were accused of graft. The county public security bureau took over the tasks of investigation and arraignment in cases involving the criminal wrongdoing of party cadres that work teams did not immediately handle.[36]

Beginning in 1954, the routine evaluation of local cadre performance was conducted by the office of the county organization department (*zuzhi bu*). Relatively small given the scope of its responsibilities, the organization department took on the tasks of transferring, promoting, and demoting county personnel, and of investigating the work situation and background of county employees. Because of the level of security involved in the handling of personnel evaluations, and of the necessity of processing a great deal of printed material, county organization department cadres generally tended to be drawn from the younger, better educated ranks of recent party recruits. Supervised by a department and a deputy department chief (*buzhang* and *fu buzhang*), organization department staff members were responsible for reviewing routine personnel evaluations for all county and sub-county agency employees, as well as for handling the organizational problems of the various agencies, cooperatives, and, after 1958, of the communes themselves. Such matters included the selection and cultivation of new candidates for cadre positions, as well as problems and issues related to recordkeeping and the maintenance of discipline.[37]

The routine evaluation process for party cadres in the mid-1950s to mid-1960s involved the compilation of an annual assessment (*jianding*) of each party cadre's record for that year. The assessment process began with a self-evaluation report that required cadres to list their accomplishments, as well as failures, over the previous year. Of primary importance were the cadres' main task assignments, and in particular the manner in which they fulfilled (or failed to fulfill) the responsibilities with which they were entrusted by the state. In practice, self-assessments tended to be modest in tone and focused more on shortcomings than on accomplishments. Each cadre was then required to frankly discuss the self-evaluation in an open meeting with his or her colleagues, and one member of that group was selected to write a brief summary of the group's opinions of the cadre's conduct. This report was then circulated to the county party branch for further evaluation and discussion, and county party branch members also added to the evaluation

36. Ezra Vogel, "Hsien (County) Organization," unpublished paper (n.p., 1964).
37. Ibid.

before passing it on to the organization department, where it was filed in the cadre's dossier.[38] Personal dossiers housed at the county organization department generally included the original application for party member-ship—for cadres who were party members—which involved a detailed auto-biographical account (*geren lishi*), a section on the individual's relatives and friends (*shehui guanxi*), thought (*sixiang*), standpoint (*lichang*), family class background (*jiating chushen*), individual class status (*geren chengfen*), and the recommendations of the individual's sponsors. For cadres who were not party members, equivalent information was included in their individ-ual dossiers. Annual evaluations for non-party cadres involved a similar process, but one that took place entirely within the individual cadre's gov-ernment work unit.[39] For both party and state cadres, the process by which these annual evaluations were prepared was also related to the selection of "advanced workers" (*xianjin gongzuozhe*), those cadres whose performance during the previous year had been exemplary and who were therefore wor-thy of emulation and reward. Each party unit was permitted to nominate a certain number of its own for consideration by higher authorities, based upon its discussions of individual records for that year.[40]

Local cadres guilty of various errors or shortcomings, on the other hand, routinely had their cases reviewed by the county supervision com-mittee (*jian weiyuanhui*). Closely related to and often physically situated near the organization department, the supervision committee personnel were responsible for urging local cadres to observe party discipline and to avoid deviation from the party line, but also for handling routine cases of cadres guilty of wrongdoing. In such cases, if the offender was a party cadre, he or she was granted the opportunity to present his or her case to a meeting of all party branch members; non-party members were generally not permitted this privilege when they were accused. The personnel of the supervision committee were entrusted with the responsibility of investigat-ing cases of wrongdoing and then, with the approval of the party branch, imposing sanctions on offenders. Often information on the conduct of the cadre in question was supplied to the supervision committee by the organization department. The most common errors routinely commit-ted by local cadres at the county levels and below included bureaucratism (*guanliao zhuyi*), commandism (*qiangpo renmin*), and corrupt lapses (*fuhua*

---

38. Barnett (1967), p. 166.
39. Ibid., p. 167
40. Martin K. Whyte, *Small Groups and Political Rituals in China* (Berkeley: University of California Press, 1974), p. 68.

zhuiluo), which generally involved sexual improprieties or careless attention to one's official duties.

However, local cadres were naturally also subjected to periodic non-
routine evaluations from both higher-level authorities and from those that
they themselves supervised, in the form of mass campaigns and rectification
movements. County administrations generally housed a county committee
special work group (*xian wei gongzuo zu*) within the county staff office to
assist in the organization of political campaigns as they arose, a unit that was
assigned additional personnel as needed by the organization department. In
the case of the campaign to root out counter-revolutionaries (*suqing fangeming yundong*) in the mid-1950s, for example, the county party committee
secretly established a special staff office to investigate cadres (*shen gan ban-
gongshi*) that incorporated cadres from the public security bureau, organization department, procuracy, court, government personnel office, finance
and trade department, and the industry and communications department.
This special staff office began its preparations by reviewing the dossiers of all
local cadres in order to determine who among them may have had "political
problems." Those with such problems who were suspected of illegalities or
other improprieties were then subjected to further secret investigations into
their background and activities. As the movement unfolded, the county
party committee expanded this special secret staff office and reorganized
it under the auspices of an open body, which was subsequently referred to
as the *su fan* staff office. Within the expanded organization, small groups
were organized to handle the specialized needs of the campaign, including
a propaganda group and an investigation team for collecting information
on cadres. The newly enlarged *su fan* staff office organized special study
groups in which all local cadres were required to participate by reviewing
materials and information about campaign goals, discussing their "political
problems," and engaging in criticism and self-criticism. At the climax of the
movement, a few cadres were selected as targets for special public criticism
at a series of mass "struggle meetings" (*douzheng hui*) at which they were
subjected to additional criticism, public defamation, and abuse.[41]

Discipline and Control in the Socialist
Education Movement

Three months after the conclusion of the Tenth Plenum at the end of 1962,
the new "socialist education campaign" was launched on a limited and
experimental basis in certain areas of the Chinese countryside. Mao's ini-

---

41. Barnett (1967), p. 170–71.

tial impetus for the launching of the Socialist Education Movement was a general concern with what he considered to be the "unhealthy tendencies" in the Chinese countryside in the aftermath of the Great Leap Forward: the reduction of the size of the communes, the adoption of the production team as the basic accounting unit, and the restoration of private plots for commune members. However, early reports from the experimental areas already carrying out the movement suggested that the crisis in the countryside was not due primarily to the possibility of a capitalist restoration, but instead to a widespread crisis in basic leadership. One report on the Fujian Lianjiang county residents revealed that the "spirit of individual enterprise" that had arisen from the economic reforms of the retrenchment period demonstrated that in fact a profound and fundamental schism had developed within their community: low-level cadres since the Great Leap period had grown increasingly reluctant to lead, and the masses increasingly reluctant to follow.

According to this report, the split originated during the land-reform campaign, when local cadres forced the landlords and rich peasants of Lianjiang county to surrender their property for redistribution. A decade after land reform had been completed, the former landlords and peasants still residing in the district were mobilizing to reclaim their confiscated property.

Since this year [1962], Xu Yisong, a landlord of Caichi in Aojiang, has not participated in collective labor, and during the War Preparation period he twice held family meetings, saying "First we want to settle accounts with the cadres, and second we want the return of our land and eighteen houses." Xu's son, taking advantage of the fear psychology of the masses during the War Preparation period, came out to tell people's fortunes, saying that the cadres' fate was [to be] "on the way out" (*waichu ming*) and the fate he saw for the poor farmers was one of "hard labor" (*laodong ming*). For the bad elements and the phony *baojia* chiefs he saw "first bitterness, later sweetness" (*xianku houtian*). He thus made everyone afraid. In the Shantang brigade there is a bad element by the name of Zeng Huoquan who in the past never spoke much but during the War Preparation period read the newspapers every day, talked about the situation, and [started] singing Fujianese folk operas and watching plays. He purposely went to the city gates to buy tobacco and tea and invited bad elements to eat and drink together. To everyone he said, "My day has come" (*wode tian xialai le*). This kind of incident became very frequent at that time, and in the June statistics, 30 to 40 percent of the Four Classes[42] arrogantly disobeyed the cadres. This is acute class struggle.[43]

---

42. The so-called "Four Classes" (*di, fu, fan, huai*), also referred to as the "Four Category Elements," included former landlords, rich peasants, counter-revolutionaries, or other assorted "bad elements" (*huai fenzi*), a catch-all term that often denoted those who had had secret-society, gang, or criminal connections prior to the revolution.

43. Wang Hongzhi, "Shiche bajie shi zhongquan hui jueyi, gonggu jiti jingji, fada nongye

In addition to the pressures faced by basic-level cadres from the disenfranchised landlords and rich peasants, the lower-level leadership in Lianjiang county was obviously uncertain about how to manage the post–Great Leap reforms in agricultural policy. Following the post–Great Leap rectification campaign, in which many basic-level cadres were roundly criticized for "commandism" and "leftist excesses," most leaders adopted a far more tentative posture toward those under their supervision. When the members of the Guantou commune Xiaqi Second Production Team openly rebelled against their team leader, refusing to plant sweet potatoes unless the household contracting system was adopted, the team leader readily acceded to their wishes, announcing: "the important thing is to get the sweet potatoes in. I'll be a nice fellow (*zuo yidian hao ren*) so that even if the Nationalists come, they will not behead me."[44]

Cadres, having forcefully urged large-scale communization in 1958, were given the nod from their superiors only a few years later to restore private plots and the system of household contract production. This dramatic shift in position left many basic-level leaders with "confused ideology," causing them to "vacillate . . . because of muddled understanding and unclear conceptions of right and wrong" (*jiexian bu qing*). One local cadre was purported to have adopted the slogan: "There is not one Chinese with an unselfish public spirit (*mei you dagong wuside*). Only under individual enterprise will efforts redouble." Thus, the report concluded that in the aftermath of the rectification struggles, there was a tendency to rely excessively on the "mass line" to the extent that

> another extreme arose within the party—that of extreme decentralization, or democracy without centralization. In all affairs, these people permit only themselves, not others, to talk; permit only the lower levels, not the upper levels, to talk; permit only the lower levels to criticize the upper, and not the upper to criticize the lower. . . . There are also some persons who have found a pretext for extreme democracy in what they call "the demands of the masses" (*qunzhong yaoqiu*) and "general opinion" (*dajia yijian*) and on these pretexts have openly opposed the upper levels. This situation also exists among the masses. They do not obey the directions of the cadre, even going to the point where they beat the cadre without being punished.[45]

---

shengchan" (Implementation of the resolutions of the Tenth Plenum of the Eighth Central Committee on strengthening the collective economy and expanding agricultural production) (1962), *Fujian Lianjiang xian feifang wenjian ji qi jiufen* (The documents of the [Communist] bandits of Fujian's Lianjiang county, with analytical notes) (Taibei: Ministry of National Defense's Bureau of Intelligence, 1964), p. 20.

44. Ibid., pp. 27–30.

45. Ibid., p. 31.

This massive crisis of confidence in the local leadership resulted in rising levels of skepticism with respect to regime policies among the ordinary commune members as well. When the Pukou commune Shantang brigade's Chen Bingyou production-team leader decided to engage in household contracting for sweet-potato production under a policy directive that encouraged such "mobilization for guaranteed output," the poor peasant members of the production team objected on the grounds that such policies would benefit only the affluent members of the team. The team leader, pressed from above to "mobilize for guaranteed output," overrode their objections, saying to poor peasant Chen Shuxiu: "You do not have to accept if you do not want to, but later we will not give you any potato seed." Reluctantly consenting to the new household contracting system, the poor peasant members of the production team said: "When you carry water in two bamboo baskets, both will be empty. Individual enterprise will starve us, but we will not be able to rely on the collective either."[46]

The author of the Lianjiang county report concluded that this widespread crisis of confidence was due primarily to the unwillingness, and in some cases, the inability of the basic-level cadres to impose the correct "party line" on the commune members they supervised following the rectification struggles of 1960–61. As a result,

There was no clear perception of the boundaries between right and wrong; there was the idea of trying to be a good fellow; there was a tendency to muddle through things; and when a tendency toward error was seen, the cadres did not dare to start criticism struggles. This failure allowed various bad tendencies to arise, such as disobedience of law and order, embezzlement and misappropriation of funds, excessive consumption, extravagance, superstition, and indiscriminate felling of trees.[47]

Shortly thereafter, the Liangjiang county party branch circulated a document that detailed extensive corruption among commune- and brigade-level cadres at Pandu commune, indicating that they suspected that the Pandu case was "not an isolated one, but that such conditions prevail in varying degrees of severity in other places in the county." The circulated document revealed that in Chishi brigade, the branch party secretary, Zhou Huojiao, had amassed a small number of local cadres, including three party members—the brigade leader, the brigade accountant, and the brigade cashier—in a collective scheme to pilfer brigade funds and materials to build a two-story, nine-room house on commune grounds. In another

46. Ibid., p. 27.
47. Ibid., p. 24.

case, the Poxi brigade chief, Chen Zhenrui, held a series of parties in order to extort money from other commune members. Initially using the pretext of his daughter's upcoming marriage, Brigade Leader Chen hosted an eight-table party and used a portion of the money given to him as gifts in order to build a home. When building costs outstripped the original investment, Chen threw another banquet, engaging commune members in a competitive struggle to see who would be able to "pledge" the greatest monetary gifts for the occasion, from which he ultimately made a profit of 730 *yuan*. In addition to extorting funds from commune members in this manner, Chen also secretly used timber owned by the brigade in building his private home. Similarly, it was discovered that Lan Yishui, assistant secretary of the Dongan brigade party branch, had likewise secretly stolen 35 cedar trees belonging to the collective in order to build himself a house. Other brigade members also helped themselves to some of the collective's camphor trees and sold the wood as boards to local shipyards. All of the cadres discovered to have committed such acts "resolved to correct their faults and to do good work."[48]

Within weeks, the Lianjiang county party branch issued a comprehensive plan for commune rectification to take place over the course of the winter and the upcoming spring, which took "socialist education" as its "essence." Dividing the county's brigades into two groups, the county party branch planned to supplant the cadres in half of the brigades for the three months projected for the movement to run its course. In all brigades the movement would begin with a round of mass meetings at which commune members would be called upon to publicly recount the conditions of their lives prior to the 1949 revolution, and then to air any complaints they may have about subsequent developments in the county. Cadres would then lead the masses in an instructive series of contrasts, comparing past to present conditions, as well as private to collective labor. Finally, participants would be called upon to "reckon accounts," assessing the nature of the changes that had taken place since the revolution, and recommitting themselves to socialism. Then all party and state organizational units would undergo a round of criticism and self-criticism sessions "to correct error and to raise the level of understanding." Clearly, the party branch's original intention for commune rectification in 1963 involved a socialist education campaign that was strictly limited in its scope and intensity. The instructions of the

---

48. Zhonggong Pandu gongshe weiyuanhui (Central committee of the Pandu commune Party branch), "Zhonggong Pandu gongshe weiyuanhui guanyu gongshe, dadui bufen lingdao ganbu de huihuo langfei he weifa luanji de baogao," December 18, 1962, Zhonggong Fujiansheng Lianjiangxian weiyuanhui (zhuanfa) in *Fujian Lianjiang xian feifang wenjian ji qi jiufen* (Taibei: Ministry of National Defense's Bureau of Intelligence, 1964), pp. 59–63.

county branch affirmed: "The emphasis in socialist education will be on party and cadre members. If the ideology of these persons can be resolved, then all work will proceed well. Therefore, education should first be conducted within the party and among the cadres. This should consist of linking it to ideology by appropriate criticism and self-criticism. The ideology of party and cadre members must be made deep and clear." Mass "struggle sessions" and "key point criticisms" were expressly forbidden, except as leveled against members of the Four Class elements.[49]

A large-scale transfer of upper-level and urban cadres to the rural communes immediately began in earnest. Cadres had been periodically "sent down" to rural areas in large numbers since the founding of the People's Republic, in large part to compensate for the overstaffing of upper-level state and party bureaucracies. The goal of the "sent-down" (*xiafang*) transfers was twofold: on the one hand, the Beijing leadership sought to reinvigorate the ranks of mid-level cadres by subjecting them to labor experiences in the communes; on the other hand, the newly unfolding Socialist Education Campaign required a reliable staff to implement educational and ideological policies at the local levels. Accordingly, the leadership selected "a number of exemplary party members, cadres, and personnel who are loyal to the cause of the revolution . . . and who are capable workers, are experienced in the practice of mass-line work, to work in the countryside over a long duration [of time]."[50] In the month of February, 30,000 provincial, district, county, and commune-level cadres in Guangdong were moved to production teams in rural areas where they were supposed to "assist production team cadres in their work leading [the masses] and in excelling at harvesting spring production."[51] Organized into work teams by the provincial party committee in conjunction with county party secretaries,[52] the sent-down cadres ostensibly were sent to learn from the experi-

49. Lianjiang County Party Branch, "Commune Rectification Plan of the Lianjiang County Committee" (January 5, 1963), in C. S. Chen and Charles Price Ridley, *Rural People's Communes in Lien-chiang* [Lianjiang] (Stanford: Hoover Institution Press, 1969), p. 152.

50. *Renmin ribao* (People's Daily), January 25, 1963.

51. *Renmin ribao* (People's Daily), "Guangdong sanwan ganbu shenru chungeng di yi xian, tong jiceng ganbu he sheyuan tong laodong tong gongzuo xieli jiejue wenti" (30,000 Guangdong cadres dig in deep for spring plowing, together with basic-level cadres and commune members to engage in work and labor together and to unite efforts to solve problems) (February 23, 1963), p. 1.

52. Wang Guangmei, "(Zhuanfa) 'Guangyu yige dadui de shehui zhuyi jiaoyu yundong de jingyan zongjie' de pishi" (Summary of the experiences of a production brigade in the Socialist Education Movement) (September 1, 1964), in *Pipan ziliao: Zhongguo He Luxiao fu Liu Shaoqi fangeming xiuzheng zhuyi yanlun ji* (Critique: the collected counter-revolutionary revisionist speeches of China's He Luxiao, spouse of Liu Shaoqi) (Beijing: Renmin chubanshe, 1967),

ences of rural residents, and to adopt their lifestyle as completely as possible under the "eat together, live together, labor together" (*tong chi, tong zhu, tong laodong*), or "three togethers" (*santong*) policy. Cadres with relatively high-level posts often adopted pseudonyms during their time on the communes and employed other measures to conceal their identities from the commune members with whom they worked.[53] However, according to party regulations, they were to receive no preferential treatment from commune members during their stays. In the early phases of the movement, sent-down work teams were to assist local residents in carrying out the "four clean-ups" campaign, involving the investigation into commune accounts, warehouses, work points, and supplies, as well as generally leading the production teams in exercises of criticism and comparison with other model units. In later phases of the movement, these work teams became instrumental in conducting secret investigations into the affairs of both local cadres and residents alike, and in leading intense and sometimes violent struggle sessions against those they deemed "reactionary" and "counter-revolutionary."

Plans to expand and intensify the movement began shortly after the Chinese New Year celebrations in January 1963. In early February, Fujian Lianjiang county party branch secretary Chen Fulong convened a meeting of party and state cadres and work-team personnel stationed in the county in order "to study how to launch a large-scale Socialist Education Movement for increased production and economy." Noting that favorable progress had been made toward the initial goals of the movement, Secretary Chen asserted, however, that "the scale of the movement that we have been conducting has not been sufficiently large, and, in particular, a large-scale mass movement has not been formed. Using up time in going through the formal motions still occurs. Ideological problems have not been solved in depth." Calling for a simultaneous deepening and widening of the movement, Chen assured his audience,

We must let our banners fly and sound our battle drums and conduct the movement with great vigor. This cannot be an ordinary movement. We must arouse the masses. We must understand clearly that if we do not conduct it on a large scale, we can neither suppress the evil tendencies of capitalism or feudalism, nor elevate the awareness of the masses and the cadres. . . . Therefore, we must conduct a large-

pp. 472-73; although excerpts from Wang Guangmei's so-called "Taoyuan Experience" report are widely available outside the PRC, I am indebted to Michael Schoenhals for sharing his copy of the complete and unexpurgated report with me.
53. Wu Xiuquan, *Huiyi yu huainnian* (Recollections and remembrances) (Beijing: Zhonggong zhongyang dang jiao chubanshe, 1991), p. 386.

scale movement in the manner of the 1953 General Line and the 1958 Great Leap Forward movements.[54]

To initiate this process, Secretary Chen recommended yet another round of struggle sessions directed against the cadres in leadership positions at the brigade and team levels. Citing the various malpractices that had already taken place in Lianjiang county, he proposed

During this stage [of the movement], cadre members at all levels who commit bad acts should be investigated, and criticism and self-criticism should be carried out. Individuals who seriously violate laws and regulations should be punished. It is at this stage that the masses have been critical of us. . . . At this point, many among the masses say: "Socialist Education is only for the masses, not for the cadres. What does this mean?" Because we have not solved the severe and predominant problems concerning the cadres, the masses are critical.[55]

Central leaders in Beijing had originally envisioned a movement that would be relatively limited in scope and short in duration, although they hoped it would have maximum impact in rooting out cadre malfeasance. At the local level, calls for ordinary commune members to mobilize against the basic-level cadres continued through 1963. In May, the party leadership in Beijing released the "First Ten Points," a document purportedly drafted under Mao's supervision, which outlined in basic terms the projected course the Socialist Education Movement would take. Noting the persistence of "bourgeois influences" at work in the Chinese countryside, the authors of the document warned local communities to maintain a vigilant watch against a potential resurgence of capitalism and targeted groups for special supervision:

1. The exploiting classes, landlords, and rich peasants who have been overthrown are always trying to stage a comeback. They are waiting for an opportunity to counterattack in order to carry out class revenge and to deal a blow against the poor peasants and lower-middle peasants.

2. Landlords and rich peasants who have been overthrown are employing all kinds of schemes in an attempt to corrupt our cadres in order to usurp the leadership and power. In some communes and brigades the leadership and power have actually fallen into their hands. In some sectors of other organizations they also have their agents.

---

54. Chen Fulong, "Jin yibu kaizhan yige da guimo de zengchan jieyue, shehui zhuyi jiaoyu yundong," in *Fujian Lianjiang xian feifang wenjian ji qi jiufen* (Taibei: Ministry of National Defense's Bureau of Intelligence, 1964), p. 47.

55. Ibid., pp. 50–51.

3. In some places landlords and rich peasants are carrying out activities for the restoration of feudalistic patriarchal rule, putting out counter-revolutionary propaganda, and developing counter-revolutionary organizations.

4. Landlords, rich peasants, and counter-revolutionaries are making use of religion and the reactionary *huidaomen* [secret, religious, and welfare societies] to deceive the masses and carry out criminal activities.[56]

When reviewing documents outlining how the mass movement ought to proceed, Mao purportedly argued for a short campaign of significant intensity, focused on "class, class struggle, socialist education, reliance on poor and lower-middle peasants, the four cleans, [and] cadre participation in labor."[57] Accordingly, the "First Ten Points" opened the way for further investigation into the activities of the "Four Class elements," but at the same time warned that "new bourgeois elements" had also arisen, "who have become rich by speculation." This new class, lurking within the revolutionary organizations and operating from within the collective economy, actively conspired with the Four Class elements to overthrow the new socialist order in the Chinese countryside: "corrupt elements, thieves, speculators, and degenerates . . . have ganged up with landlords and rich peasants to commit evil deeds. These elements are a part of the new bourgeoisie, or their ally." Citing the experience of Hebei's Baoding Special District Committee, whose rural investigations revealed dissatisfaction on the part of many ordinary commune members with the allocation of work points and the maintenance of commune accounts, the report called for a two-pronged attack on corruption in rural China. First, poor and lower-middle peasant associations were enjoined to carry out a thorough investigation and "cleaning up" of the administration of four aspects of their collective existence: granaries, property, account books, and the work-point allocation system, a process referred to as the "Four Cleans" campaign. Second, local cadres were urged to "put down their burdens" by confessing their wrongdoing in these areas, "washing their hands and bodies" to make certain they were "clean of hand and foot." Cadre confessions were to be strictly voluntary and were not to be compelled; those accused were to be given the opportunity to defend themselves publicly against the charges. Once they admitted their errors and, if necessary, made restitution of any collective materials misused or misappropriated, cadres would be considered successfully redeemed, with the expectation that they would set about their work with renewed vigor.[58]

In September, the party Central Committee released a revised report on the progress of the Socialist Education Movement, subsequently known as

56. Baum and Teiwes (1968), pp. 60–61.
57. Bo (1993), p. 1108.
58. Baum and Teiwes (1968), pp. 61–67.

the "Later Ten Points," which enjoined not only team, brigade, and commune cadres, but also those serving at the county, district, and provincial levels as well, to carry out a thorough "hand-washing" to purify themselves before continuing to press rectification on their subordinates. This document, purportedly drafted under the supervision of Deng Xiaoping and Peng Zhen but with corrections and revisions made by Mao,[59] also delineated an emerging role for the work teams sent down to the communes over the previous year. For areas in which members of the "Four Classes" had already taken formal control by occupying positions of responsibility, work teams were given license to remove the guilty parties from power and take control over those units themselves; for the remaining units, the work teams were to serve as "staff" to the basic-level cadres, assisting them in planning, providing guidance and assistance, and "enlightening" them "in the analysis of problems and the determination of policies and methods." The work-team members were again warned against convening "struggle rallies," and were enjoined against promoting physical violence against targets of the campaign; however, at the same time, they were instructed to investigate the class backgrounds of local cadres and commune members alike and to carefully monitor those who were of the "Four Classes."

Those who have committed violence . . . should be arrested and punished according to law immediately. Other "four elements" engaged in obstructive activities should be dealt with by adopting the basic principle of "killing none and arresting few" (under five percent). The few "four elements" engaged in obstructive activities who warrant immediate arrest should also first be put to a process of struggle conducted among the masses, so as to expose the enemy and educate the masses. At an opportune time they are to be taken into custody according to law after due examination and authorization. The arrest of an offender should be strictly carried out under two conditions: first, the crime is serious, the evidence is clear, and the offender shows no repentance; and second, the majority of the masses demand the arrest. By observing these two conditions, we cannot make mistakes in the arrest of offenders. . . . There will also be some individuals whose executions are demanded by the masses. These are altogether necessary.[60]

While the "Later Ten Points" was subsequently denounced as a piece of revisionist propaganda during the Cultural Revolution, it evinced a fundamental continuity with the policies set forth by the previous document and at the same time clearly called for an intensification of the mass movement already under way in most areas of China in late 1963. Work teams were implicitly given more leeway than before to conduct their investigations

---

59. Frederick C. Teiwes, *Politics and Purges in China: Rectification and the Decline of Party Norms, 1950–1965* (New York: M. E. Sharpe, 1979), pp. 521–22.
60. Baum and Teiwes (1968), pp. 102–17.

into the class backgrounds and activities of both cadres and commune members and were encouraged to apply appropriate sanctions in cases in which they were warranted. At the same time, the "Later Ten Points" advocated an increasingly hostile and suspicious attitude toward the already troubled class of basic-level cadres. Whereas the "First Ten Points" had argued for a thorough "clearing of accounts," the "Later Ten Points" implicitly pushed this process a step further, strongly suggesting that cadres found guilty of malpractices should be treated as class enemies engaged in an antagonistic contradiction with socialist revolutionary forces.

Not surprisingly, as the rhetoric began to wax in intensity, so too did the work teams pick up the pace of their activities in the rural counties to which they were assigned. With the cadre problem defined as an antagonistic contradiction by central authorities in Beijing, work teams in the countryside began turning up record numbers of cases of cadres who had committed either corruption and graft or associated wrongdoing.

POLITICAL CORRUPTION AND THE SOCIALIST EDUCATION MOVEMENT

During the Socialist Education Movement, each province established a provincial socialist education movement work union (*shejiao gongzuo tuan*) with the provincial party secretary as its leader. Beneath the provincial level existed a network of branch unions (*fentuan*), each in charge of monitoring the work-team activities within a county. The branch unions supervised work brigades (*dadui*) that were responsible for Socialist Education Movement activities within a given commune, and the branch brigades (*fendui*) beneath these organized the movement into individual production teams. Leaders of work teams assigned to production-team units, generally speaking, were members of the commune-level (*dadui*) or county-level (*fentuan*) work union branches. Often, the majority of members assigned to a given work team originated from the same provincial-level work unit (*danwei*), and so were already well acquainted and accustomed to working together prior to being dispatched to the countryside.[61]

Charges pressed against local cadres and team leaders during this period, as in the past, generally reflected the designs of central state-makers in Beijing. Allegations raised either directly by work-team members or by ordinary commune members under the direction of work-team personnel

---

61. Ren Junmo, "Yi Jiaonan xian shejiao yundong yi jiao" (A recollection of the Socialist Education Movement in [Shandong] Jiaonan county), in *Shandong wenshi ziliao, di ershiliu ji*, ed. Shandong wenshi ziliao weiyuanhui (Jinan: Shandong renmin chubanshe, 1989), p. 253.

initially more or less conformed to the "Four Uncleans" formulation of the "First Ten Points": employing haphazard or false accounting procedures, sloppy or bogus recording of work points for both cadres and team members, inadequate upkeep of granary supplies, and misuse of collective materials, all of which were considered by central authorities to have resulted in slowed agricultural productivity and subsequently diminished procurement levels. In 1966, statistics compiled for the previous year revealed that in some 80 Guangxi communes involved in carrying out the Socialist Education Movement, no fewer than 11,650 basic-level cadres were found to have varying degrees of problems associated with the "Four Uncleans," representing altogether no less than 80.5 percent of the basic-level cadres in Guangxi. Of these 11,650 cadres, some 586 (4 percent of the total pool of basic-level cadres in Guangxi) were discovered to have committed serious "Four Uncleans" errors.[62] In Shaanxi's Jiandong county, 9,638 cadres of various ranks, out of a total of 16,100 cadres in the county (accounting for 59.9 percent of the total), had "Four Uncleans" problems, of which just over 1,500 received some sort of sanctioning from the party.[63] In the four communes of Guangdong's Luoding county, 3,202 "Four Uncleans" cadres were discovered, comprising 42.7 percent of the cadres in that county. Of the 3,202 cadres, the minority was found to have "serious economic problems" and appropriate punishment was meted out to them; however, the majority was found guilty only of minor attempts to "take more than they were entitled to" (*duo chi duo zhan*).[64] In Guangdong's Foshan municipality, more than 3,000 workers were dispatched into eleven work teams to investigate basic-level cadres and discovered 1,765 cases of corruption, graft, and speculation that involved a combined total of over 118 million *yuan*, as well as cases of "extravagance and waste" involving over 45 million *yuan*.[65]

Other charges not directly related to the specific mishandling of commune accounts, work points, granaries, and tools were also pressed against cadres. In Xiamen's Fuqing municipality, 130 cases of cadre corruption

---

62. Huang Ruhai, "Guangxi nongcun shehui zhuyi jiaoyu yundong chutan" (Preliminary investigation into the Rural Socialist Education Movement in Guangxi), in *Yongding wenshi ziliao*, no. 6, ed. Yongding wenshi ziliao weiyuanhui (Nanning: Guangxi renmin chubanshe, 1989), p. 53.

63. Zhang Yihui, ed., *Jiandong xianzhi* (Jiandong county gazetteer) (Shanghai: Shanghai renmin chubanshe, 1991), pp. 669–70.

64. Literally, to "eat more and grab more"; see Zhang Jianxing, *Luoding xianzhi* (Luoding county gazetteer) (Guangdong: Guangdong renmin chubanshe, 1994), pp. 391–92.

65. Wang Maosong and Cai Yaojin, eds., *Zhongguo Gongchandang Foshan shi zuzhi zhi* (Gazetteer of Chinese Communist Party organizations in Foshan municipality) (Guangdong: Guangdong renmin chubanshe, 1991), p. 72.

were reported to local officials, of which 20 were pursued against a total of 56 individuals. Of these 56, 24 were cadres in businesses and enterprises and 32 were basic-level rural cadres. Their combined crimes included taking advantage of their power and position (*liyong zhiquan*) in collaboration with other cadres as well as ordinary citizens in order to fabricate receipts (*danju*) and bills (*fapiao*), file fraudulent applications and claims *(xubao maoling)*, embezzle grain rations (*kekou kouliang*), and to use other means to defraud the public and enrich themselves (*jiagong jisi*). The value of the moneys and property embezzled totaled over 5,000,000 *yuan*. Nineteen cases of this sort were tried in Fuqing during 1963, involving 45 individuals. Six were arrested and arraigned, two were cashiered, and 26 were required to return the misappropriated items or sums of money.[66]

However, considerable regional variations make it difficult to generalize about the nature of corruption charges filed against basic-level cadres during this period. For example, in Jilin province, the anti-corruption drive of 1963–66 was conducted not under the auspices of the Socialist Education Movement or the "Four Cleans" campaign, but instead in response to a directive from the provincial party secretary: "Notification regarding the active participation of supervisory organs in the anti-corruption and graft, anti-departmentalism, and anti-bureaucratism (also known as the new 'Three Antis') movement." This directive resulted in a total of 1,369 charges of corruption, of which 756 were investigated, and 601 actually resulted in cases that led to the arrest of some 296 individuals, 177 of whom were disciplined for their crimes.[67] In September 1963, the Central Committee's Organization Department first secretary, An Ziwen, called for a new anti-corruption drive in all central party organs, as well as in schools, enterprises, and other cultural work units;[68] in many locales, this anti-corruption effort became conjoined with the ongoing Socialist Education Movement, or with the "Four Cleans" movement, with a good deal of overlap in both campaign goals and personnel.

Thus, in Hunan and Hebei in 1963, while the "Four Cleans" campaign was being carried out in rural areas, a simultaneous urban-based anti-cor-

---

66. Qiu Yuqing, ed., *Fuqing shizhi* (Fuqing municipal gazetteer) (Xiamen: Xiamen daxue chubanshe, 1994), p. 686.

67. The directive under which this series of investigations was undertaken apparently originated in the party's Central Committee, and was handed down to the Jilin provincial party committee, which delivered the order to the provincial investigation division (*sheng xiancha yuan*). Yang Xiaohong and Zhang Zongxin, eds., *Jilin shengzhi (sifa gongan zhi)* (Jilin provincial gazetteer [law and public security]) (Changchun: Jilin renmin chubanshe, 1992), *juan* 12, pp. 128–29.

68. Bo (1993), p. 1111.

ruption campaign was undertaken, referred to as a "five-antis" movement (*wufan yundong*). The targeted activities of this movement included corruption and graft, speculation (*touji daoba*), extravagance and waste, departmentalism (*fensan zhuyi*), and bureaucratism.[69] In Guangdong's Foshan municipality, the 1963 "five-antis" targeted "four investigations" (*sicha*), including investigations into "loopholes" (*loudong*), waste, loss, and "trickery" (*shangdang*).[70] In Henan's Zhumadian municipality, the 1963 "five-antis" movement was initially carried out in two experimental locations involving 36 work units: 639 cadres were investigated and ultimately "put down their burdens" (*fang baozhuang*), confessing to various wrongdoings before the movement was brought to a close in September. Less than a year later, in August of 1964, the party provincial secretary ordered Zhumadian municipality to complete the work of the previous year (*saowei gongzuo*), and 186 people employed in 8 different work units again were mobilized in order to conduct intensive study, to "wash their hands," "take baths," and again "put down their burdens" for a total of 35 days. The following month, the provincial party secretary selected 91 cadres and divided them into two work teams: the first work team (a total of 53 cadres) was dispatched to Zhengzhou city to participate in an urban "five-antis" movement there; the second group of 38 cadres was sent to Xinyang county to participate in rural Socialist Education Movement work teams. In Zhumadian, it wasn't until October 1965 that these activities came to be associated with the "Four Cleans" movement, when the city established a Four Cleans Work Leaders Small Group, beneath which Four Cleans Work Offices were set up, and 195 cadres were sent down to various levels in the countryside to practice the "three togethers" (*santong*). This final stage of the movement in Zhumadian wasn't concluded until June 1967.[71]

However, most cadres who received some sort of sanctioning during the "Four Cleans" movement appear to have committed what were generally considered to be rather mild infractions. Common violations of this sort were seen as falling into two basic categories of error: mismanagement of collective economic or material resources, and errors associated with "bureaucratism," or those pertaining to incorrect or improper "work styles" (*zuofeng*). Errors of the first type generally included the sloppy management or supervision of either the work-point system or of collective

69. Zeng Xianghu, ed., *Hunan shengzhi zhengfa zhi* (Hunan provincial political and legal gazetteer) (Changsha: Hunan chubanshe, 1995), p. 169. See also Li Zhanling et al., eds., *Pucheng xianzhi* ([Hebei] Pucheng county gazetteer) (Beijing: Zhonghua shuju, 1994), p. 685.
70. Wang Maosong and Cai Yaojin (1991), p. 71.
71. Henan Zhumadian shi shizhi bianmu weiyuanhui, ed., *Zhumadian shizhi* (Zhumadian municipal gazetteer) (Zhengzhou: Henan renmin chubanshe, 1989), pp. 102–3.

resources such as tools, farm implements, and raw materials. Wrongdoing associated with "bureaucratism" or poor "work styles" generally included basic-level cadres "taking more than they were entitled to" (*duo chi duo zhan*), "issuing confusing orders" (*xia zhihui*), "riding roughshod over [the wishes of] the people" (*qiya qunzhong*), and "restraining the positive social-ist impulses of the peasant masses" (*nongmin qunzhong de shehui zhuyi jiji xing shoudao yayi*).[72] In the Shangshan brigade of Lianjiang county's Aojiang commune, in March 1963, a total of 113 brigade and production-team cadres, 33 of them party members, were found guilty of committing the foregoing types of error. Forty-two cadres, including the branch party secretary, were accused of misappropriating 3,412 *yuan* of public funds. Twenty-three of these cadres had already made complete restitution in March; the remaining cadres were permitted to wait until after the sweet-potato sale, or the summer harvest distribution, to repay requisite sums. Nine individuals misappropriated a combined total of 1,786 catties of col-lective food, approximately half of which was immediately returned, the other half to be returned to the collective in installments. Forty-one people were found to have been occupying a combined total of 10.8 *mou* of collec-tive lands: those who had already planted crops on the occupied land were permitted to harvest their crops before returning the land; lands not yet planted were immediately returned. Forty-seven individuals were guilty of having engaged in excessive consumption of food and fertilizer, and six people slaughtered hogs in excess; virtually all these individuals immedi-ately made restitution of the amounts consumed. In addition, eleven com-mune members abandoned agriculture in favor of trade, twelve individuals were found to have engaged in occasional gambling, and one person was discovered to have used his access to the collective's facilities to privately manufacture brick and lime. All these individuals underwent "thorough self-examinations and recognized their errors" and none were formally punished.[73]

In accordance with the directives framed in Mao's "First Ten Points," corruption charges were most often pressed at local levels against those who had been classified as the political enemies of the new regime, and who had previously been designated as the appropriate targets of class struggle. These groups, listed in the "First Ten Points," included landlords and the socioeconomic elite in the countryside under the previous regime, as well as former Nationalist Party and secret-society members and those who had

72. He Ruling, *Zhengdang zhengfeng jianghua* (Discussion of party and work-style rectifica-tion) (Shenyang: Lianoning renmin chubanshe, 1984), p. 153.
73. Chen and Ridley (1969), pp. 230–32.

collaborated with counter-revolutionaries. Thus, generally speaking, cadres accused of crimes during the "Four Cleans" also tended to have bad class backgrounds, having been designated as landlords, rich or middle peasants during the process of land reform, or to have had some kind of connection to the Nationalist Party or invading Japanese forces during the Civil War period. On one commune in Changzhi village in Shanxi's Lucheng county, for example, most of the cadres accused by the work teams were of suspicious class origin: the shopkeeper for the Fourth Production Team, a former rich peasant, admitted to having misappropriated several bushels of wheat, which he then shared with the Third Production Team's accountant, a former member of the allegedly counter-revolutionary underground Catholic organization, the Legion of Mary; a buyer for the Sidelines Team, described as a rich peasant "struggle object," was found to have kept sloppy accounts, failed to collect on accounts due, and misappropriated more than 1,000 *yuan*; the brigade's chief accountant, who had served during the Anti-Japanese war as the captain of the puppet police, was relieved of his position when he was accused of having misappropriated about 100 *yuan*.[74] In Shaanxi's Jiandong county, members of no fewer than five local secret societies—the Three Treasures Sect (Sanbao men), Great Road Sect (Dadao men), Double Fragrances Sect (Shuangxiang men), One Heart Heavenly Road Longhua Sheng Church (Yi xin tiandao longhua sheng jiaohui), and Mingxin Benevolence Society (Mingxin shanshe)—were all specifically targeted for suppression (*qudi*) during the Socialist Education Movement. Public security forces investigated a total of 54 leaders and 865 followers of these sects within the context of the movement; all were interrogated, forced to register with the authorities, and then to renounce their ties to these groups.[75]

More serious crimes of corruption were also reported, and these also tended to involve a combination of economic and political crimes, often committed by individuals with questionable political backgrounds. One such case that came to light during the "Four Cleans" movement in Shaanxi's Xi'an municipality involved some seven individuals in a far-flung corruption scheme of misappropriation and illegal sale of privately produced goods outside the purview of the state supply and marketing cooperatives. At the center of this case was Li Yinggui, a 32-year-old Shandong Jiyang county native, who served as the department head of the Xi'an Metal-lurgical Machine-Building and Repair Factory's Materials Department, and

---

74. William Hinton, *Shenfan: The Continuing Revolution in a Chinese Village* (New York: Random House, 1983), pp. 338–39.
75. Zhang Yihui, ed. (1991), p. 518.

was arraigned on charges of "corruption, graft, and plotting to betray the nation" (*tanwu daoqie panguo*). The case against Li established that from March 1959 until the end of December 1960, he bought, sold, and otherwise made use of items outside the purview of the state monopolies in a vast profit-making enterprise that earned him a profit of more than 24,000 *yuan*. His accomplices included purchasing agents employed at the Anshan Instrument and Meter Plant, the Shenyang Railway Machines and Tools Purchasing Department, and the Liaoning Lingyuan Xinsheng Mining Company, as well as a host of other "counter-revolutionary" and "bad elements." The charges against Li included the fact that he organized this corrupt band of purchasing agents to collude in a scheme involving graft, theft, and seditious activities and can be loosely arranged into three general categories of wrongdoing: economic crimes (involving graft and misappropriation), moral corruption (involving unethical behavior), and political crimes (involving anti-state and anti-party activities).

The charges of graft and misappropriation against Li stemmed largely from his circumvention of the state-controlled market to engage in speculative sales and purchases of products and materials. In collaboration with various other purchasing agents and low-level cadres, Li made a series of secret purchases and sales of steel products, pig iron, cement, lumber, and 168 different items worth a combined total of well over 3,000,000 *yuan*. Li's two main accomplices, purchasing agents Wang Jianke and Liu Ziting, also earned a combined total of nearly 50,000 *yuan*, of which approximately 18,000 *yuan* had yet to be recovered by state authorities by the time the case went to trial.

With respect to the charge of corruption, the evidence against Li included the fact that he had previously hosted lavish banquets, proffered expensive gifts, and gave and accepted bribes in order to carry out his secret business deals. In his circumvention of the law, he furthermore was accused of having attempted to curry favor with corrupt (*fushi*) state cadres, and swindled and bluffed (*zhaoyao zhuangpian*) a host of innocent law-abiding citizens. In addition, Li, Liu, and Wang all reportedly made frequent trips to Shanghai, where they "squandered public funds (*huihuo gongkuan*), frequented exclusive cocktail lounges and expensive restaurants, lavishly eating and drinking (*dachi dahe*) and generally indulging themselves in dissipation (*huatian jidui*). Their depravity was without limit, surpassing every extreme, leading the debauched lifestyle of the capitalist class . . . and spending time with criminal seducers and salacious women (*weixie*)."

Finally, while in Shanghai and Shenyang, Li was purported to have engaged in counter-revolutionary activities, and of "launching an evil and poisonous attack on the socialist system." The primary evidence supporting the charge of sedition was the fact that he was alleged to have said, "There is no freedom in China; the most freedom is to be found in capitalism"; "A third world war is an inevitability (*fei bu ke*), the Communist Party will be destroyed, Jiang Jieshi [Chiang Kai-shek] will come back and put them down, and slaughter most of the Communists"; and was once heard to "wildly scream" out: "If there is ever a day that I seize the reins of power, I'll kill most of the damned bunch [myself]." He was also purported to have stolen official seals and five blank official document forms from three different work units (*danwei*)—the party branch office at the Xi'an Metallurgical Plant, the personnel department of the railway's Number Six Engineering Office, and the Personnel Department of the Shaanxi Provincial Government—and planned to use them in "carrying out destructive activities." However,

most serious of all, Criminal Li and Wang Jianke, Liu Ziting, and others, while in Shanghai, Hangzhou, Shenyang, Anshan, and other places, had conducted numerous secret meetings, obviously plotting to hijack an airplane to escape out of the country, to betray the nation and defect to enemy [territory]. In October 1960, one of the cohort contacted authorities with some information [about this plot]. Criminal Li, in fear that his criminal behavior would be exposed, along with Liu Ziting, threatened their fellow collaborators, preventing them from confessing [to the authorities], and instigated their escape, moreover planning to poison them, and furthermore planned to take the account books of the Xi'an Metallurgical Machine-Building and Repair Factory's Materials Department, and to throw them into the fire so as to destroy all evidence of their crimes.

Thus the charge that Li and his accomplices had "betrayed the nation" was linked, at least in the foregoing summary of the legal case against them, with their intended betrayal of their fellow criminals, and underscored the treachery of those involved. Their refusal to permit their fellow accomplices to confess and reform furthermore indicated to the authorities who tried the case that Li himself was entirely unrepentant and could not be reformed, either through education or labor. The Xi'an Intermediate People's Court sentenced Li to death on January 1, 1963.[76]

A synopsis of the case was subsequently published in a compilation of legal cases representing the broad range of corruption charges handled during the Maoist era, and in particular within the context of the Socialist Education Movement, and embodies several key themes of the period. First, as noted above, in the economic retrenchment that followed the Great Leap period, the Beijing leadership simultaneously moved to decentralize agricultural production by lowering the primary accounting unit

---

76. Jiao (1994), pp. 405–6.

to the production team and to exercise greater control over the marketing of commodities through the expansion of supply and marketing cooperatives. The secret purchases and sales conducted by Li Yinggui and his accomplices clearly circumvented the state monopoly on industrial products and raw materials, and obviously represented an important conduit through which goods and products found their way onto the black ("free") market, over which central authorities sought to increase control in the early 1960s. Second, with respect to the charge of corruption, the trips to Shanghai taken by Li and his cohorts occurred in 1959 and 1960, two of the years during which famine conditions prevailed throughout most of rural China; the wasteful and extravagant nature of these trips stands in marked contrast to the increasingly stringent austerity measures under which most of the country labored during that period, and serves to justify the intervention of state authorities in the punishment of Li's crimes. One goal of the "Four Cleans" was to shift at least some of the responsibility for the massive shortages incurred during the Great Leap to the pilfering and mismanagement of the basic-level cadres, and to redirect public attention away from the role played by central state planning authorities. Third, the plot to escape to "enemy territory" appears to have been hatched in late 1960, when increasing numbers of refugees from the mainland flooded into Hong Kong. Party leader Tao Zhu was roundly criticized for having permitted massive waves of migration by failing to maintain vigilance over the Guangdong–Hong Kong border, which ultimately contributed to crippling labor shortages in the southern Chinese countryside. During the retrenchment period, the labor shortages (caused both by famine deaths and massive emigration) were so severe in Guangdong that a major campaign was launched to increase the numbers of cows being raised for use as draft animals. In the spring of 1962, Guangdong officials temporarily relaxed border controls, with even more disastrous results than before, and tens of thousands of farmers and urban residents living near the border rushed into Hong Kong, creating the largest single migration wave since the founding of the People's Republic. In the aftermath of the crisis, stiff border controls were reinstituted and discipline was tightened over the summer.[77]

Official anxiety over the numbers of otherwise compliant rural and urban residents seeking to flee the country, engage in secret schemes, and practice dissimulation burgeoned during the series of local investigations conducted in the early 1960s. Such apprehensions, while certainly heightened by sporadic mass emigrations and the occasional discovery of local

77. MacFarquhar (1997), pp. 205–6.

networks engaged in smuggling or pilfering scarce commodities and food-stuffs, grew to endemic proportions among the Beijing leadership in the aftermath of the Great Leap. The heightened paranoia among party and state leaders over the possibility of large-scale "recruitments" of members of the "five red classes" to the "enemy camp" was reflected not only in official documents that set the course for the Four Cleans and Socialist Education Movements but also increasingly in the reports of their investi-gations into actual conditions in the countryside.

Timur Kuran suggests that revolutionary regimes across the board suc-cumb to such suspicions because of the widespread practice of what he refers to as "preference falsification" under authoritarian rule: "Since peo-ple's public and private preferences may differ, a revolutionary regime is justified in suspecting that its supporters include many would-be turncoats, people who participated in the revolution even though they privately favored the old regime."[78] It is hardly surprising, then, that as the disjunc-tion between the representational and objective realities of class struggle during the Socialist Education Movement sharpened,[79] a deepening para-noia began to permeate the official discourse of class struggle.

POLICING STATE AND SOCIETY UNDER MAO

Definitions of political corruption and associated crimes pursued by cen-tral state authorities in the aftermath of the acute crisis of the Great Leap Forward were primarily shaped by the twin needs to reassert central con-trol over the state and economy and to restore the moral legitimacy of the regime. The goal of economic recovery and of increased production necessitated the extension of basic monitoring and control mechanisms in all state industrial and agricultural enterprises. Similarly, the attempts of state and party leaders to shore up existing state monopolies on certain commodities and to oversee the sale and purchase of others through the workings of supply and marketing cooperatives translated into stricter sur-veillance on the purchase and use of a wide variety of goods by rural col-lectives and urban enterprises alike. These goals created a political agenda that linked administrative discipline at the lower levels of state and party bureaucracies to the control over certain types of unethical and undesir-able behavior, particularly graft, larceny, speculation, extravagance, and waste. At the same time, the Beijing leadership sought to shore up the

---

78. Timur Kuran, "Sparks and Prairie Fires: A Theory of Unanticipated Political Revolution," *Public Choice* 61 (1989): 27.
79. Huang (1995).

legitimacy of the regime through employment of mass mobilization, small-group criticism sessions, and mass political education during the Socialist Education Movement. Whether the rectification of work-styles at the lowest levels of rural and urban enterprises resulted from an attempt to deflect responsibility for the disastrous failures of the Great Leap away from the upper echelons of the Beijing leadership, or from a genuine concern that basic-level cadres were largely incapable of providing proper leadership, the dispatching of thousands of work teams to carry out socialist education represented an intensive effort to penetrate political society down to the level of the production team and to remold both cadre and mass norms in the context of socialist production.

Yet these measures, pursued throughout most of the country during 1962 and 1963, failed to satisfy the collective aims of the Beijing leadership. Local communities did not readily accept the leadership of the dispatched work teams, and frequently attempted to subvert, sabotage, and derail their efforts to penetrate and remake the local political scene. The accounts of those "sent down" to the villages and factories during this period reveal that ordinary commune members and workers, as well the basic-level cadres who were targeted for "clean up" during the Socialist Education Movement, frequently resisted, sometimes violently, attempts to monitor, educate, and correct them. As central authorities became aware of the extent to which local communities had become resistant to such efforts, they moved to employ a new set of techniques to ferret out and suppress such resistance on a broad scale, and to reconfigure local practices in accordance with the normative agenda of Maoism.

SEVEN
Local Variations in the "Big Four Cleans"

The course of the Socialist Education Movement took an unexpected and dramatic turn over the summer of 1964. In the fall of 1963, Wang Guangmei, the spouse of then-president Liu Shaoqi, volunteered to participate in a "Four Cleans" work team headed for the Taoyuan brigade in Hebei's Funing county. Her decision to do so was apparently not a popular one within the upper echelons of the Beijing leadership. In April 1967, reflecting on the events that preceded her being "sent down" to the countryside, Wang would admit: "Many people were against my going to Taoyuan; only Liu Shaoqi . . . [and] Chairman Mao backed me up."[1] Nevertheless, in November 1963, Wang adopted the pseudonym Dong Pu, and, carrying personal documents that identified her as an employee of the Hebei Provincial Public Security Department (Gongan ting) and clad in the clothing of an ordinary worker, she departed Beijing for Taoyuan. Although she originally intended to remain in Funing county for three months, the normal period of service for "Four Cleans" work teams at the time, she reported that "the more we did, the more complicated [the situation] became; in actuality we took five months to carry out [the movement], and only then had we carried it out thoroughly."[2] In her report to the Central Committee on her experiences in Taoyuan, delivered on July 5, 1964, but more widely disseminated in September of that year,

1. Richard Baum, *Prelude to Revolution: Mao, the Party and the Peasant Question* (New York: Columbia University Press, 1975), p. 89.
2. Wang Guangmei, "(Zhuanfa) 'Guangyu yige dadui de shehui zhuyi jiaoyu yundong de jingyan zongjie' de pishi" (Summary of the experiences of a production brigade in the socialist education movement) (September 1, 1964), in *Pipan ziliao: Zhongguo He Luxiao fu Liu Shaoqi fangeming xiuzheng zhuyi yanlun ji* (Critique: the collected counter-revolutionary revisionist speeches of China's He Luxiao, spouse of Liu Shaoqi) (Beijing: Renmin chubanshe, 1967), pp. 472–74.

Wang painted a bleak portrait of local-level politics in the Chinese countryside, and of the Socialist Education Movement as it was then being implemented.

In short, her report argued that the "Four Cleans" movement was being hastily carried out in most areas, barely scratching the surface of what she perceived to be a complex web of petty corruption, graft, and counter-revolutionary activities and attitudes that ensnared local cadres and ordinary commune members alike. The processes of socialist production and political mobilization in the rural communities beneath and around the roots of the party were poisoned by widespread dissimulation, feigned compliance, and subterfuge. Furthermore, this web of corruption extended much further up the bureaucratic hierarchy than previously expected. In contrast to the earlier assumptions of the "First Ten Points" and "Later Ten Points," both of which suggested that upward of 95 percent of the basic-level rural cadres and residents were fundamentally good and treading the correct path, Wang's investigations uncovered malfeasance in the performance of more than half of all the local officials she examined, including principal cadres such as the secretary and deputy secretary of the brigade party branch. In a letter written by Liu Shaoqi to Wang in the spring of 1964, Liu concluded on the basis of her account that "The Taoyuan party branch basically does not belong to the party . . . it is basically a two-faced counter-revolutionary regime." Liu instructed Wang to "publicly criticize, struggle against, and where necessary dismiss and replace the 'rotten' cadres in the brigade." As a result, 40 out of 47 brigade and production-team cadres in Taoyuan, or 85 percent of the total, received some sort of sanction, resulting in a virtually complete turnover in local political leadership.[3] Wang Guangmei's widely publicized experiences set in motion a chain of events that was to alter the progress of the Socialist Education Movement and moreover opened the way for the massive inversions of political power that occurred during the Cultural Revolution.

One immediate consequence of Wang Guangmei's Taoyuan report was the release of a new document that dictated several key changes in the implementation of the Socialist Education Movement and the "Four Cleans" campaign policies being pursued in the countryside. In August 1964, shortly before Wang's findings were made widely available, Mao lamented: "In our state at present approximately one-third of the power is in the hands of the enemy or of the enemy's sympathizers. We have been going for fifteen years and we now control two-thirds of the realm. At present you can buy a [party] branch secretary for a few packs of cigarettes, not

---

3. Baum (1975), p. 86.

to mention marrying his daughter."⁴ The following month, the Central Committee issued a new revision that subsequently became known as the "Revised Later Ten Points." However, unlike the two "Ten Point" formulations that preceded it, the September 1964 document advocated a far more intensive investigation into the overall rural situation than had previously been prescribed. While rhetorically still maintaining that upward of 95 percent of both the cadres and the masses were "without problems," the authors of this document noted,

Our view on the vast number of basic-level cadres should be thoroughly and not fragmentally analyzed. Among basic-level cadres, many have committed big or small mistakes. They have not only committed the Four Uncleans economically, but also failed to draw the line between friend and enemy, lost their own stand, discriminated against poor and lower-middle peasants, hid their backgrounds and fabricated history, and so forth, thus committing the Four Uncleans politically and organizationally. The mistakes committed by some of them are more serious in nature. Some have even degenerated into agents and protectors of class enemies. Besides, a few landlords, rich peasants, counter-revolutionaries, and undesirable elements have also infiltrated the ranks. The problem, as we see it, is indeed serious.⁵

Accordingly, in the fall of 1964, the Beijing leadership officially shifted the focus of the Four Cleans from the investigation into crimes of petty corruption to investigation of errors that were more fundamental in nature. Moreover, whereas earlier directives limited these investigations to the activities of basic-level cadres, the "Revised Later Ten Points" noted that the experience of the upper-level leadership "revealed that cadres in basic-level organizations who have committed serious mistakes are usually connected with certain cadres of higher-level organizations . . . and are instigated, supported, and protected by them. In such cases we must go to the origin and get a hold of the responsible persons."⁶

The widening of the movement's targets inaugurated a new phase of the campaign, which subsequently became known as the "Big Four Cleans," in contrast to the earlier, more restrained "Small Four Cleans" of the preceding year. The "Big Four Cleans," rather than confine itself to the clearing up of work points, granaries, account books, and collective property, ultimately embraced a far more ambitious course of action: the aim was nothing less than a complete rectification of politics, economics, local orga-

---

4. Teiwes (1979), p. 536.
5. Richard Baum and Frederick C. Teiwes, *Ssu-Ch'ing: The Socialist Education Movement of 1962–1966* (Berkeley: University of California, Center for Chinese Studies, 1968), pp. 112–13.
6. As cited by Teiwes (1979), p. 544.

nizations, and ideology, and resulted in a purge of the party and state ranks that engulfed upward of 70 to 80 percent of sub-village leaders across the Chinese countryside,[7] and culminated in nothing less than a total schism within the upper echelons of the party and the state.[8]

Following on the heels of Mao's increasingly broad and subjective reformulations of the meaning of class struggle, the "Big Four Cleans" was designed not merely to revisit the issue of class status in the aftermath of collectivization, but to reenact the rituals and dramas of the land-reform campaign of more than a decade before. The return of private plots, sideline occupations, and free markets during the post-Leap period stimulated not only economic recovery but also the apparent resurgence of traditional social customs centered in family and clan networks, signaling to some that the revolutionary gains of the past had been largely overturned. The Socialist Education Movement, also dubbed the "Second Land Reform,"[9] attempted to reverse such trends by restaging the ritual dynamics of rural class struggle that defined the Communist victory in the countryside. Class labels were investigated exhaustively in order to correct cases in which a family's true status had been "overlooked" (*louhua*) or wrongly assigned at the time of land reform, and rectification was undertaken on a mass scale, among grassroots cadres and ordinary commune members alike.[10]

Socialist education not only involved the re-creation of the local past in accordance with the new party line, but the rewriting of it as well: tens of thousands of college and middle-school students and urban cadres were "sent down"' (*xiafang*) to rural communities throughout the countryside in a campaign within the campaign to compile local histories that highlighted the "class sympathies" and "roots of bitterness" of the revolutionary past. Participants in this mass exercise to recall and record the so-called Four Histories—of families, villages, communes, and industries—were instructed to focus on the themes of social suffering, class struggle, and the contradictions between socialism and capitalism in a vast effort to set personal experience and local histories within the overarching narrative framework constructed by the party. The ultimate goal, according to a July 1964 *People's Daily* editorial, was to encourage China's youth

not only to acquire knowledge of revolutionary struggle through the revolutionary history of a village, a commune, a factory, or a family . . . [but to] understand the

---

7. Michael Oksenberg, "Local Leaders in Rural China, 1962–65: Individual Attributes, Bureaucratic Positions, and Political Recruitment," in *Chinese Communist Politics in Action*, ed. A. Doak Barnett (Seattle: University of Washington Press, 1969), p. 184.
8. Dittmer (1974).
9. Huang (1995), p. 128.
10. Bo (1993), pp. 1130–36.

history of the struggle of the great proletariat and the great Chinese Communist Party of our fatherland (*zuxian*) so that they will take their own destinies and the destinies of the proletariat and people who labor and link them inseparably together (*jinmi lianxi qilai*).[11]

The meticulous production of these new local histories was a monumental undertaking shaped by an impressive number of hands. In southeastern Shanxi, the party district committee sent thousands of students into rural villages, where they compiled no fewer than 70,000 family histories. A carefully selected editorial committee culled these down to a sample of 96 representative accounts that were then rewritten by a team of writers whose ideological credentials were beyond reproach. Finally, the manuscripts were circulated to local party branches, as well as to the party district committee, for final approval before publication and distribution.[12] The local histories and family genealogies of the past were thus completely overwritten to serve the needs of the present; when historical realities proved resistant to the political concerns of the present, they were obliterated in a movement that subsequently became known as the attack on the "Four Olds." As Shi Chengzhi noted of the Four Histories campaign, "it was a struggle between new and old, between a new historical consciousness (*yishi*) and the old historical consciousness, between a new political ideology (*yishi xingtai*) and an old political ideology . . . the actual fuse [that ignited] the Cultural Revolution."[13]

For rural residents the consequences of this exercise were profound. Relying upon Wang Guangmei's model of undercover investigation, work-team members infiltrated rural communities as though they were actual "enemy encampments" that concealed their true natures behind a revolutionary socialist façade. Counseled to "strike roots and link up" (*zhagen chuanlian*) with the ideologically reliable poor peasants, work teams collected detailed information on the day-to-day practices of local cadres, as well as on their personal backgrounds. Eventually, grassroots cadres and the presumed "old class enemies" who aided and abetted them were subjected to grueling "back-to-back" (*bei kao bei*) interrogations, before both were subjected to public struggle sessions during which they were attacked "face to face" (*mian dui mian*). Ordinary commune members were helped along in building the "contrast of past misery with present happiness" (*yiku*

---

11. Shi Chengzhi, "Shilun 'sishi' yu 'wen'ge'" (Discussing the "Four Histories" and the "Cultural Revolution"), *Mingbao yuekan* (December 1971): 9.
12. Stephen Uhalley, Jr., "The 'Four Histories' Movement: A Revolution in Writing China's Past," *Current Scene* 4:2 (January 15, 1966): 6.
13. Shi (1971), p. 13.

sitian) by their participation in the mass history-writing project, and were encouraged to "speak bitterness" (*suku*) in a series of emotionally charged mass rallies that frequently lasted for several days.

Given such tactics, it is hardly surprising that the intensification of the Socialist Education Movement in late 1964 and 1965 resulted in increasing levels of violence and social unrest as central state authorities sought to redefine the normative practices of both local cadres and commune members around the pivotal theme of ongoing class struggle. The broader and more radical political agenda of the "Big Four Cleans" and the strategies it necessitated dramatically altered the dynamics between the moral authority of the party and the bureaucratic pragmatism embodied by the state. Driving the "spearhead" (*maotou*) of continuing class struggle—first downward into rural communities, and then upward into the cadre ranks—set in motion a cataclysmic series of dislocations, not only for the central state-makers in Beijing, but for the nation as a whole.

THE TAOYUAN BRIGADE MODEL

The Taoyuan brigade, consisting of four production teams involving 217 families (slightly more than 1,000 people) collectively farming just over 2,000 *mou* of land, was part of the Luwang Village commune on the Hebei plain. At the time of Wang Guangmei's visit, of the 217 households belonging to the Taoyuan brigade, two had previously been classified as landlord families, and two as rich peasants. Taoyuan had two brigade chiefs, one of whom was female, and a party branch secretary. The "Four Cleans" movement had been carried out under the direction of the basic-level leadership during the previous spring, and had revealed no particular problems with the brigade leadership. The brigade's party branch secretary, Wu Chen, was an illiterate but very capable poor peasant, well liked by the brigade members and widely regarded as politically "loyal and reliable." With a relatively small household, his income was considered adequate to his needs, and thus there was little incentive for him to engage in graft or petty corruption. The "Four Cleans" investigations of the previous spring had turned up only one case of a low-level conscript in the local people's militia (*minbing*) who had apparently removed approximately 200 *yuan* from an account he had been overseeing at the time. However, aside from this one minor case, the investigations turned up no other evidence of malfeasance, graft, or misappropriation; a few instances of waste and of "taking more than one is entitled to" (*duo chi duo zhan*) were discussed. At the same time there were also a few scattered reports of brigade members who had engaged in "superstitious practices," gambling, and other undesirable behavior. The ordinary brigade members were said to have received the movement with enthusiasm, and were already milling rice and butchering meat in preparation for the arrival of the new "Four Cleans" work team.[14]

The plan of the work team, which numbered 20 cadres sent down from the provincial, district, and county levels, was to "establish roots and link up" (*ligen chonglian*) with the local brigade members, to convene meetings to discuss the principles of the two "Ten Points" documents, and then to organize poor and lower-middle peasant associations. Following these preliminary organizational and educational measures, the work team intended to begin carrying out the "Four Cleans" in earnest, investigating charges of misconduct among basic-level cadres in a series of private "back-to-back" (as opposed to "face-to-face") meetings with individual brigade and team members, encouraging them to reveal the wrongdoing of others they had witnessed. Cadres were urged to confess openly their own errors to the work-team members, to "put down their burdens" and "take a warm bath" by sharing detailed analyses of their own attitudes and ways with the work team. Those who failed to "pass the gate" by not confessing their mistakes, or those whose confessions were considered to be less than complete and totally sincere, faced yet another stage in the rectification process, during which they would be openly "struggled against" as "enemies" of the people. Once these mass rallies had concluded, and all mistakes had been rectified, the brigade would enter the final stage of the process, manifested by rising productivity. Both Wang Guangmei and the leadership of the work team anticipated that this entire process, from start to finish, would take three months.

However, Wang Guangmei and her work-team colleagues reportedly encountered several serious obstacles right from the outset. Despite the assurance of the party branch secretary Wu, the ordinary brigade members were not enthusiastic about the arrival of the work teams in Luwang Village, nor did they demonstrate any interest in the underlying principles of the movement. According to the conversations she had with her initial informants, Wang reported that the members of the brigade were more concerned about how to make the commune resources stretch to accommodate the needs of the new arrivals with their grand political objectives than they were with the principles underlying the two "Ten Points" documents. They appeared to have no opinions about the activities of the landlords and rich peasants who lurked in their midst, nor were these members of the community despised and reviled as class enemies. When pressed for more information, the occasional worker

---

14. Wang [(1964) 1967], pp. 472–74.

or student might offer up a bold statement or two, but as Wang commented:

Even these were still under the control of their parents, or their wives were holding them back (*laopo la houtui*). All of them had family members who were afraid of starting something (*pa shi*), and would call them back, not permitting them to interact [freely] with us, saying "You come back here with me, don't go stirring up trouble!" Others, if you asked one question, you got back three "I don't knows." If you asked them how they divided up [the brigade's] food, how much was eaten, nobody knew. "I don't pay attention to them!" (*wo buguan jia ya*), "I'm not sure!" Those who would talk a little were still afraid, "If I tell you, you'll have to keep it quiet" and then they'd say something once, but when we looked for them again, they'd avoid us. We then began to feel that the masses were apprehensive, and that things weren't right.[15]

Wang also had her suspicions raised by the conduct of the basic-level cadres within the brigade, all of whom "frequently came to ask us if we were too cold or too warm, appearing to be very solicitous of us." The female brigade chief, Yuan Shouying, in particular earned her distrust by checking up on her several times a day in order to make certain she had enough lamp oil, or to see if her bedding was too cold (*kang leng bu leng*), or whether she had enough blankets. Wang would often press her for her opinions when she came to visit, but she remained reticent. Another told her that Brigade Chief Yuan had had some serious "Four Uncleans" problems, but didn't dare say more, all of which apparently piqued Wang's curiosity further.[16]

In attempting to piece together the situation before her in Luwang Village, Wang felt that her greatest obstacle was locating reliable informants. "It wasn't as if the good ones and the bad ones had it written on their faces, not like in [traditional Beijing] opera where as soon as one steps out onto the stage it's obvious from the clothes and makeup and we derive an impression—this person is eight-tenths good or bad."[17] Her first step was to attempt to return to the records of class backgrounds compiled by the Luwang Village cadres during the land-reform campaign, so that she could easily identify those of the proper class background in the commune, and to begin to "sink roots and link up" with poor and lower-middle peasants. However, much to Wang's disbelief, when the work team requested the commune records they were told that they had been lost long ago, and that although the class backgrounds (*chengfen*) of the residents and cadres alike

---

15. Ibid., p. 476.
16. Ibid., p. 477.
17. Ibid., pp. 475–76.

had been revised at least once since land reform, there were no written records available for the work team to use.

In the absence of written records, Wang and her colleagues were forced to ask the residents and cadres themselves for the information. However, this solution was highly unsatisfactory in Wang's view:

> In letting the masses report their own class status, they would lower it in any case, [saying] it's not high; asking the cadres, [having] cadres say who is of what class status, would be far more certain. But how do they arrive at this determination? It's a minority of cadres secretly conferring and consulting together (*yi niegu yi heji*), then determining who has what class label, it's hard to discriminate between the genuine and the false [ones].[18]

Wang's basic distrust of the cadres only deepened over time. In carrying out her investigations, she came to believe that the local cadres were either withholding information or offering her carefully rehearsed answers. This impression was based largely on the fact that when one local cadre would offer an opinion or respond frankly to one of her questions, Wang found that another would as well:

> If this cadre would say a bit, then that one would say it, too; it seemed as if they were all observing a standard (*duiguo biaode*), but behind [my] back issuing orders [to each other]: should they talk or not, they'd go back and report [to each other] and together they'd agree they'd talk about this, then later they'd talk about that. It had that kind of feeling about it (*jiu zhenme ge weidao*).[19]

Likewise, Wang began to adopt a particular pose as "a city person who had seldom visited the countryside, and there was much that I didn't understand about peasant life, this being my first time in the village, I didn't understand the situation." By feigning complete ignorance, Wang claimed that she began to hear "real talk," and slowly began piecing together what ultimately became, in her eyes, a massive conspiracy involving several levels of the commune and county administration, and a local society befouled by what she identified as two "black winds" (*hei feng*): fighting and gambling. Of the former, Wang noted that it was common for production-team cadres in the Taoyuan brigade to beat and curse ordinary commune members without the slightest provocation. Some production-team members had apparently been seriously wounded as a result of such scuffles in the past. Of the latter, Wang commented:

> Why is this gambling wind so serious? It is precisely because the cadres set the

---

18. Ibid., p. 476.
19. Ibid., p. 477.

example (*dai tou*). When the cadres gamble, they tell the party members to stand guard. People bring them midnight snacks, and when they've eaten their fill, they gamble again. During the day they sleep, and their work points are duly recorded. I heard once that commune [authorities] had come to nab the gamblers, and one cadre tried to jump over a wall to escape, and broke his leg. [He was] injured for 28 days, and for those 28 days he still recorded work points. And it's not only the village cadres who gamble; Assistant District Leader (*fu quzhang*) Su Zhangji often comes to the village to gamble, and he has even brought the county party branch office manager, Wang Shoujing, here for gambling. Higher-level cadres come to participate, and the lower cadres who started gambling feel even more justified (*geng youli le*), and nobody intervenes. Little children are also gambling. Once a child calling on [Brigade Party branch secretary] Wu Chen caught him gambling, and Wu Chen said, "You throw me a 4–5–6, and if you succeed, I'll let you go." What luck, that moment [the kid] threw a 4–5–6. Wu Chen said, "You're lucky, get out of here!" and the child was released.[20]

Wang noted that once she and the other work-team members had identified these "black winds," they simply "traced them back to their origin": brigade party branch secretary Wu Chen. Despite the initial assurances she received from the county party branch secretary that Wu Chen was of unimpeachable political integrity, Wang was convinced that he was in fact the root of the evil that had infected the Taoyuan brigade.

Initial attempts at mobilizing the residents of Luwang Village to "struggle" against Wu Chen were not successful. Their reluctance to do so puzzled the work team until they were approached by a local activist, who berated them, saying:

How can you trick us! The "Four Cleans" is only going to be carried out for 20 days, and then it will end [and] you will leave. In the past didn't you claim that you wouldn't leave if things weren't "cleaned up"? . . . There are people who say that the "Four Cleans" will last 20 days, we'll suffer through it, [but] once the "Four Cleans" is over, the cadres will still be the cadres and the commune members will still be the commune members.[21]

In attempting to trace the source of this rumor, Wang Guangmei finally concluded it had come from Wu Chen's wife, acting at the behest of her husband. Wu Chen had attended an earlier commune-wide meeting on the "Four Cleans" at which the 20-day figure had been discussed. Fearful that his gambling and bad temper had already come to the attention of the work team, Wu and his wife connived to use this fact as a "magic weapon"

---

20. Ibid., pp. 491–92.
21. Ibid., p. 492.

(*fabao*) to "pour cold water on the masses" and squelch their participation in the movement.[22]

At this point the work team was split in its opinions about precisely how to proceed. Some of the work-team members felt that the errors they had uncovered, including Wu Chen's gambling and violent outbursts, were not sufficiently serious as to merit a total mobilization of the masses against them. Others feared that mass criticism sessions and public rallies would destroy the morale of the basic-level cadres and render them unable to function again as positive contributors to the brigade's well-being in the future. Some work-team members pointed out that if the masses "toppled" the cadres, there would be no appropriate leadership to take the place of the "Four Unclean" officials, and that would leave the brigade in a chaotic state. However, Wang Guangmei was determined to push ahead with the mass rallies, arguing that the process of having the masses topple the cadres and having the work team re-educate them was fundamental to the process of socialist revolution. When Assistant Party Branch Secretary Zhao Shuchun heard that he was among those to be publicly struggled against, he fell ill and took to his bed, reportedly unable to face the prospect of such a humiliation. The work team visited him at his home and once again explained the principles of the two "Ten Points" documents to him, finally urging him on by saying: "You're the assistant party branch secretary—if you want to revolutionize your [political] awareness, then pick up your head!" Zhao, however, remained unmoved. Finally, the work team informed him that they were taking leave of the brigade to carry out the movement elsewhere, and that they wished him well. When he turned up a few days later to "see them off," they naturally concluded that he had been using his illness as a pretext, and were "made clear" that he was willing to struggle once again with their help. They then informed him that they had decided to stay.[23]

However, one aspect of the work team's investigations into the cadre situation continued to puzzle Wang: how was it possible for Wu Chen, whose crimes far outweighed in their severity those of other cadres, to have fallen prey to such temptations, particularly in light of his own class status as a poor peasant? The social diagnosis outlined in the two "Ten Point" documents suggested that "Four Unclean" cadres were primarily of two types: either they themselves had come from questionable class backgrounds, or they had come under the influence of the so-called "Four Classes" (landlords, rich peasants, counter-revolutionaries, and bad elements). With his poor peasant background, Wu Chen seemed an unlikely target for "Four

---

22. Ibid., pp. 492–93.
23. Ibid., pp. 497–98.

Cleans" rectification. However in the course of her investigations, Wang uncovered evidence that Wu Chen's father had in fact been a small business-owner prior to the revolution and not a peasant at all. Wu Chen himself had become a peddler and a "troublemaker" whose business had gone under, with the result that he became a traveling trader working on his own, spending his money on food, prostitutes, and gambling, and who finally fell in with a bunch of hooligans prior to 1949. With no property of his own, he was quickly classified during the land-reform campaign as a poor peasant, and had been leading a duplicitous life ever since. Wang furthermore discovered that of the 31 ordinary brigade members whom he had allegedly beaten over the years, only one had been the son of a rich peasant. The remaining 30 who had suffered his ire had all been poor and lower-middle peasants. Thus exposed, Wu Chen represented an ideal target for mass struggle, and the work team continued to carry on the campaign.[24]

Although the Red Guards subsequently challenged Wang Guangmei's assertions during the Cultural Revolution, the report of her experiences at the Taoyuan brigade was interpreted by the Beijing leadership as a pessimistic evaluation of the progress of socialist revolution in the Chinese countryside. Generalizing her conclusions to extend to every brigade and commune across the nation, Liu Shaoqi undertook the project of revising the "Later Ten Points," allegedly at the behest of Chairman Mao.[25] Although the revised document did not fundamentally alter the principles of the earlier version of the directive and did not propose new methods, the period of time allotted for work teams to carry out the movement was changed from three months to six months or more. In addition, work teams were warned against relying on local cadres for information or assistance in carrying out the movement; instead, the work teams were instructed to circumvent the local power structure and to "link up" directly to the masses. In addition, the revised plan called for a re-examination of class backgrounds assigned during the land-reform campaign, with the masses openly participating in a simultaneous re-evaluation of the class ranks of all residents in order to rectify any past mistakes in the assignment of class labels. Struggle sessions were not to be avoided, either "because of the fear of 'hurting' cadres' feelings, affecting the unity of the cadres, or of the cadres' quitting work"; real unity could be achieved only once all errors had been confessed and all wrongs had been righted.[26]

Wang Guangmei was not alone in reporting such practices. Chen Boda's report on the movement's progress in Tianjin's Xiaozhan district

24. Ibid., pp. 503–4.
25. Teiwes (1979), p. 542.
26. Baum and Teiwes (1969), pp. 106, 112.

uncovered no fewer than three "counter-revolutionary cliques" that had engaged in "counter-revolutionary restorationist activities for a long time." Subsequent updates on the Xiaozhan case were increasingly alarming, and in October, the Central Committee mandated that "in all cases in which local political power had been rigged or usurped by enemies, or local leadership had been wrested away by morally degenerate elements, it is imperative to struggle to seize power, otherwise, serious mistakes will be committed."[27]

Collectively, such reports suggested that the process of socialist transformation had only superficially altered traditional rural society. Despite the establishment of broad-scale collective organizations, pre-revolutionary power dynamics continued to prevail. Compliance with the policies of the new regime took place only on the surface: the old patterns of domination and submission continued, albeit more covertly than they had under the old society. The revolution had not eliminated the evils of traditional village life, but had merely driven them further underground, where they continued to fester and chip away at the process of socialist production. With no sure method of discerning who were the genuine enemies of the revolution, the only way for the new regime to strike back was to mobilize outside work teams to "squat" in the village communities for long periods of time, carrying out elaborate and secret investigations, involving dissimulation and subterfuge if necessary, in order to expose the truth.

LOCAL PERSPECTIVES ON THE ROLE OF WORK TEAMS

Following the promulgation of the revised "Later Ten Points," increasing numbers of mid-level cadres were mobilized and "sent down" to carry out the "Four Cleans." Prior to their departure for various communes and villages in the countryside, these groups underwent fairly extensive training sessions, during which they studied and discussed all of the "Ten Points" documents, as well as Wang Guangmei's Taoyuan brigade report. In carrying out the movement, organization was considered key: within the communes to which they were dispatched, work teams were to organize the leaders of all branch teams serving smaller units in a supervisory body, with a team at the county or district level overseeing all work teams sent down to production teams.

In Guizhou's Zunyi county, the first task of the work teams dispatched to the villages of Xiazi district (qu) was to "wipe out contradictions" by exposing elements still supposedly loyal to the Guomindang, branding the

---

27. Bo (1993), p. 1124.

district as a whole a "local bandit lair" (*tufei wo*). Work-team members were to be ever vigilant of coming into contact with the enemy. As two former work-team members recalled:

Some [work-team members] feared exposing their identities, and changed their first and last names. Entering Xiazi district we were wide-awake and never at peace (*xingxing bu an*), saying: "it is like entering enemy territory," and moreover concocted imaginary fears [as well]. If a breeze blew and the grass moved, we would want to go investigate, creating an atmosphere of terror, as if the enemy were everywhere. There were two work-team members who went to the Three Crossings Collective restaurant for a meal, and were discovered by the work-team leader. Aside from criticizing them severely, he educated us all, saying: "Don't you all know, that's a restaurant opened by the Nationalist Party!"[28]

With respect to their interactions with local cadres, the work-team members sent down to Xiazi district were given a list of "nine forbiddens" to disseminate among village cadres. Local cadres were instructed, among other things, not to avoid shouldering their responsibilities during the campaign, not to collude with one another to cover their errors, not to strike back in retaliation, and not to obstruct the mobilization of the masses by the work teams. Before long, word had been disseminated to all the work teams in the area that the "Xiazi district party committee is a Nationalist Party committee." The atmosphere became so tense that among the work-team members, word passed about the district cadres: "if we pick one can, the whole pile will come tumbling down—there's not a good one in the bunch," and the local leaders they were sent to investigate were collectively known as "bad cadres"; moreover, an informal regulation was observed within the sent-down teams: "With respect to any cadre above [the level of a work-point] recorder, as a rule they cannot be relied upon."

With respect to their interactions with local residents, work-team members were told that ordinary commune members were not to be trusted either until their true class backgrounds had been fully established. This work required the highest level of secrecy, and work-team members were instructed to investigate each resident going back three generations before "linking up and striking roots" with those who were proven to be poor and lower-middle peasants. Families in the district were informally classified by work-team members into four types of "roots" based upon their supposed political reliability: family members of cadres absolutely could not be trusted; if any members of a family were either related to or friendly

---

28. Li Jianren and Zhao Fumin, "Xiazi qu 'Siqing' yundong shimo" (The whole story of the Xiazi district's "Four Cleans"), in *Zunyi wenshi ziliao*, ed. Zhengxie Zunyi xian xuexi wenshi weiyuanhui, di wu ji (Guiyang: Guizhou renmin chubanshe, 1990), p. 62.

with a cadre, then the family as a whole could not be trusted, either. Among the work-team members it was said that "selecting a root is like picking out a son-in-law" (*xuan genzi xiang tiao nuxu neiyang*). Gradually, the numbers of households upon whom the work-team members could rely dwindled. Once the team had completed its investigations into the 34 families of the Heping brigade on Qingshan commune, only 7 were considered trustworthy.[29]

Having discerned which of the villagers were politically reliable, the Xiazi district work teams set about inciting the ordinary residents to inform on the cadres. With respect to cadres' errors, commune members were told: "It doesn't matter if it was seen, heard, or even [just] suspected, all can be revealed." However, even with such lax standards of evidence, the work teams experienced obstacles in inducing the commune members to criticize their leaders, and the sense of solidarity among local residents presented a formidable obstacle to the work-team members. As one informant from Guangdong recalled,

There were also commune cadres who came to my team to "squat" (*dundian*). A cadre named Jian from the commune Armed Forces Department came to my team to "squat," but he did not live in the team. He stayed at the brigade and usually came to the team during the day. He could not solve any problems, and did not achieve anything worthwhile because my team is of one mind toward outsiders.[30]

Work teams attempted to overcome their distance from the local residents by practicing the so-called "three togethers" (*santong*) policy of "eating together, living together, and laboring together" (*tong chi, tong zhu, tong laodong*). As one former work-team member recalled,

Usually, we were sent to commune members' homes to eat. According to party regulations, the family whose turn it was to receive us was to prepare food no better than tofu to serve us; we were only to eat a common peasant family's ordinary meal. [But] the local peasants led lives so hard that their only food [except for rice] was pickled sour cabbage, and eating tofu was considered a good meal.[31]

Another work-team member noted that the regulations regarding meals were so strict that when the assistant leader of the production team once sent them food to eat at their own living quarters (presumably to curry favor with them), they were forced to refuse it. When other commune

---

29. Li and Zhao (1990), pp. 62–63.
30. Steven B. Butler, "People's Communes in China: The Functioning of an Administrative Unit," in *Select Papers from the Center for Far Eastern Studies*, 4, ed. Tsou Tang (Chicago: University of Chicago Press, 1981), pp. 198–99.
31. Wu (1991), pp. 386–87.

members hosted them for dinner, if they were offered corn flour cakes, they were permitted to accept them; if the steamed buns served at dinner were made from white flour (ground millet), or if they were served noodles, they would graciously decline, since the peasants themselves only ate such foods at special occasions and during Spring Festival.[32] One former work-team member in Guangxi recalled that in his team one member had once bought some hot pepper sauce to put on his food, and had shared it with his host. He was immediately reported and criticized for his lapse.[33] In Zunyi district, work-team members were prohibited from eating chicken, fish, pork, or eggs, and one work team went so far as to promulgate the slogan that their members "had best not even drink boiled water," so as to preserve the little firewood local residents had on hand. The stiff regulations caught even the host families in a bind: if a local resident offered the work team any kind of superior food, the family background of that resident was investigated by the work team to determine whether or not the family had any connections to local cadres. On the other hand, if the food given to the work team was considered substandard, another investigation would be launched to determine if the family of the host had any reason to want to drive the work teams away.[34] At the height of the "Four Cleans," one work-team member was often heard to grumble: "In carrying out this 'Four Cleans' there are really [only] 'three words': the first one is 'receive' (we receive the resentment of the masses, receive criticism of our comrades, receive the 'three togethers' regulations); the second one is 'hard' (the work is hard, and the life is hard); and the third is 'not enough' (we don't eat enough, sleep enough, and don't have enough freedom)."[35]

Yet despite these efforts to draw nearer to the masses, the distance between the work teams and their host communities was wide and presented considerable obstacles to mobilization. Local residents generally avoided active participation in the movement whenever possible. One report on the Socialist Education Movement in several Jiangsu counties, including Dantu, Yixing, and Danyang, noted that a key problem in carrying out the movement was the reluctance of cadres to "go downstairs" (xialou) to actively carry out investigations. Alleged misconduct reported to commune officials were alternately not scrutinized, or partially rectified and partially ignored. In a small number of cases, cadres turned on the commune members who brought the allegations and counter-attacked. One

---

32. Ren (1989), pp. 255–56.
33. Huang (1989), p. 57.
34. Li and Zhao (1990), p. 63.
35. Huang (1989), p. 57.

commune member quoted in the report reflected in rhyme: "Whoopee, what fun, every year a new one; fresh campaign, same old rules, the cadres retaliate, and we're the fools." Another less poetic commune member retorted to a work-team member: "Let's not start by opposing our capitalist [tendencies]; let's take the party members and cadres and oppose them a bit instead!"[36]

To overcome precisely this type of reluctance among the commune residents, the Xiazi work teams offered various material incentives. The unit overseeing the work teams began a campaign "to distribute relief winter clothing," during which 4,787 articles of winter clothing were distributed to area residents, an average of one article of clothing per four people in some brigades. Before beginning the process of "struggling" against cadres in Qingshanbao Brigade, work teams held "distribution of relief winter clothing" meetings; later on, they convened "struggle sessions for those wearing new padded clothing to participate in." Alternatively, the provincial administration allocated large sums of money for distribution to the counties and districts for their various "relief" efforts. On occasion, Zunyi county received 100,000 *yuan* from the Guizhou provincial government, of which the supervisory work-team board allocated 50,000 *yuan* to Xiazi district. Even so, work-team members had to inflate the numbers of those said to have participated in "Four Cleans" struggle sessions in order to produce acceptable statistics for the organs supervising the work teams.

Even once the work teams managed to secure the participation of local residents in the mass struggle rallies, local residents often were unclear about what was expected of them.

Members of the five bad elements were brought up to the podium and forced to kneel before the crowd. There was a middle-aged woman among the bad elements. The high-level cadre from the prefecture signaled a poor peasant to come and asked him within earshot: "Is that a landlord's wife (*dizhupo*)?" The poor peasant answered: "Yes, cadre," and went up to that woman and pressed her head down to the floor throughout the struggle session. At the end of the meeting the high-level cadre asked this poor peasant, "Why did you force that woman's head down for so long? I thought that this campaign was supposed to avoid unnecessary physical abuse." The poor peasant answered: "But, cadre, I thought you had given me the order to force her head down (*dizhetou*)!" You see, this high-level cadre was from north China and his accent in spoken Mandarin was barely understandable. With poor peasants with limited education and ability to understand directives from the central government, abuses were inevitable.[37]

---

36. *Neibu cankao* (hereafter, *NBCK*), no. 3480 (March 29, 1963): 5.
37. Huang Shumin, *The Spiral Road* (Boulder: Westview Press, 1989), p. 77.

In contrast to the "soft wind and gentle rain" tactics of the "Small Four Cleans," the work teams who studied the Taoyuan brigade report were encouraged to employ more heavy-handed measures with those cadres and commune members deemed to be appropriate struggle targets. Those accused were subjected to severe punishment and were treated like criminals for the duration of the struggle process. In Zunyi county, cadres to be subjected to struggle were placed under special armed guard by the local people's militia units and were accompanied by armed escorts whenever they needed to be moved from one location to another. The local people's militia detention centers were used to hold the struggle sessions, and the family members of all cadres targeted for struggle were placed under military surveillance. In many cases, accused cadres had their homes searched and property confiscated. Two grain storehouses were converted into prisons staffed by public security bureau personnel in order to house cadres detained for questioning and mass struggle. During the winter of 1964–65, there were always several tens of cadres imprisoned there, some for longer than three months at a stretch. One poor peasant production-team chief from Xiazi commune who was accused of having sold rapeseed oil was labeled a "speculator" and incarcerated in the former granary for 105 days; his household property was confiscated and the eight members of his family were turned out of their home. One Lansheng commune work team incarcerated all 172 cadres serving the commune. The commune secretary, whose father had been a labor-union organizer before the revolution and who had only been accused of some minor infraction, was placed under surveillance for more than 20 days, during which time he was forced to chop wood and dig ditches up in the nearby mountains while under armed guard. When one day he accepted a bowl of hot pepper oil that was offered to him, he was accused of "continuing to lead a corrupt lifestyle" and was again struggled against for three days.[38]

In many instances, those who were subjected to mass criticism and struggle were accused on the basis of their unfavorable class backgrounds. In Xiazi district, during the effort to rectify class status, the members of 45 cadre households were classified as having "escaped being labeled as landlords or rich peasants" (louhua zhufu) and had their status revised accordingly. All in all, 538 households had their class ranks re-evaluated. "Elements" subsequently subjected to criticism or punishment included: the new "landlord elements," new "rich peasant elements," "alien class elements" (jieji yifi fenzi), "morally degenerate elements" (tuihua bianzhi fenzi), and "opportunist elements" (touji badao fenzi). Of the 69 people thus reclas-

---

38. Li and Zhao (1990), pp. 69–70.

sified, 25 underwent re-education and surveillance following mass struggle, and 12 were prosecuted in criminal trials; most of these were cadres or family members of cadres. The brigade chief of Mingxin brigade of Zunyi's Qingshan commune, whose widowed mother married into a family that subsequently became classified during land reform as "rich peasants," had been classified as a "middle tenant peasant" because his family owned 2.8 *mou* of farmland. During the "Big Four Cleans," however, he was accused of leading a "lavish rich peasant life" (*houshou funong shenghuo*), reclassified as a rich peasant, expelled from the party, and relieved of his post.[39] In early 1964, the district party secretary of Jiangxi's Duchang district (*qu*) was accused of having "class problems." During the "Big Four Cleans," a county work team, relying on hearsay, determined that for three years prior to the 1949 revolution he had earned more than 25 percent of his income from exploiting others and claimed he had "escaped being classified as a rich peasant." Accused of being a class enemy, he was struggled against. One production-team leader from Sichuan Chongqing's Shiqiao commune was accused of destroying collective property when an aged cow he had been tending died. The "Big Four Cleans" work team found that he had engaged in small handicraft labor prior to revolution and raised his class status to "rich peasant." Subsequently accused of being a "subversive rich peasant element," he was forced to submit a written confession and was turned over to the county's political-legal department for further investigation. Upon his release, he committed suicide.[40]

SOCIAL VIOLENCE AND RETRIBUTION

It is not surprising that the harsh tactics of the work teams and the climate of fear and suspicion generated during this phase of the movement produced rising levels of social unrest. In Sichuan's Guanghan county, it was the "Big Four Cleans" movement that gave way to the "Four Greats" (*sida*) phenomena, involving grand public gestures of mass participation: "speaking out freely, airing views fully, holding great debates, and writing big-character posters" (*da ming, da fang, da zibao, da pinglun*). This great public ferment was originally encouraged by work teams in order to expose the errors of the "Four Uncleans" cadres and "Four Classes," as well as other "cow ghosts and snake demons." Guanghan county cadres were divided into categories: "good" ones, those who were "comparatively

---

39. Ibid., pp. 73–74.
40. Wen Lu, *Zhongguo 'zuo' wu* (China's "leftist" errors) (Beijing: Chaohua chubanshe, 1993), p. 399.

good" (*bijiao haode*), those who "had problems" (*you wentide*), and those with "serious character [problems]" (*xingzhi yanzhongde*). This process continued in Guanghan county through 1966 and on into the Cultural Revolution period.[41]

One recurring problem associated with public criticism sessions was that local residents used them as opportunities to exact retribution for previous slights. Documents from the Socialist Education Movement period are replete with examples of ordinary commune members threatening to take revenge upon cadres during future struggle sessions. In Fujian's Aojiang commune, one member (formerly the regional party secretary under the Nationalists, later branded a counter-revolutionary) threatened a cadre, saying: "When our day comes, we will reckon accounts with the cadres" (*you womende tianqi, yao gen ganbu yao suanzhang*). He purportedly turned on the team chief as well, saying: "You should take a little care. When the time comes, there will be a good play to watch" (*yao xiaoxin dadian, dao shihou you haoxi kan*). Members of a different production team on Aojiang commune grew restive when their cadres attempted to persuade them against adopting the system of household contract production, which it was widely believed would increase the overall level of production in the units in which it was adopted. During one production-team meeting, after all of the cadres but one openly rejected the proposed system, one commune member blurted out: "Not to engage in household contract production is all very well, but you cadres will be responsible for making good any deficiency in production" (*Bu 'baochan daohu' ye keyi, pei chan yao ganbu fuze*).[42]

Many local cadres were understandably reluctant to participate in the movement, and many attempted to obstruct its progress in any way possible. An August 1963 report from Weiting commune in Jiangsu's Wu county detailed a wide variety of fears preventing full cadre participation in the Socialist Education Movement, including "fear of punishment, fear of demotion, fear of being expelled from the party, fear of being struggled, fear of losing face, fear of being divorced by their wives."[43]

"Retributive attacks" (*dadao baofu*) became increasingly common, and the growing violence associated with the Socialist Education Movement

---

41. *Guanghan xianzhi* (Guanghan county gazetteer) (Chengdu: Sichuan renmin chubanshe, 1992), p. 395.

42. Wang Hongzhi, "Shiche Bajie Shi Zhongquan hui jueyi, gonggu jiti jingji, fada nongye shengchan" (Implementation of the resolutions of the Tenth Plenum of the Eighth Central Committee on strengthening the collective economy and expanding agricultural production) (1962), *Fujian Lianjiang xian feifang wenjian ji qi jiufen* (The documents of the [Communist] bandits of Fujian's Lianjiang County, with analytical notes) (Taibei: Ministry of National Defense's Bureau of Intelligence, 1964), p. 26.

43. *NBCK*, no. 3533 (August 1, 1963): 3.

began to destabilize many rural communities. Bo Yibo notes that as early as January 1963, the Party Central Committee issued a directive strictly forbidding the use of physical punishment during the Socialist Education Movement. The notice was circulated after the committee received word that in Hunan's Changde district, there had been numerous cases of "the reckless pursuit of struggle" against targets that included physical beatings, "reckless investigations," haphazard "retraining" of accused individuals, the "reckless assignment of labels" or "hats" against those accused of wrongdoing, and the "wanton issuance of fines or punishments." In Hubei's Macheng county, 331 people had reportedly been struggled against, including 21 who had been beaten, 65 who had been bound or forcibly restrained, 3 who were hanged, and 42 who had been forced to kneel for long periods during struggle sessions. By the end of February in Hunan alone, a reported 76 to 97 people had committed suicide as a result of the Socialist Education Movement. Yet such directives apparently did little to curb the rising waves of violence. By the conclusion of the first wave of experimental Socialist Education Movement criticism sessions, more than 2,000 people had committed suicide; the second wave of struggle sessions, which lasted only 25 days, resulted in an additional 74 deaths. During the experimental phase of the Socialist Education Movement in Guangdong, which transpired during the autumn and winter of 1963, a reported 602 people attempted suicide, the majority of whom succeeded.[44]

The roots of many of these cases of retribution reached back several years, or even decades, before the "Big Four Cleans" movement began, and involved extensive political maneuvering by several factions within a locale. For example, when Sichuan's Guanghan county was amalgamated with neighboring Shifang county in April 1960, the original Guanghan County Party Committee called a meeting of mid-level cadres to arrange for transfers and to discuss the problems of Guanghan's "backwardness" and the "work-style problems" of some of Guanghan's cadres. At the meeting, the county party branch leaders were criticized for having done "superficial work" in the past and for having had "opinions." In 1962, when the party committee convened another meeting to discuss the rectification measures proposed in Mao's "Seven Thousand" cadres speech, these criticisms were again raised by participating county and basic-level cadres. In April 1963, when the county launched the "new Five-Antis" movement, the county party branch organized work teams to go to the local communes and factories, and the investigation committee apparently dispatched some personnel specifically in order to investigate those same cadres who had

---

44. Bo (1993), pp. 1111, 1114–15.

previously raised criticisms against the county party branch. The county investigation committee treated these as "special cases," and collectively classified the investigations as "cases of disorganized activities" (*fei zuzhi an*), in which possible charges of subversion were explored. That year, at least 50 people were accused of possible "anti-organizational activities" and the relevant suspects were hauled in for extensive questioning. In August 1965, during the "Big Four Cleans" movement in Guanghan, these individuals were again accused, but this time of organizing their own small groups (*xiao zhizu*). The county party committee's secretary of the investigative sub-committee, Li Zhuanxin, was purged of his party membership on the grounds that his "serious capitalist class individualist tendencies" had run amok, that he had ultimately created a "sect" (*zongpai*) in the party and had subverted the will of the party by carrying on small-group activities. The assistant secretary of Guanghan county, Gao Deqing, was found guilty of "harboring another [criminal] engaged in anti-party activities"; and the head of the former county legal department, Zhang Guanghua, was found guilty of having "participated in Li Zhuanxin's sect within the party, and of continuing erroneously to carry on small-group activities." Once all had been struggled against, the former party committee's secretary of the investigative committee, Li Zhuanxin, retired to Yaan to convalesce. Later that year, he was hauled back to Guanghan and placed under house arrest on the grounds of his former workplace, the county bureau of investigation, until he succumbed to illness and died a few months later.[45]

In Shaanxi province, no fewer than 728 "retributive attack" cases involving some 850 individuals were received from October 1964 through September 1965, the period of the "Big Four Cleans" campaign. Virtually all of these cases involved either "mean-spirited defeated class enemies" or "resolutely unrepentant" "Four Uncleans" cadres,

wantonly counterattacking to settle old scores (*fangong dasuan*), ruining the collective economy, and moreover employing every type of method to attack and harm the workers, poor and middle peasants, and other revolutionaries. Some of them knocked out the teeth of the poor and middle peasants, pulled out their hair, or broke their bones to the point that they crippled them for the rest of their lives. Some even went to the extent of secretly poisoning others and committing murders.[46]

In Shaanxi's Ankang county, two poor peasants, a husband and wife, were allegedly beaten to death by the son of a landlord when the peasant

---

45. *Guanghan xianzhi* (Guanghan county gazetteer) (1992), p. 393.
46. *Shaanxi shengzhi* (Shaanxi provincial gazetteer) (Xi'an: Shaanxi renmin chubanshe, 1994), pp. 361–62.

removed a few ears of corn from the latter's private plot. In Chen'gu county, "Four Uncleans" cadre Xi Cunde, "harboring hatred in his heart from when the poor peasants exposed his corruption and theft during the rectification phase of the Socialist Education Movement," awaited his opportunity to take revenge. After the campaign had ended, he poisoned them in retribution. In Jiangxi's Longnan county, Liao Caicun, a former production brigade accountant from Taojiang commune, slaughtered 24 fellow commune members and cadres in retribution for their having struggled against him during the Socialist Education Movement. During his tenure as the brigade accountant, Liao purportedly pocketed 500 *yuan* of brigade funds. After his crimes of the previous year were exposed during a Socialist Education Movement struggle session in 1963, Liao was relieved of his post and ordered to make restitution. However, after the movement concluded in Longnan, Liao repudiated the debt and further-more filed an appeal with the county Socialist Education Movement secretary's office, the county procuracy, and the local court. When his claims were denied, Liao pilfered some dynamite, detonating caps, and fuses from a local irrigation project site and built an explosive device. When his last appeal was denied, he rigged the brigade meeting hall during an evening conference, killing 24 of the 30 commune members in attendance. Liao was apprehended the next day and sentenced for his crimes.[47]

Cases of violent retribution were so numerous in Shaanxi by the latter half of the "Big Four Cleans" movement that provincial leaders and judicial officials hurriedly convened a conference in order to discuss the problem, and dispatched special work teams specifically to investigate the manner in which "retributive" cases were being handled in Xianyang, Weinan, Huayang, Dongguan, and Hua counties. Apparently, local courts were divided about how to deal with such cases: some local judicial officials felt that most such incidents should be processed as routine civil disputes and were treating them accordingly. However, with the help of the newly dispatched work teams and "after study raised their penetrating insight into class struggle, their handling [of such] cases had [new] direction." All such disputes involving so-called "Four Elements" or "Four Uncleans" cadres were subsequently investigated for evidence that those involved may have been seeking retribution for having been exposed or criticized during the Socialist Education Movement; if such evidence could be found, such cases were classified as instances of "anti-party, anti-people, anti-socialist expressions of anti-revolutionary activ-

---

47. *NBCK*, no. 3675 (September 4, 1964): 20–21.

ity," and those involved faced even more severe penalties than they might have otherwise.[48]

According to judicial officials in Shaanxi's Liquan, Yongshou, and Hua counties, the rapid escalation in social unrest and crime there during the Socialist Education Movement was largely due to "errors" (*piancha*) in the manner in which the campaign was pursued by work teams in the counties. First, the targets of the movement were too broadly defined, causing widespread attacks at the local level. The sheer numbers of individuals targeted for investigation, criticism, and struggle were so large that arrests skyrocketed, far exceeding the numbers projected by provincial authorities. Second, the implementation of movement policies was unstable (*bu wen*),

confusing two essentially different kinds of contradictions (*hunxiao lianglei butong xingzhi de maodun*). The spearhead of the attack was not precise, lumping together those who were engaged in destructive activities with landlords, rich peasants, counter-revolutionaries, and bad elements, who had already been punished following liberation, and who for many years had not engaged in counter-revolutionary activities. However, merely because of petty corruption, they were prosecuted for counter-revolutionary and corruption crimes. In some cases, the words and deeds or the hopes of some landlord elements that reactionary rule would be restored were all regarded as crimes, [and] used to counter-attack against them. In other cases, commonplace bets and scuffles among peasants were treated as crimes [and] prosecuted under the laws against gambling and as violations against their personal rights (*qinfan renshen quanli*).[49]

Finally, lax legal and judicial standards permitted countless individuals to be punished for crimes that they had not committed, simply on the basis of information collected by work teams, or of information that emerged during mass struggle rallies. In other instances, cases were tried in the absence of the relevant judicial authorities, and without conducting any further investigations into the nature of the cases, both violations of the organic laws establishing the "people's courts."[50]

The heightened vigilance and tension created by the activities of outside work teams in some locales led to resistance against work-team directives. One former Sichuan Santai county resident noted that on Luban commune during the "Big Four Cleans," conflict erupted between the local leadership and the "sent-down" work-team members over the manner in which the movement ought to proceed in their community, with the result that the work team ultimately used the movement as a pretext for settling scores

---

48. *Shaanxi shengzhi* (Shaanxi provincial gazetteer) (1994), p. 361.
49. Ibid., p. 362.
50. Ibid.

with the local leadership. According to his account, the local leadership had opposed the work team's policy of "rectifying" the class backgrounds of all of the households within the commune and had argued, in accordance with the earlier "Ten Points" documents, that the vast majority of the local cadres were basically good and did not require re-education, criticism, or rectification. With respect to the first, the resident noted:

Now, under the directive of "making class struggle the key point," to again bring up issues from nine years ago, and moreover to widen their significance in relationship to other events, just isn't [reflective of] objective reality. . . . The large-scale mass movement was carried out in this manner, investigating class ranks and checking them back three generations, rooting out "class enemies" . . . and associating the economic inequalities between peasants following land reform with the employment situation of their grandfathers and grandmothers, using this as the measure to establish class ranks. Those who were classified as poor and middle peasants, industrialists, and their employees during the period of land reform were again marked off as landlords, rich peasants, capitalists, and bogus officials.[51]

Agreeing with the former leadership of the commune, the local resident cites several cases of fellow commune members who were reclassified as either rich peasants or wealthy landlords as a result of work-team investigations. These reclassifications appear to have been related, not to the socioeconomic status of the families involved prior to the 1949 revolution, but instead were made on the basis of gains made under the new regime.

For example, Wu Ruhai, during land reform classified as a poor peasant, has always had his whole family engaged in painstaking labor, building up his family's savings. One day, suddenly in the middle of this movement, without bringing to light the realities of his exploitation prior to liberation, and using the transference of feudally owned landlord properties under land reform, he is now classified as a landlord. His son, upon graduating from school, was notified by the work team that he had to return home immediately to undergo criticism, and lost the opportunity to put in for a work assignment. Or take Kang Youquan, classified during land reform as a middle peasant, who has a big family with good labor power, very enterprising, and his life is much better now than before liberation, but no one brings out the reality of his exploitation. Because he was the accountant and because his brigade selected a labor-poor household as the standard, when now they calculate his work points and grain rations, they decide he's corrupt, reclassify him as a rich peasant, and fine him 770 *yuan*. When he contests the charge they investigate him again and accuse him of the crime of "counter-attacking to settle old scores" (*fangong daosuan*), and

51. Tang Hongyi, "Luban 'shejiao' yundong" (Luban's Socialist Education Movement), in *Santai wenshi ziliao xuanji*, no. 8 ed. Santai wenshi ziliao weiyuanhui (Chengdu: Sichuan renmin chubanshe, 1989), p. 86.

reclassify him again as a landlord, and then they take the three younger brothers in his family back in 1954 and reclassify them as landlords, too.[52]

With respect to the second criticism of the work team—that it ostensibly ignored the official declaration that the vast majority of cadres were basically good and had no "problems"—the commune resident noted that the work team took the earlier voluntary self-criticisms offered by both the ordinary commune members and cadres alike, and later used that material to brand certain individuals in Luban as "capitalist roaders" and "class enemies." Thus, attitudes that should have merely been exposed and then corrected became classified as crimes and labeled as targets of "revolutionary and class struggle." Local cadres who may have displayed evidence of "bureaucratism," along with local party members who were found to have "capitalist roader" tendencies, were all exposed to the "strong winds and violent rain" tactics of "penetrating class struggle" as conducted by the outside work teams. In all, in addition to the party branch secretary of Luban commune, ten production-team branch secretaries and most of the brigade leaders and party members were all undeservedly removed from their posts and subjected to violent struggle.[53]

The New National Model: State-Sponsored Localism

In mid-December 1964, several months after the widespread publication of Wang Guangmei's Taoyuan brigade report, the party branch secretary of the Dazhai brigade in Shaanxi's Xiyang county departed for Beijing in order to participate in the First Session of the National People's Congress (NPC) as a member of the Shaanxi provincial delegation. The 83-household brigade, located in a remote northern corner of Shaanxi, had previously risen to national prominence for having made astronomical gains in agricultural productivity following collectivization, experiencing annual grain harvests of more than 800 *jin* per *mou* of farmland in the early 1960s, as compared to the pre-revolution average of only 150 *jin* per *mou*. These increases, moreover, had apparently been accomplished without the benefit of state aid, and therefore the brigade was heralded not only as a model of the types of advances that were made possible under socialist agricultural production but also as a model of self-reliant economic development. Local communities across the nation were being

---

52. Ibid., p. 86.
53. Ibid., pp. 86–88.

urged to "hold high the red banner of Dazhai," and low-level cadres were urged to study the experiences of Brigade Party Secretary Chen Yonggui. Originally the founder of a labor-poor mutual-aid team in the village, Chen had risen first to local and then to regional prominence as a loyal and dedicated local activist and had in 1964 been rewarded for his efforts by being elected to serve as a deputy to the Xiyang county people's congress. As a member of the provincial delegation to the NPC, he left Dazhai not long after the "Big Four Cleans" work team arrived there and began its activities to mobilize the local residents against the cadres in earnest. However, soon after his arrival in Beijing, Chen took the opportunity during a private meeting he had with Chairman Mao to offer him a local perspective on the manner in which the Socialist Education Movement had developed in Xiyang county and to criticize the techniques of the work team that had been dispatched to Dazhai. His account of the Socialist Education Movement in Dazhai purportedly altered Mao's assessment of the progress of the movement as a whole, and contributed to Mao's abrupt change in course with the promulgation of the so-called "Twenty-three Articles" in January of 1965. This document, along with Mao's subsequent shift in attitude, signaled his shift to a very different vision of the situation in the countryside than had been adopted in Wang Guangmei's Taoyuan brigade report. Attacking many of the tactics employed by Wang and her work team in Taoyuan, Mao argued for a more open investigation process, smaller work teams, and far greater involvement from local leaders in managing the movement in their communities.[54] His subsequent embrace of the Dazhai model over the more central state-focused critique of local-level politics implicit in the Taoyuan brigade report radically shifted the power dynamics of the Socialist Education Movement and ultimately contributed to the massive devolutions in the authority of central government structures during the Cultural Revolution period.

In the autumn of 1964, Shaanxi provincial officials dispatched a work team to Dazhai to carry on intensive investigation into the local political scene there. Their decision to do so was prompted by the embarrassing Shenshi brigade incident in which a "Four Cleans" work team had exposed extensive corruption, crime, and heavy-handed tactics at the national model brigade in Guangdong, and unmasked the brigade's party branch secretary, Chen Hua, as a brutal rapist who often violently abused the ordinary commune members and had them living in fear for their lives. When two elderly peasants informed the work team of the wrongdoing of the Shenshi brigade party branch secretary, his superiors at the com-

---

54. Teiwes (1979), pp. 558-59.

mune level criticized Chen for his "improper work styles," although they took no other action against him. During the subsequent brief absence of the work team, he purportedly had his two accusers brutally beaten; although the two did not inform the work team after it returned of the beating they suffered, the two peasants secretly wrote a letter to provincial authorities detailing the incident and Chen's prior abusive behavior. After another work team that had been dispatched to investigate the accusations against Chen Hua failed to turn up any evidence against him, the two suffered yet another beating at the behest of Chen. Finally, the two elderly peasants wrote directly to the General Office of the Party Central Committee with their story; a third work team was dispatched to conduct a highly secretive and sensitive investigation of the affair, this time headed by Wang Guangmei herself. When Chen Hua learned of the existence of the new work team and the identity of its leader, he attempted to escape with a handful of his co-conspirators in a midnight motorboat ride to Hong Kong, but authorities intercepted them within minutes of their departure. Chen and his accomplices were returned to the brigade, where they underwent mass criticism and were punished for their crimes. Shortly thereafter, Chen Hua died when he either threw himself or was thrown against a high-voltage electrical transformer at the brigade.[55]

With the embarrassment of the Shenshi incident still fresh in their minds, soon after arriving in Xiyang county, the work-team members dispatched to the national model Dazhai brigade to carry out the "Big Four Cleans" suspended the activities of the local party branch and informed all of the county cadres that they would be required to be set aside and to submit to rectification. In part due to the allegations that had surfaced against the Shenshi brigade secretary, it appears that the work team took a particular interest in investigating the activities of Brigade Secretary Chen's family. His son, Chen Mingqu, the leader of the Dazhai Youth League, was immediately relieved of his post. Chen's daughter-in-law, a clerk in the commune cooperative store, was charged with misappropriating collective funds and the store was closed down. Chen's wife was charged with stealing pig feed from the brigade's pig farm where she was employed. Other local cadres were similarly accused.[56] In early December, in light of their investigations the work team announced: "There are grubs in the staff of the red banner of Dazhai. If they are not eliminated, it cannot be raised high." The brigade accordingly lost its sta-

55. Baum (1974), pp. 114–15.
56. Hinton (1983), p. 320.

tus as an "advanced" work unit and was reclassified as a "brigade that had serious problems."[57]

The report of the work team raised several charges against the brigade leaders, alleging that they had used a variety of techniques to over-inflate their per *mou* crop yield. One early charge was that the actual land being farmed at Dazhai was in fact much greater than reported, accounting for the high grain yields; the extensive surveys of the arable land in Dazhai conducted by the work team did indeed disclose that the peasants had been farming more land than had been reported to the state. Another accusation centered on the moisture content of the grain weighed to calculate the harvest, and whether or not the grain had been adequately dried; work-team members discovered that the brigade had not been observing state regulations regarding the procedures for drying grain. The work team also took on the issues of work-point and grain-ration allotments in Dazhai, and accused the brigade cadres of recording work points for themselves on one occasion that they had not actually earned, and of distorting national policies on calculating grain rations by allowing larger rations to be allocated for laborers; in fact, Dazhai had developed a local policy concerning the distribution of grain rations that deviated from the nationally mandated standard. Finally, the work team accused brigade authorities of failing to properly implement some of the post–Great Leap reforms formulated by central state authorities, including the institution of controlled free-market trading of certain commodities and the lack of private plots for commune members.

Chen Yonggui's responses to the allegations of the work team, which were later widely publicized during the Cultural Revolution, represented a localist critique of central policies, one that was overtly anti-bureaucratic, radically egalitarian, and, to a certain extent, anti-state as well. When the work team alleged that Dazhai's high production rates had been manufactured by underreporting the land under cultivation there, Chen strenuously asserted that not only had all of the original land farmed been reported to state authorities, but that the enterprising brigade members had managed to make extensive use of labor-intensive terracing in order to open up new fields. However, when further surveying continued to reveal a discrepancy, Chen asserted that their extensive terracing efforts had allowed them to retire less fertile fields and to plant fruit trees on them, with the final result that their tilled acreage had remained roughly the same throughout. In response to the criticisms that their corn had not been fully dried before the harvest was calculated, the brigade authori-

---

57. *China Pictorial*, no. 1 (January 1968), p. 27.

ties were forced to admit that the national regulation mandating a certain deduction be calculated for corn that retained moisture was one that "Dazhai people had never heard of." The work-team members had alleged that the local cadres, by not observing the mandatory deductions for moisture, had overtaxed the peasant harvests, leaving them with smaller shares and had probably retained the surplus thus extracted for their own use. Apparently some of the commune members were convinced that this type of graft had in fact occurred in Dazhai and pressed this charge at a public rally to criticize the basic-level cadres. However, the local cadres argued to the work team that their violation of state regulations ought to be forgiven in light of the fact that their increasing yields translated into higher annual procurements for the state. To the peasants, the local cadres defended their actions, claiming:

We didn't deduct for moisture because our corn was dry. Aren't we getting bigger crops than ever before? Aren't you all getting larger shares than ever before? Of course. But they are telling you that we aren't harvesting big crops on the one hand and on the other they are telling you that we cadres have misappropriated so much that when it is divided up you'll get more than you ever got in the land reform. Does that add up![58]

On the issue of allotting work points, one production-team cadre was in fact able to produce records that showed that a group of team cadres had reported to work an hour late on a certain occasion, but brigade records showed that they had in fact been granted work points for the missed hour. To the work-team members, the cadres who had received the extra work points argued that they had been delayed by a provincial-level cadre who had "demanded full reports on many subjects," and that they had typically "reported to him during their noon break and at night after working hours. On the day that he left they still had not completed their reports. They talked through and beyond their noon hour, so that nothing would be left out and reported for work one hour late." At this point, according to Chen's account, the brigade members indicated that they felt that under the circumstances, the work points were probably deserved. Furthermore, the rank and file then turned on the work team, saying:

When you work in your office eating the people's millet, have you ever been one hour late to work? Have you never been off sick for one day? Have you ever paid for medical care? You say you don't miss an hour a year? What nonsense! Not ten, not one hundred would be enough to cover what you yourselves miss![59]

---

58. Hinton (1983), p. 321.
59. Ibid., p. 322.

Mao's adoption of the Dazhai model of radical local self-reliance, and its overtly anti-bureaucratic critique of state authority as manifested by "Big Four Cleans" work teams during the Socialist Education Movement, represented an early signal of what would develop into a full-blown schism in the upper echelons of party and state leadership during the Cultural Revolution period. Regardless of the reliability of Chen's account of the Socialist Education Movement in Dazhai,[60] Mao read in the experiences of the Shaanxi brigade a lesson in populist political ethics that may have prompted him to authorize the January 1965 "Twenty-three Articles," which repudiated many of the underlying principles of the "Revised Later Ten Points." This final document pressed for a more careful and clear distinction to be drawn between the minority of cadres who had "serious problems" and the vast majority of those who did not; it also stressed the importance of a work team's sensitivity to local needs and particular conditions in the villages, and urged far greater leniency overall in dealing with those who may have made errors. While these reforms were by no means solely the result of Mao's meeting with Chen Yonggui, as Chen later indicated, Mao clearly signaled his support at their 1964 meeting: "Chairman Mao was best able to understand us [Dazhai cadres], and he showed the greatest concern for us. At the crucial moment of the struggle, he received me in audience and gave me important instructions concerning work in Dazhai. . . . To us this was the greatest encouragement, the most intimate concern, and the most powerful support."[61]

Following the January 1965 release of the "Twenty-three Articles," Mao became increasingly critical of the manner in which the work teams had pursued their targets during the Socialist Education Movement, and in particular of the Taoyuan brigade model. Even before the new document had been disseminated, in a talk on the subject of the "Four Cleans" movement, he complained: "Four Cleans means . . . cleaning up a few people. Where there is something unclean, clean it up; where it is clean, no cleaning up will be necessary. There must be some clean people! Where there are no lice on a person, how can you find lice?" Even more to the point, he attacked the notion of sending outside work teams, and in particular the large outside work teams characteristic of the "Big Four Cleans" period, into the villages to conduct the cadre purges: "18,000 people were concentrated in a county of 280,000 people. . . . Why didn't you rely on the

---

60. Chen Yonggui's later speeches and the subsequent versions of the Dazhai story retroactively attribute certain negative elements of the Dazhai experience to the early workings of the alleged "Liuist faction." See Lowell Dittmer, " 'Line Struggle' in Theory and Practice: The Origins of the Cultural Revolution Reconsidered," *China Quarterly*, no. 72 (1977).
61. Baum (1974), p. 120.

280,000 people of that county? . . . If you had relied on the right people, it would have been sufficient to send a dozen or more people to each county. . . . Terrible! Such a waste of time!"⁶² According to Liu Yuan, the son of Liu Shaoqi and Wang Guangmei, by 1965 Mao openly mocked elements of the Taoyuan model by referring to it as representing "the philosophy of hairsplitting and the strategy of the human sea" (*fansuo zhexue, renhai zhanshu*) and "strike roots, link up, and perpetrate mystification" (*zhagen chuanlian, gao shenmihua*). In summing up their respective approaches to the movement, Liu suggested:

What Mao emphasized was an attack on class polarization (the means of production had by that time been collectivized), and moreover the emergence of a capitalist class and other capitalist roaders; what Liu emphasized was the abolition of stratification (the ever-present danger of the isolation of those in power), and moreover the emergence of a privileged bureaucratic stratum. What Mao opposed was the restoration of capitalism (China never experienced a stage of capitalist development); what Liu opposed was the restoration of feudalism (China inherited several thousand years of feudal society). Mao wished to settle the contradictions between us and the enemy; Liu wanted to solve, among the many contradictions that existed, first those among the people, to the extent that "if there is a problem to be solved, then solve it." Mao advocated, with respect to the enemy, attacking the antithesis, eliminating the antithesis in isolation, a "fight to the death"; Liu advocated, with respect to the people on our side, the expansive aspect of education, the unifying aspect of education, the liberation of the majority, and an education that was both broad and deep.⁶³

Regardless of what the aims of the central leadership may have been, or how they may have diverged, the Socialist Education Movement can hardly be counted as a success for the regime. The release of the "Twenty-three Articles" and Mao's repudiation of Wang Guangmei's Taoyuan brigade model signaled an inconclusive end to the "Four Cleans." Six months later, with numerous work teams still laboring in the countryside, Mao announced that the movement had already concluded, stating: "The 'Four Cleans' movement was wound up in the year [1964] and has been fundamentally completed; [only] medical and health work in the villages has not yet been completed."⁶⁴ At the same time, Chen Yonggui's star continued to rise, and his career in national-level politics culminated with seats on

---

62. Ibid., pp. 122–24.
63. Liu Yuan and He Jiadong, " 'Siqing' nituan" (The "Four Cleans" ball of mud), in Liu Yuan et al., *Ni suo buzhidaode Liu Shaoqi* (The Liu Shaoqi you never knew) (Shijizhuang: Henan renmin chubanshe, 1999), pp. 118–19. Not surprisingly, this interpretation of Liu Shaoqi's presumed aims is an overwhelmingly positive and generous one.
64. Dittmer (1977), p. 699.

the State Council and the Politburo, both of which he was able to hold for only a brief period. The story of the Dazhai brigade, in various versions, also moved to the fore, and was studied and discussed widely for many years as a model of revolutionary localism, before being discarded and discredited in 1980.[65]

Popular evaluations of the "Four Cleans" and Socialist Education Movement are overwhelmingly negative. As one rural resident who summed up the collective experience of the movement in Guangxi Yongding county noted,

From early 1963 to early 1966, towns and villages throughout the nation developed the Socialist Education Campaign (also called the "Four Cleans" movement, in order to clean up politics, clean up thought, clean up organization, and clean up economics). At this point, it had already gone from being propagandized as a spectacular "one-time great revolutionary movement" to [being a movement to] "take seriously the struggle to educate the people anew." "After the education movement is over, the entire nation will be the picture of prosperity (*xinxin xiangrong*)." . . . As the test of historical experience shows, we should say, "although with respect to solving cadre work styles and difficulties encountered with enterprise management, it certainly proved to be of practical use, but due to various and sundry problems, we all [now see] that it was a reflection of class struggle or of inner party struggle, and many basic-level cadres that were harshly criticized were wrongly attacked (*bu yingyou dadao*)"; then it "subsequently developed into the leading battles of the Great Proletarian Cultural Revolution." From the foregoing summary, we can now say, the Socialist Education Movement was fundamentally a failure.[66]

WRITING AND REWRITING THE MAOIST STATE

The Socialist Education Movement can be read as a vast and sustained effort to increase the scope of central state supervision over local practices, and thereby to restore the moral agency of the Maoist party-state in the aftermath of the disastrous Great Leap Forward. Clearly, the moral force of Communist victory in 1949 was rooted in the party's claim to represent the collective material interests of the peasant and proletarian majority. However, the catastrophic institutional and organizational failures of the climactic fulfillment of Mao's transformative vision during the Great Leap effectively nullified the early promise of the revolutionary regime. The economic recovery that followed served to underscore the insufficiency of the Maoist program in meeting the material needs of the peasants and

---

65. Other national models are discussed by Norma Diamond in "Model Villages and Village Realities," *Modern China* 9:2 (April 1983): 163–81.
66. Huang (1989), p. 54.

workers whom the party claimed to represent. The growing disjunction between the party line on the one hand and the lived experience of the majority of rural residents on the other achieved a new salience during the Socialist Education Movement. Whereas the "Big Four Cleans" work teams sought to anchor cases of corruption in the official rhetoric of continuing class struggle, the terms that dominated the political discourse of the move-ment—"counter-revolutionary," "revisionist," "capitalist-roader"—did not correspond in any meaningful way to the material context of rural life in the aftermath of communization. The instrumental manipulation of these concepts by work teams, cadres, and local residents ultimately served only to deepen the sense of moral alienation and disaffection already experi-enced by most survivors of the famine.

With the benefit of hindsight, Mao's fateful 1962 call to continue class struggle signaled a critical shift in the normative agenda of the regime. If the party's socioeconomic agenda had manifestly failed to secure even the most basic material interests of rural residents during the Leap, the regime nonetheless ruthlessly demonstrated its willingness to wrench compliance where it had failed to obtain consent. No longer able to reliably elicit the voluntary support of the majority on whose behalf it claimed to rule, Mao offered a new, non-material standard by which to assign political status: behavioral compliance with the party line as measured by routine expres-sions of loyalty for the regime. With work teams acting as their agents, cen-tral authorities defined new types of political subjects in the wake of eco-nomic recovery, and invested them with political power as moral agents either supporting or opposing the agenda of the regime. During the cam-paign, the heightened level of surveillance to which individuals and com-munities were subjected required private citizens not only to demonstrate their own compliance, but furthermore to police the behavior of others who might conceivably attempt to "recruit" them to the opposite side.

Viewed collectively, the mass campaigns of the Maoist era thus repre-sent a new technology of governance that aimed to produce self-disciplin-ing individuals for whom the larger agenda of the state provided a moral framework for both intention and action on a day-to-day basis. The state-mandated practices of diary-keeping, small-group discussion meetings, and criticism sessions fused individual and collective identities to an unprec-edented degree. One recent survey tracking political slogans in the Peoples' Liberation Army newspaper during the 1950s and 1960s documented the systematic incorporation of the private by the collective: whereas the onset of communization was heralded as an organizational manifestation in the spirit of "all for one and one for all" (*renren wei wo, wo wei renren*), over time, commune members and cadres alike were enjoined to "[in service to] the public, forget the self" (*gonger wangsi*), and then, finally, to "magnify the public and obliterate the private" (*dagong wusi*).[67] Unlike the disciplinary practices of earlier Chinese regimes, which were more limited in both scope and intent, the process of "socialist education" under the rubric of the "Four Histories" required not only cadres but participants of all backgrounds to produce and parrot genealogical narratives recording how their lives had been transformed under socialism.

The process by which the public realm steadily consumed the private realm was not merely manifest at the level of institutional or organizational change; it mandated transformations at the personal level as well. Individuals were called upon not only to comply with the party's reshaping of history but to conform their own personal histories to the larger narrative framework of collective revolutionary change. One such case that was published and distributed to a cadre readership under the title "The Use of Revolutionary History" was the excerpted diary of Wang Zhongchuan, a nineteen-year-old commune resident from Qiangcheng village in Shanxi's Lucheng county. The prefatory comments describe Wang as the son of a poor peasant at the time of land reform who had nonetheless not warmly welcomed the developments of post-revolutionary Qiangcheng. Instead, Wang recorded in his diary that he felt that he had become a mere "beast of burden driven by a small pack of blood-sucking devils" beginning in August 1961, when he became a full-fledged laborer in the commune. In one January 1962 entry, he complained of the numbing cold he was forced to endure, and the fact that he had been assigned to pull a cart that was so heavy that he could barely move it: "While I was a student in school, we felt that seven people to pull one cart wasn't enough, it wouldn't budge, and now how is it that two people pulling this cart are supposed to make it move?" His bitter entry on the first day of spring records his continuing disillusionment with commune life:

I truly have become a beast of burden. I really don't understand: why have the few been changed into blood-sucking parasites (this of course is the minority), [and] the majority have become beasts of burden? Of course, I am but one among

---

67. *Dagong wusi*, a classical aphorism, was frequently invoked by the Confucian literati during the imperial period and was resurrected as a Mao-era political slogan. See Qian Gang, "Hongse ciyu de boxing he liubian (1956–69)" (The rise and spread of red words [1956–69]), an unpublished manuscript. Qian Gang maps the shift in slogans (from "*wo wei renren, renren wei wo*" during the Great Leap, to "*gonger wangsi*" and "*dagong wusi*" during the Cultural Revolution); see especially Section Four, pp. 30–39; see also Qian Gang, "Cong 'Jiefang junbao' (1956–69) kan 'jieji douzheng' yici de chuanbo" (The dissemination of the phrase *jieji douzheng* [class struggle]: a case study of *PLA Daily* [1956–69]), *Ershiyi shiji* (Twentieth-century China), no. 77 (June 2003): 50–60.

many others. Although I am a youth of eighteen, yet I grow old, my energy saps, [and] sometimes in my dreams I appear as a wan and sallow shadow with my brow furrowed in worry. I am afraid, how long can I go on like this?

It is unclear precisely how the county party committee obtained the diary, but excerpted portions note a dramatic change in attitude within days after the movement launched. During the campaign meetings, Wang's father is invited to "recall the bitterness" of his former life as a poor peasant under the old society, a tale that greatly moved his son. Wang's father announced that "under the old society, the landlords wanted us to die; under the new society, the Communist Party wants us to live and moreover, to live well. The Communist Party is our savior. We must not forget our old sufferings, we must not fall prey to the landlords' tricks; we have now arrived at a fork in the road." Moved to tears by his father's speech, the following morning Wang concludes that the blame for all of his earlier suffering belongs to Li Dongbao, a former landlord in Qiangcheng village:

My mistake was that I mistook poison for honey and ate it, falling prey to the landlord's tricks. My two earlier diary entries would have earned the praise of Landlord Li Dongbao, I can see him saying sweetly, "Zhongchuan, these two entries are very well-written, you are better than any of the high-school graduates from this village of ours, you have written words of sincerity and truth." I'm so stupid, I took such words as a compliment.

It is unclear from the text whether the conversation between Wang and the landlord was a real or imagined event, yet its repercussions prompted him to act. No longer able to contain his fury at the landlord, Wang not only denounced Li Dongbao at a subsequent meeting of the poor and lower-middle peasant association, but, with great difficulty, examined the error of his own ways: "I took a firm foothold, drew a clear line of class demarcation, and will never again fall prey to the tricks of the landlord class." The final excerpt has Wang extolling the importance of clearly allocating work points to commune laborers, in complete accord with the new party line.[68]

In the end, not unlike the Nationalists before them, the Communists produced a state-building effort riven by paradoxical impulses: a profound ideological commitment to social mobilization on the one hand, and increasing anxiety, even paranoia, about the results of that process on the other. Yet if the Nationalist regime's corporatist re-organization of local communities ultimately proved ineffective in building widespread popular support, the Maoist party-state managed to weave a complex web linking

---

68. *NBCK*, no. 3533 (August 1, 1963): 9–12.

compliance, complicity, and presumed consent down to the level of the individual. Having effectively ensnared civil society, the Maoist party-state sporadically expended enormous efforts to reanimate it under the auspices of a normative agenda that, over time, carried less and less weight with the majority in whose interest it presumed to rule. In a massive demonstration of coercive power, the Maoist regime virtually supplanted the dynamics of popular consent with those of its own narrowly defined political will, all the while claiming, triumphantly, to have reinvented society.

EIGHT

Conclusion: The Moral Language of State-Making

It does not matter that discourse appears to be of little account, because the prohibitions that sur-round it very soon reveal its link with desire and with power. . . . Discourse is not simply that which manifests (or hides) desire—it is also the object of desire; and since, as history constantly teaches us, discourse is not simply that which translates struggles or systems of domination, but is the thing for which and by which there is struggle, discourse is the power which is to be seized.

—Michel Foucault, "The Order of Discourse"

In his work on the theater state in nineteenth-century Bali, Clifford Geertz notes that the term "state"—"that master noun of modern political discourse"—encompasses at least three distinct etymological themes. First, "status, in the sense of station, standing, rank, condition—*estate*"; second, "pomp, in the sense of splendor, display, dignity, presence—*stateliness*"; finally, "governance, in the sense of regnancy, regime, dominion, mastery—*statecraft*."

And it is characteristic of that discourse, and of its modernness, that the third of these meanings, the last to arise (in Italy in the 1540s; it was not even available to Machiavelli), should have so come to dominate the term as to obscure our understanding of the multiplex nature of high authority. Impressed with command, we see little else.[1]

The historical process of state-formation, as well as those subsequent efforts to extend and deepen centralized power that we refer to as state-making, unquestionably involve the application of coercive force. Yet within the broad spectrum of instruments and resources at the disposal of the modern nation-state, coercion represents only a relatively narrow band of possible expressions of power, as recent discussions regarding the importance of "soft power," suggest.[2] In the preceding chapters, I have sought a fuller account of what Geertz refers to as "the multiplex nature of high

---

1. Geertz (1980), p. 121.

2. The term "soft power" was coined by Joseph Nye, who described it as a form of "co-optive power," or "the ability to set the political agenda and determine the framework of debate in

authority" by exploring how, under the guise of three distinct regimes, the modern Chinese state made and remade itself in its quest to transform society while meeting varying levels of resistance and accommodation from those who presumed to speak on behalf of local communities.

As the preceding chapters have shown, the process of state-making in modern Chinese history is a profoundly normative one: regimes have not only sought to define and then impose moral standards on the behavior of those both in- and outside the state but have also attempted to redraw state boundaries so as to exclude or expel agents and forces not in keeping with their shifting moral agendas. The historical construction of the state as a moral agent arises from particular social imaginary significations: shared understandings about the nature of the regime and how it operates, as well as collective perceptions of the larger society in which it is embedded. Moreover, I argue that the normative dimensions of the state-making process are recursive: in crafting policies to address perceived social problems and bureaucratic dysfunction, central authorities not only articulate and impose particular norms, but also construct the state itself as a moral agent. Those historical episodes we refer to as periods of intensive state-making are precisely those critical junctures in which central authorities translate normative prescriptions into new institutional practices under the auspices of state control. Moreover, this process cuts to the very core of precisely what it is that states do. "States," Corrigan and Sayer observe, "if the pun be forgiven, *state*";

The arcane rituals of a court of law, the formulae of royal assent to an Act of Parliament, visits of school inspectors, are all statements. They define, in great detail, acceptable forms and images of social activity and individual and collective identity; they regulate, in empirically specifiable ways, much—very much, by the twentieth century—of social life. Indeed, in this sense "the State" never stops talking.[3]

Chinese regimes throughout history have attempted to capture and wield monopolistic control over the legitimate production of political meanings through their command over language. In China in particular, the act of writing, from the time of its invention down to the present, defined not only those who wielded power but the scope and type of power they wielded as well. The ability of regime elites to maintain family genealogies, record cadastral surveys, annotate territorial maps, and construct historical narratives was not simply a manifestation of elite domination; it was also the medium through which political power was consolidated, exercised,

---

a way that shapes others' preferences." Joseph S. Nye, Jr., "Soft Power," *Foreign Policy* 80 (1990): 166.
3. Corrigan and Sayer (1985), p. 3.

and seized. Contests over how accounts of the past were to be ordered, and by whom, formed a central part of the Chinese history of state-making. Etienne Balazs's oft-cited observation that imperial Chinese historiography is a sort of history "written by officials for officials"[4] underscores the imbrication of the processes of Chinese state-making and history-writing: each of the three regimes under consideration in the preceding chapters strove to produce moral narratives variously designed to conceal, reveal, and, most important, to reproduce the power of the state by recording accounts of events those in power wished to commemorate and by expunging those they sought to suppress.

Yet despite the persistent efforts of central authorities to create, control, and police appropriate forms of political expression, alternative discursive traditions proved difficult to contain. The complexity of these struggles is part of the written historical record, partially cloaked in debates concerning the various arrangements of power between center and periphery that formed the backdrop for more formal discursive exchanges between those in positions of authority and those contending for power at the margins. Tensions between bureaucratic and feudal models of imperial statecraft, state tutelage, and local self-government during the Nanjing decade and the "revisionist" and "radical" versions of mass-line politics under Mao each, in their time, served as normative frames within which local actors sought to anchor competing claims for power and influence. Central authorities frequently responded to such challenges by interpellating such subjects as enemies of the state, political labels that became sites of political contestation, struggle, and resistance.

The moral languages of Chinese state-makers, grounded as they were in legal and political institutions that valorized the needs of the central state, represented one type of normative vocabulary within which evaluations of official and, increasingly, mass conduct were constructed. The terms and concepts of this normative vocabulary, as Quentin Skinner points out, "must not be viewed simply as propositions with meanings attached to them; they must also be thought of as weapons (Heidegger's suggestion) or as tools (Wittgenstein's term)."[5] As such, the legal concepts and political labels employed by central state authorities to a large extent defined the reach of their state-making efforts:

Thus the problem facing an agent who wishes to legitimate what he is doing at the same time as gaining what he wants cannot simply be the instrumental problem of tailoring his normative language in order to fit his projects. It must in part be

4. Etienne Balazs, *Chinese Civilization and Bureaucracy: Variations on a Theme* (New Haven: Yale University Press, 1964), pp. 132–35.
5. Quentin Skinner, "What Is Intellectual History?" *History Today* 35 (1985): 51.

the problem of tailoring his projects in order to fit the available normative language.[6]

As the preceding chapters demonstrate, the discursive projection of the state as a moral agent invited contest, both from those within and those outside the shifting conceptual boundaries of official control. Disenfranchised agents and marginalized social forces were not always content to retreat silently from the advancing forward line of the state. Rather, those collectively and individually interpellated by central authorities through a process of (mis)recognition and (mis)representation at times sought redress, and found support, in a discursive tradition that celebrated the solidarity and moral superiority of local communities over and against the remote coercive machinery of the central state. Localist discursive traditions, as Hunt notes in the French case, were "used rhetorically to build a sense of community and at the same time to establish new fields of social, political, and cultural struggle";[7] they were woven into the tapestry of family genealogies, unofficial histories, local gazetteers, and newspaper accounts. Taken as a whole, such texts shed light on the ongoing push and pull between the moral agendas of center and periphery. They portrayed, often in bold and dramatic terms, the heroic dimensions of contests waged over the loyalties of local officials; but they also record, in terms no less significant to those involved, the same struggle reflected in the quotidian practices of calculating and then recalculating "that which belonged to Caesar" under the watchful eye of the state.

IMAGINED STATES IN COMPARATIVE PERSPECTIVE

As noted in the introduction, Philip Abrams argues forcefully for the conceptual disaggregation of the state in scholarly analysis, recognizing on the one hand the manifestly disorganized institutional maze of the "state system"—an uneven, sprawling web of agencies, actors, and coalitions that are, more often than not, "divided against one another, volatile and confused"—and the existence, on the other hand, of what he refers to as "the state idea," "an ideological artifact attributing unity, morality, and independence to the disunited, amoral, dependent workings of the practice of government."[8] I have argued that state-making represents an attempt to impose a particular, historically contingent "state idea" upon the quotidian workings of a given "state system," thereby rendering the

---

6. Quentin Skinner, *The Foundations of Modern Political Thought* (Cambridge, Eng.: Cambridge University Press, 1978), vol. 1, pp. xii–xiii.
7. Hunt (1989), p. 17.
8. Abrams (1988), pp. 76–77, 81.

routine practices of governance accountable to an idealized projection of the state as moral agent. As the preceding chapters have demonstrated, each of the three regimes under consideration sought to accomplish this by exercising what I refer to as the "boundary-drawing capacity of the state" on two levels. First, all three of the regimes in question sought to extend the institutionalized power of the state into those intermediate realms of political practice where local officials governed. This involved, in each case, the drawing of a conceptual boundary to demarcate those actors whom the state recognized as the legitimate agents of its power, and those who operated beyond the recognized scope of formal government.

A second and related manifestation of the boundary-drawing capacity of each regime involved the interpellation of political subjects on either side of that dividing line based upon an evaluation of their conduct. That is to say, for each regime in question, central state-makers first undertook to distinguish "state" from "non-state" forces operating at the local level, and then imposed and enforced respective normative boundaries prescribing specific types of conduct that would be tolerated from each. These interrelated boundary-drawing exercises were integral to the projection of the state in its capacity of what Durkheim refers to as "above all, supremely, the organ of moral discipline";[9] at the same time, a central finding of this study of the normative dimensions of state-making supports Mitchell's claim that such boundaries constitute lines that are "drawn internally, within the network of institutional mechanisms through which a certain social and political order is maintained."[10] In other words, a comparison of the respective boundary-drawing capacities of the late imperial, Republican, and Mao-era states reveals that while these regimes were naturally embedded within the larger societies they governed, their relative ability to present themselves as bounded, coherent entities standing apart from and above society—and, to a certain extent, the more mundane and ephemeral considerations associated with locality and historical time—constituted an important resource during each of the periods in question. Individual states, which are of course products of idiosyncratic historical processes, may succeed or fail on the basis of their ability to perpetrate a vast web of mystification that conceals their own boundedness in space and time. Even regimes that ground their claims to legitimacy in contingent historical and material processes, as Marxist-Leninist regimes do, expend considerable resources to project a sense of moral agency that is both translocal and ahistorical.

In all three cases, central state-makers presented themselves as presiding over a social world that was internally fractured and fragmented, and per-

---

9. Durkheim (1957), p. 72.
10. Mitchell (1991), p. 90.

haps therefore both morally inferior and hostile to the normative agenda of the state. Over time, these internal divisions increasingly preoccupied central leaders, finally emerging during the Maoist era as an official discourse that presumed the existence of widespread anti-regime conspiracies simmering just beneath the surface of post-revolutionary society and endangering the continued survival of the party-state at every turn. These successively "imagined societies" suggest the unfolding of larger, generational shifts in the manner in which central state-makers understood the internal dynamics of social life. During the late imperial era, as Murata notes, the primary internal divisions that differentiated the peoples of the Qing imperium were not "indices of race, ethnic group, religion or language, but the presence or absence of the ritual system of 'culture'"; even those marginal "barbarian" races that "fell outside the civilized sphere, once they became favored with the grace of *wenhua*, they might all be incorporated into the world of *tianxia*." As the discursive focus shifted during the final years of the Qing from *yitong chuishang* (uniform order in the realm) to *lieguo jingzheng* (competition among the powers),[11] the key political forces of the Republican era were precisely those that threatened to destroy the fragile unity of the nascent sense of Chinese nationhood—namely, regional warlords in the early years of the Republic. These perceived enemies of the state were eclipsed by the less powerful but far more numerous and equally troubling "local bullies" and "evil gentry," who constituted a particularly colorful genus of the rich political bestiary of the Nationalist regime. Such social categories were gradually replaced by a concept of socioeconomic class (*jieji*) that, even among early Communist activists during the 1920s, had more in common with traditional Confucian concepts than with the notions of socioeconomic class that dominated Western discourse at the time.[12] By the early 1960s, this too gave way to a more fungible conception of class that linked normative assessments of political behavior not to categories defined by inherited socioeconomic status but to routine expressions of support for the regime and its policies.[13] Thus, over time, the manner in which successive central regimes read the presumed social consent to state rule shifted from the absence of overt resistance to the imperial will to limited participation in the ceremonies and rituals associated with Republican

11. Murata Yujiro, "Dynasty, State and Society: The Case of Modern China," in *Imagining the People: Chinese Intellectuals and Concepts of Citizenship, 1890–1920*, ed. Joshua A. Fogel and Peter G. Zarrow (Armonk, NY: M. E. Sharpe, 1997), p. 117.

12. Kuhn (1986), p. 19.

13. Stuart Schram, "Classes, Old and New, in Mao Zedong's Thought," in *Class and Social Stratification in Post-Revolution China*, ed. James L. Watson (Cambridge, Eng.: Cambridge University Press, 1984), pp. 29–55.

citizenship[14] to the routine expressions of mass loyalty demanded under Maoist rule.

Despite such differences, some patterns persisted over time. All three of the regimes in question were self-limiting, not merely in terms of elaborating specific mechanisms and codes of bureaucratic procedure and control, but also in terms of containing the overall size of the state with respect to society. As G. William Skinner points out, the number of county-level units relative to population declined steadily from the Han to the Qing dynasties: if the late imperial state maintained the size of its field administration relative to the population at the ratio established in A.D. 180, the late Qing imperium would have required "a field administration with nearly 10,000 subprovincial yamens, not counting those of circuit intendants."[15] Each expansion of formal state power in question was the result of an inherently conservative calculus that weighed incremental increases in the size and scope of the state apparatus against the projected costs levied against collective resources required to support it. All three of the regimes in question observed, albeit with varying degrees of fidelity, the traditional dictum that valorized a minimalist state that was lean in terms of its overall bureaucratic structure, but nonetheless capable of pursuing maximalist cultural, political, and economic outcomes through the vigorous but voluntary mobilization of social resources. While this tendency was most clearly in evidence during the Yongzheng reign, even the involutionary Nationalist state of the Nanjing decade and the totalizing Mao-era state of the 1960s sought to mobilize social forces within local communities in order to control, police, and monitor themselves. The primary goal of central Chinese state-makers in each case was not to refine or expand the coercive apparatus of state extraction but to organize social resources—communities, decimal hierarchies, and collectives—capable of meeting the needs of the state.

Second, all three of the state-making efforts under consideration failed, at least in the short-term. The Yongzheng emperor's strenuous efforts to rationalize local fiscal administration were overturned by his son and successor; the Nationalist reorganization of county administrations quickly unraveled under mounting pressures from the Japanese on the one hand and the internecine struggle against the Communists on the other; and, finally, efforts to recentralize and standardize the planning process in the aftermath of the Great Leap Forward again succumbed to the centripetal dynamics of the Cultural Revolution. State-making is by definition a ter-

---

14. See, for example, Henrietta Harrison, *The Making of the Republican Citizen, 1911–1929* (Oxford: Oxford University Press, 2000).
15. G. William Skinner, "Introduction: Urban Development in Imperial China," in *The City in Late Imperial China*, ed. G. William Skinner (Taibei: SMC Publishing, 1977), p. 20.

minal process: initiatives aimed at administrative centralization, increased social penetration, bureaucratization, and rationalization have historically been realized within a specific time horizon or have succumbed prior to implementation to the forces of organizational resistance or bureaucratic inertia. Over the longer term, however, the effective reach of the state certainly expanded, even if the size of its field administration did not keep pace with the size of the population it governed.

Third, each of the episodic transformations described in the preceding chapters occurred in the wake of a crisis. The massive investigation into local government accounts and the policy of "returning the meltage fees to the public coffers" was triggered by Yongzheng's discovery of significant deficits in the imperial treasury. Local administrative reform under the Nationalist regime was designed to consolidate centralized control over widespread social violence, spawned in part by years of protracted struggle by regional warlords. The Socialist Education Movement was an attempt to investigate and regulate the accounting practices and leadership styles of grassroots cadres in the aftermath of the disastrous Great Leap Forward. Whereas the Western European history of state-making appears to have been largely driven, as Tilly argues, by the attempts of various European rulers to acquire the means to make war, in the Chinese case, armed conflict with external rivals did not provide the spur for the robust state-building initiatives described in the preceding chapters. Certainly, war-making and its attendant preparations were never absent from the scene. The Yongzheng emperor engaged in several campaigns to rout various groups mobilized along the southwest frontier and elsewhere; the Nationalists under Jiang Jieshi's administration not only took several years to defeat internal rivals but soon thereafter faced encroachment by Japanese forces in the north and the east; and the heightened tensions across the Sino-Indian border certainly helped to set the context for Mao's 1962 emphatic pursuit of domestic class struggle. Yet, in contrast to Tilly, I would argue that in the Chinese case, military mobilization played only a supporting role in the state-making process. Instead, the catalyst behind these sporadic efforts to extend the reach of the Chinese state were the crises themselves, either real or manufactured by central authorities in order to build support for, and minimize overt resistance to, various policy agendas designed to empower certain political actors while disenfranchising others. By framing particular problems as crises that required state intervention, central authorities actualized ideological preferences as specific plans for government action; the linking of such crises to the activities of political enemies—litigious clerks and corrupt runners, local bullies and evil gentry, or the "five bad elements"—mobilized actors at the outer margins of the state by duplicating at the local level the cleavages of power envisioned by those who occupied the center.

Finally, the state-making process itself is driven by contradictions, because paradox is integral to the nature of statehood. If a state is to successfully monopolize the legitimate use of physical force within its jurisdiction, it must at some level be perceived as applying its powers of extraction and coercion in service to the greater good. State-making, which by definition involves an extension of such powers, invariably involves the application of the instruments of institutionalized violence against some of those on whose behalf, and in whose interest, the state claims to rule. The paradox inherent in the minimalist late imperial state with maximalist aims, or the tutelary democracy of Nationalist party-state, or the perpetuation of violent class struggle a decade after the successful Communist revolution, presented conundrums for the central leaders of respective Chinese regimes who shaped policies at the national level. Yet these contradictions were nowhere more vexing than at the margins of power, where the local agents of the state applied, on a day-to-day basis, the instruments of extraction and coercion against residents of the local communities they inhabited, and in whose interests they claimed to wield power. One critical finding of this analysis of Chinese state-making is that the local state agents frequently numbered among the first victims of the state-making process. Caught in the fundamental contradictions between the shifting ideological orientations of central leaders and the material realities of local communities over which they presided, the states' first line of defense against the encroachment of social forces, no less than intransigent local elites, were often the first to fall.

VIRTUE AND VIOLENCE

In an oft-cited essay on the historical dynamics of Western European state-making, Tilly remarks: "If protection rackets represent organized crime at its smoothest, then war making and state making—quintessential protection rackets with the advantage of legitimacy—qualify as our largest examples of organized crime." Criminal protection rackets by definition threaten grave danger and personal harm to businesses and individuals operating within their jurisdictions, but also offer relief and protection from violence to those willing to pay. Insofar as modern states seek to organize and monopolize violence within the societies they govern, and offer protection from that violence for those who comply with state demands, modern states bear strong functional similarities to far-flung criminal protection rackets. The chief difference, moreover, lies not in their respective manners of operation, but rather, in the relative ability of states and criminal rackets to imbue their deployment of coercive force with a sense of legitimacy. "Eventually, the personnel of states purveyed violence on a larger scale, more effectively, more efficiently, with wider assent from their subject populations than did the personnel of neighboring organizations."[16] The bounty of legitimacy accorded states, therefore, was the historical by-product of their comparatively greater efficiency in wielding violence against certain groups and agents while shielding others from the same, and the various technologies they developed to differentiate between those groups.

The respective uses of state juridical power to enforce new norms did not merely involve new attempts to interpellate, police, and eliminate real and imagined rivals for political power, but also provided a rationale for vesting authority in groups of actors that those in positions of authority sought to mobilize. The Yongzheng emperor's massive investigation into the condition of local accounts and granaries deployed hundreds of degree-holders and expectant officials in the effort to investigate and police bureaucratic practices at the margins of Qing officialdom; many of these went on to replace those they ousted. The National Revolutionary Army forces traveled with Nationalist Party workers who oversaw the countless transfers of power at the local level between warlord forces and new administrations loyal to the Nationalists. The young students and cadres "sent down" to the countryside to carry out the Four Cleans and Four Histories campaigns participated not only in a reshuffling of power in those locales, but also in a vast program of "socialist education" designed to produce a new cadre of state and party leaders schooled in the modes of bureaucratic conduct preferred by the post-Leap central leadership. By reframing the category of political corruption, each of the regimes in question not only effected mass transfers of power at the margins between state and society, but furthermore devised new political economies of crime and control. As Foucault notes of the deployment of juridical power,

Penality would then appear to be a way of handling illegalities, of laying down the limits of tolerance, of giving free rein to some, of putting pressure on others, of excluding a particular section, of making another useful, of neutralizing certain individuals and of profiting from others. In short, penality does not simply "check" illegalities; it "differentiates" them, it provides them with a general "economy." And, if one can speak of justice, it is not only because the law itself or the way of applying it serves the interests of a class, it's also because the differential

16. Tilly (1985), pp. 169–73.

administration of illegalities through the mediation of penality forms part of those mechanisms of domination.[17]

I would argue that it is precisely this mechanism—of deploying penality to transform social practices—that has allowed Chinese state-making to succeed over the long term, even where it has failed in the short term. Following Abrams, it is possible to understand historically situated states as regimes that have always operated at two levels. At the first level are the external manifestations of power, of coercive sanctions broadly associated with the repressive organs of the state. This level, "a palpable nexus of practice and institutional structure centered in government and more or less extensive, unified, and dominant in any given society," which Abrams refers to as the "state system," is certainly real enough, for its executors as well as its victims. But it does not and cannot exist of its own accord: these institutions "conspicuously fail to display a unity of practice—just as they constantly discover their inability to function as a more general factor of cohesion. Manifestly they are divided against one another, volatile and confused." This far-flung net of coercion and extraction must be supported by a second level, which Abrams refers to as the "state idea," wherein its true believers, members, and agents actualize the idea itself through their activity. The power of the state is therefore based both on the repressive and coercive machineries of violence, externally manifested in its myriad institutional forms, and internally upon the collectively imagined "state idea," which is not merely conceptual but is also concretely manifested in everyday activities and behavior that, in turn, construct and reconstruct the state itself.[18] Thus, if the institutional re-ordering of power during sporadic bouts of state-making failed to create lasting change, the impregnating effect of the new disciplinary techniques introduced during the state-building process succeeded, breaching the boundaries policed between those in- and outside the state in such a way as to give birth to new forms of political power.

MARKETING MORAL ANXIETY IN THE ERA OF REFORM

In contrast to the three periods of intensive state-making described in the preceding chapters, the post-Mao era has been driven in large part not by the expansion and intensification of the power of the central state, but rather by its gradual but steady retreat to allow for the advance of free-market forces. The simultaneous softening of numerous boundaries—between pri-

---

17. Michel Foucault, *Discipline and Punish: The Birth of the Prison*, trans. Alan Sheridan (New York: Vintage Books, 1979), p. 272.
18. Abrams (1988), pp. 75–79.

vate, local government, and state-owned industries; between local governments and township and village enterprises; and between state and market
forces—has resulted in rising popular and official concern about the pervasive nature of political corruption during the process of reform. Perceived
endemic corruption and widespread nepotism within the Communist Party
were clear concerns among the students who demonstrated in Tiananmen
Square in the spring and summer of 1989. Published statistics suggest that
such widespread popular concern was not without merit: reported corruption cases climbed steadily after the introduction of reforms in 1978,
and exploded dramatically in 1989 before the implementation of a much
publicized year-long anti-corruption campaign, after which the number
of reported cases has tended to remain within a relatively stable range,
although the severity of such cases has continued to intensify.[19] Nearly
seven years later, international businessmen ranked the PRC first among
twelve Asian nations and territories in both the scale and scope of bureaucratic corruption, prompting Jiang Zemin to assert: "If we cannot resolve
our corruption problem, we will lose the masses, and will be unavoidably
forsaken by history."[20] In 1998, Chen Xitong, the former mayor of Beijing,
was sentenced to sixteen years in prison in the first open sentencing of a
Politburo member since the infamous "Gang of Four" trial in 1980.

The reform era has witnessed a resurgence of public discourse about
political corruption that rivals the media attention paid to the topic during the 1960s and 1970s under Mao, although it is vastly different both in
content and in form. A new and burgeoning tabloid industry has grown up
around the current public fascination with scandal, lurid official behavior,
and sensationalized crime.[21] Popular fascination with the topic has resulted
in several made-for-television extended historical dramas (*lianxuju*) on anti-
corruption efforts, including one extremely popular miniseries detailing
the policies of the Yongzheng emperor. Lü and Bernstein recently detailed
the scope of the entrepreneurial and often predatory strategies of revenue
enhancement pursued by local government officials across the countryside
during the reform era;[22] Li and O'Brien richly document the rising level

---

19. Andrew Wedeman, "Anticorruption Campaigns and the Intensification of Corruption in
China," *Journal of Contemporary China* 14 (February 2005): 94–95.

20. Foreign Broadcast Information Services Report (FBIS-CHI-96-088), 3 May 1996, "PRC:
Jiang Zemin's Remarks on Corruption."

21. See, for example, Richard Levy, "Corruption in Popular Culture," in *Popular China:
Unofficial Culture in a Globalizing Society*, ed. Perry Link, Richard P. Madsen, and Paul G.
Pickowicz (Lanham, MD: Rowman and Littlefield, 2002), pp. 39–56.

22. Thomas P. Bernstein and Xiaobo Lü, *Taxation Without Representation in Contemporary
Rural China* (Cambridge, Eng.: Cambridge University Press, 2003).

of frustration among the rural residents who constitute the majority of the victims of predatory state strategies in recent years, and, perhaps not surprisingly, a concomitant popular nostalgia among them for the anti-corruption campaigns of the Mao years, particularly the Four Cleans movement.[23] Caroline Hsu's recent survey of the reform-era press maps a dramatic rise in the numbers of articles addressing political corruption during the 1980s and 1990s, an increase of more than 400 percent in 1993 over those reported in 1978.[24]

Yet the recent wave of popular fascination with political corruption, unlike the cases detailed in the preceding chapters, has sprung up in the discursive space created by the steady withdrawal, and not the extension, of centralized state power. The reform era has not witnessed concerted and sustained efforts by central state-makers to identify targets and impose new normative standards on the scale attempted during the three periods discussed here. By contrast, corruption discourse during the reform era is more diffuse and less politicized than was the case during these three time periods and relies more heavily on the language of the market than on political categories defined by the state. The images of political corruption that predominate in reform-era tabloids are frequently intermingled with lurid descriptions of criminal and deviant sexual behavior, and offer very little by way of political analysis as to possible causes or potential cures. As the state has receded to make room for market forces, corruption discourse itself has become commodified, eschewing the categories of class and status, and caters to a new set of manufactured popular desires. The unofficial narratives of corruption of the Deng and post-Deng eras can therefore be seen as one band of the larger spectrum of what Barmé refers to as a "dissident genre" of cultural products that emerged during the 1990s. Such products were uniquely designed to take advantage of the multiple softening boundaries of state and society during the period of reform, seeking to provoke authorities enough to prompt their disapproval and perhaps a mild rebuke, but without moving them to go so far as to actually ban the material. Official disapproval, either actual or perceived, can impart a niche-market value to cultural products completely unrelated to their artistic value. This has resulted in an explosion of what Barmé has termed "bankable dissent"

---

23. Li Lianjiang, "Support for Anti-Corruption Campaigns in Rural China," *Journal of Contemporary China* 10:29 (2001): 573–86; see also Kevin O'Brien and Li Lianjiang, "Campaign Nostalgia in the Chinese Countryside," *Asian Survey* 39:3 (May/June 1999): 375–93.

24. Caroline Hsu, "Political Narratives and the Production of Legitimacy: The Case of Corruption in Post-Mao China," *Qualitative Sociology* 24:1 (June 2001): 25–54.

in the public sphere.[25] The lurid tales of official corruption that dominate the burgeoning tabloid industry in China today represent a type of popular anti-state critique insofar as they sell to the reading public an image of the state that is riddled with moral failings and that has strayed far from its explicit ideological moorings.

This manufactured desire for corruption discourse, now driven by the widening consumer market, caters in part to the unique political subjects created during the Mao era: an aging public of self-reflective self-disciplining individuals, weaned on the social dynamics of public confession and rituals of repentance, for whom the larger agenda of the party-state provided a moral framework for both intent and action. Decades later, with the implosion of Maoist revolutionary norms and the withering away of the central state as the "organ of moral discipline," post-revolutionary political subjects serve as a captive audience for the carnivalesque unfolding of political corruption in the age of reform. Indeed, many have remarked on the theatrical nature of anti-corruption efforts during the reform era, which Wedeman recently likened to "a form of Beijing Opera in which the actors rush about the stage amid great sound and fury in a drama that ultimately signifies nothing because, after the din dies down and the actors leave the stage, corruption abides."[26]

Likewise, although popular discourses of corruption after the suppression of the 1989 student demonstrations in Tiananmen Square have proliferated and become increasingly graphic in their depictions of bureaucratic excesses, they appear no longer to wield critical moral force. Increasingly shaped by the political and economic ambiguities inherent in the collective pursuit of "market socialism," lurid tabloid tales of scandalous corruption compete for popular attention alongside glossy gossip magazines produced in Hong Kong. Just as the party itself continues to adhere, if only in name, to the tenets of Marxism-Leninism, popular narratives of political corruption during the reform era are themselves reduced to hollow shells of "bankable dissent" in no small part because the purveyors of such spectacles are themselves complicit in their production. Members of the reading public are increasingly inured to the normative ramifications of such tales, and those who peddle them can hardly be counted upon to express moral outrage. As Václav Havel notes of life in "post-totalitarian" Czechoslovakia, "Because the regime is captive to its own lies, it must falsify everything. It falsifies the past. It falsifies the present, and it falsifies the

---

25. Geremie Barmé, "Soft Porn, Packaged Dissent, and Nationalism: Notes on Chinese Culture in the 1990s," *Current History* 93 (September 1994): 270–75.
26. Wedeman (2005), p. 94.

future." Certainly, individual citizens cannot be required to believe such elaborate mystifications, but because the state retains its monopoly on the instruments of violence, they must behave as though they do or face repercussions. Thus, in countless everyday ways, they assent to "live within the lie"; and, in so doing, they "confirm the system, fulfill the system, make the system, *are* the system."[27]

Caught in the net woven between compliance and complicity under post-totalitarian rule, the public sphere is no longer the realm characterized by rational discourse and common interests described by Habermas. It becomes pathological, driven by inchoate emotional appeals to human instinct. Prevented from articulating collective interests autonomous of state control and from producing independent organizations to represent those interests, the contemporary public sphere is instead saturated by political narratives that trade in the more accessible currencies of popular fear, suspicion, and desire. Reform-era corruption discourse, circulated by the mass media but still censored and therefore partially shaped by state and party agents, is rife with graphic depictions of sadistic violence, moral decadence, and sexual excess that both titillate and repel the contemporary reading public. Moreover, these mass-produced corruption narratives serve to manufacture another sort of popular desire, one that serves to legitimize, and even render desirable, the existing system of rule. Revisionist historical dramas that were wildly popular during the 1980s and 1990s featured autocratic and austere central rulers who struggled against endemic corruption within the ranks of middle- and low-level bureaucrats, spawning what some have referred to as waves of "totalitarian nostalgia." State agents not only play a role in the production of these historically based teledramas (*lianxuju*); central leaders also let it be known that they, too, are ardent consumers of such cultural products and that they identify closely with the historical autocrats depicted therein. The wildly popular *Yongzheng Dynasty* (*Yongzheng wangchao*), which aired in 1999, was widely seen as a thinly veiled endorsement of former Premier Zhu Rongji, who had a reputation for taking a hard line against bureaucratic malfeasance, and who broadcast widely his approval of the series.[28] Not only does the reform-era state have a hand in staging such spectacles, but its agents also number among its most avid consumers. Spectacle, as Rogin notes, "is itself a form of power and not simply window dressing that diverts attention" from

27. Vaclav Havel, "The Power of the Powerless," in *Living in Truth* (London and Boston: Faber and Faber, 1986), pp. 45, 52. Italics in original.
28. Ying Zhu, "*Yongzheng Dynasty* and Chinese Primetime Television Drama," *Cinema Journal* 44:4 (Summer 2005): 3–17.

more traditionally recognizable exercises of political power: it diffuses the boundaries between the public and the private in service to power.[29]

The salacious and alarming accounts that frequently circulate in the popular press describing the criminal activities of decadent state and party officials also serve as implicit reminders of the state's capacities for violence and extraction, even when such narratives are framed by assurances, as they often are, that corruption is indeed being monitored and stemmed by the increased surveillance of central authorities. Perhaps more important, popular media images of endemic corruption fuel what Lipschutz has referred to as a "political economy of danger"[30] by conjuring a social world saturated with moral ambiguity, potential threats, and the ever-present possibility of violence. The pervasive anxiety that contemporary Chinese society hovers on the brink of chaos serves to legitimate existing power relations and engenders begrudging popular support for the regime precisely because it appears to offer the best hope for maintaining social stability.

Of course, such dynamics are by no means the exclusive terrain of post-totalitarian systems: as Havel reminds us, this mode of governance was originally "built on foundations laid by the historical encounter between dictatorship and the consumer society," the roots of which lie in "the general unwillingness of consumption-oriented people to sacrifice some material certainties for the sake of their own spiritual and moral integrity."[31] It stands as a warning to those in the West and wherever else those in power may seek to silence dissent and muster popular support by spinning narratives of suspicion and fear.

---

29. Michael Rogin, "'Make My Day!': Spectacle as Amnesia in Imperial Politics," *Representations* 29 (Winter 1990): 100.

30. Ronnie D. Lipschutz, "Terror in the Suites: Narratives of Fear and the Political Economy of Danger," *Global Society* 13:4 (October 1999): 411–39.

31. Havel (1986), p. 54.

Reference Matter

Works Cited

Abrams, Philip. "Notes on the Difficulty of Studying the State." *Journal of Historical Sociology* 1:1 (March 1988): 58–89.

Ahn, Byung-joon. *Chinese Politics and the Cultural Revolution: Dynamics of Policy Processes.* Seattle: University of Washington Press, 1976.

Alitto, Guy. "Rural Elites in Transition: China's Cultural Crisis and the Problem of Legitimacy." *Select Papers from the Center for Chinese Studies.* Chicago: University of Chicago Press, 1979.

Althusser, Louis. "Ideology and the State." In Louis Althusser, *Lenin and Philosophy and Other Essays.* Trans. Ben Brewster. New York: Monthly Review Press, 2001.

Anderson, Benedict. *Imagined Communities: Reflections on the Origins and Spread of Nationalism.* London: Verso, 1991.

Anhui Jingde xianzhi (Anhui Jingde county gazetteer). Jiaqing 13 (1808) edition. 1925 reprint.

Antony, Robert J. "Subcounty Officials, the State, and Local Communities in Guangdong Province." In *Dragons, Tigers, and Dogs: Qing Crisis Management and the Boundaries of State Power in Late Imperial China,* ed. Robert J. Antony and Jane Kate Leonard. Ithaca, NY: Cornell University Press, 2003.

Antony, Robert J., and J. Kate Leonard, "Dragons, Tigers, and Dogs: An Introduction." In *Dragons, Tigers, and Dogs: Qing Crisis Management and the Boundaries of State Power in Late Imperial China,* ed. Robert J. Antony and Jane Kate Leonard. Ithaca, NY: Cornell University Press, 2003.

Archives of Central Political Council (Zhongyang zhengzhihui), Nationalist Party History Committee (Dangshihui). Yangmingshan, Taiwan.

Archives of Internal Administration Department (Neizhengbu). Number Two Historical Archive. Nanjing, PRC.

Archives of the Yu-E-Wan sansheng jiaofei zong siling bu (Henan-Hubei-Anhui Provincial Central Bandit Extermination Headquarters). Number Two Historical Archive. Nanjing, PRC.

Atwood, Christopher P. "National Questions and National Answers in the Chinese Revolution." *Indiana East Asian Working Paper Series*, no. 5 (Winter 1994).

Bachman, David. *Bureaucracy, Economy, and Leadership in China: The Institutional Origins of the Great Leap Forward*. New York: Cambridge University Press, 1991.

Balazs, Etienne. *Political Theory and Administrative Reality in Traditional China*. London: School of Oriental and African Studies Press, 1965.

———. *Chinese Civilization and Bureaucracy: Variations on a Theme*. New Haven: Yale University Press, 1964.

Barfield, Thomas J. "The Shadow Empires: Imperial State Formation Along the Chinese-Nomad Frontier." In *Empires: Perspectives from Archaeology and History*, ed. Susan E. Alcock, Terence N. D'Altroy, Kathleen D. Morrison, and Carla M. Sinopoli. Cambridge, Eng.: Cambridge University Press, 2001.

Barkan, Leonore. "Patterns of Power: Forty Years of Elite Politics in a Chinese County." In *Chinese Local Elites and Patterns of Dominance*, ed. Joseph W. Esherick and Mary Backus Rankin. Berkeley: University of California Press, 1990.

———. "Nationalists, Communists and Local Leaders: Political Dynamics in a Chinese County, 1927-1937." Ph.D. dissertation, University of Washington, 1983. 2 volumes.

Barmé, Geremie. *In the Red: On Contemporary Chinese Culture*. New York: Columbia University Press, 1999.

———. "Soft Porn, Packaged Dissent, and Nationalism: Notes on Chinese Culture in the 1990s." *Current History* 93 (September 1994): 270–75.

Barnett, A. Doak. *Cadres, Bureaucracy, and Political Power in Communist China*. New York: Columbia University Press, 1967.

Bartlett, Beatrice. *Monarchs and Ministers: The Grand Council in Mid-Ch'ing China, 1723–1820*. Berkeley: University of California Press, 1991.

Baum, Richard. *Prelude to Revolution: Mao, the Party and the Peasant Question*. New York: Columbia University Press, 1975.

Baum, Richard, and Frederick C. Teiwes. *Ssu-Ch'ing: The Socialist Education Movement of 1962–1966*. Berkeley: University of California, Center for Chinese Studies, 1968.

Bernhardt, Kathryn. *Rents, Taxes, and Peasant Resistance: The Lower Yangzi Region, 1840–1950*. Stanford: Stanford University Press, 1992.

Bernstein, Thomas P., and Xiaobo Lü, *Taxation Without Representation in Contemporary Rural China*. Cambridge, Eng.: Cambridge University Press, 2003.

Bevan, L. R. O. "China's Constitutions." 4 parts. *Chinese Social and Political Review* 2:4 (December 1917), 3:2 (June 1918), 5:1 (March 1919), and 5a:3 (September 1920).

Bianco, Lucien. "Peasant Uprisings Against Poppy Tax Collection in Suxian and Lingbi (Anhui) in 1932." *Republican China* 21:1 (November 1995).

————. "Peasant Movements." In *The Cambridge History of China*, vol. 13, *Republican China 1912–1949*, pt. II, ed. John K. Fairbank and Albert Feuerwerker. Cambridge, Eng.: Cambridge University Press, 1986.

Billeter, Jean-François. "The System of 'Class-Status.'" In *The Scope of State Power in China*, ed. Stuart Schram. New York: St. Martin's Press, 1985.

Birrell, R. J. "The Centralized Control of the Communes in the Post-'Great Leap' Period." In *Chinese Communist Politics in Action*, ed. A. Doak Barnett. Seattle: University of Washington Press, 1969.

Bo Yibo. *Ruogan zhongda juece yu shijian de huigui* (Recollections of some important policies and events). Beijing: Zhonggong Zhongyang dangjiao chubanshe, 1993.

Brugger, Bill. *China: Liberation and Transformation, 1942–1962*. Totowa, NJ: Barnes and Noble, 1981.

Butler, Steven B. "People's Communes in China: The Functioning of an Administrative Unit." In *Select Papers from the Center for Far Eastern Studies*, 4, ed. Tsou Tang (1979–80). Chicago: University of Chicago Press, 1981.

Cavendish, Patrick. "The 'New China' of the Kuomintang." In *Modern China's Search for a Political Form*, ed. Jack Gray. London: Oxford University Press, 1969.

Chang, C. M. "A New Government for Rural China: The Political Aspect of Rural Reconstruction." *Nankai Social and Economic Quarterly* 9:2 (July 1936).

Chang, Ray. "Trends in Chinese Public Administration." *Information Bulletin of the Council of International Affairs* 3:5 (Nanjing, 1937).

Chang, Sidney H., and Ramon H. Myers, eds. *The Storm Clouds Clear over China: The Memoir of Ch'en Li-fu, 1900–1993*. Stanford: Hoover Institution Press, 1994.

Chen Boxin. *Zhongguo de difang zizhi ji qi gaige*. Nanning: Guangxi jianshe yanjiuhui, 1939.

Chen Chi-yun. "Orthodoxy as a Mode of Statecraft." In *Orthodoxy in Late Imperial China*, ed. Liu Kwang-ching. Berkeley: University of California Press, 1990.

Chen Fulong. "Jin yibu kaizhan yige da guimo de zengchan jieyue, shehui zhuyi jiaoyu yundong." In *Fujian Lianjiang xian feifang wenjian ji qi jiufen*. Taibei: Ministry of National Defense, Bureau of Intelligence, 1964.

Chen Hansheng and Feng Fengyi, eds. *Jiefang qian de dizhu yu nongmin: Huanan nongcun weiji yanjiu* (Landlords and tenants before liberation: research into the crisis in Huanan's rural villages). Beijing: Xinhua shuju, 1984.

Chen, C. S., and Charles Price Ridley. *Rural People's Communes in Lien-chiang* [Lianjiang]. Stanford: Hoover Institution Press, 1969.

Cheng, Joseph Kai Huan. "Chinese Law in Transition: The Late Ch'ing Law Reform, 1901–1911." Ph.D. dissertation, Brown University, 1976.

Ch'ien Tuan-sheng. *The Government and Politics of China*. Cambridge, MA: Harvard University Press, 1950.

China Pictorial.

Ch'ü T'ung-tsu. *Local Government in China Under the Ch'ing.* Cambridge, MA: Harvard University Press, 1961.

Cixian xianzhi (Ci county gazetteer). Taibei: Chengwen chubanshe, 1968.

Cohen, Jerome A. "The Chinese Communist Party and Judicial Independence." *Harvard Law Review* 82:5 (1969).

Cooper, Frederic, and Ann Laura Stoler, eds. *Tensions of Empire: Colonial Cultures in a Bourgeois World.* Berkeley: University of California Press, 1997.

Corrigan, Philip, and Derek Sayer. *The Great Arch: English State Formation as Cultural Revolution.* Oxford and New York: Basil Blackwell, 1985.

Crossley, Pamela. *A Translucent Mirror: History and Identity in Qing Imperial Ideology.* Berkeley: University of California Press, 1999.

Da gong bao.

Da Qing huidian. Yongzheng edition.

Da Qing lüli huitong xinzuan. Taibei: Wenhai chubanshe, 1966.

Dai Yanhui. *Tang lü tonglun* (A comprehensive discussion of Tang dynasty law). Taibei: Zhengzhong shuju, 1965.

Diamond, Norma. "Model Villages and Village Realities." *Modern China* 9:2 (April 1983).

Dittmer, Lowell. "Public and Private Interests and the Participatory Ethic." In *Citizens and Groups in Contemporary China,* ed. Victor C. Falkenheim. Ann Arbor: University of Michigan Press, 1987.

———. "'Line Struggle' in Theory and Practice: The Origins of the Cultural Revolution Reconsidered." *China Quarterly,* no. 72 (1977).

———. *Liu Shao-ch'i and the Chinese Cultural Revolution.* Berkeley: University of California Press, 1974.

Diyi lishi dang'anguan, ed. *Yongzheng chao hanwen zhupi zouzhe huibian* (Chinese vermillion endorsements and edicts of the Yongzheng emperor). Nanjing: Jiangsu guji chubanshe, 1989.

Dong Ruzhou. "Zhongguo nongcun bengkui ji qi jiuji fangfa" (The collapse of China's countryside and some methods of economic recovery). *Jianguo yuekan* (Nation-building monthly) 8:4 (April 1933).

Duara, Prasenjit. *Culture, Power, and the State.* Stanford: Stanford University Press, 1988.

Durkheim, Emile. *Professional Ethics and Civic Morals.* Trans. Cornelia Brookfield. London and New York: Routledge, 1957.

Eastman, Lloyd. *The Abortive Revolution: China Under Nationalist Rule, 1927–1937.* Cambridge, MA: Harvard University Council on East Asian Studies, 1974.

Elias, Norbert. *Power and Civility.* Trans. Edmund Jephcott. New York: Pantheon Books, 1982.

———. *The Civilizing Process: The History of Manners.* Trans. Edmund Jephcott. New York: Urizen Books, 1978.

Elvin, Mark. "Female Virtue and the State in China." *Past & Present* 104 (1984).

———. *The Manchu Way: The Eight Banners and Ethnic Identity in Late Imperial China.* Stanford: Stanford University Press, 2001.

Esherick, Joseph W., and Mary Backus Rankin, eds. *Chinese Local Elites and Patterns of Dominance*. Berkeley: University of California Press, 1990.

Etienne-Will, Pierre, and R. Bin Wong. *Nourish the People: The State Civilian Granary System in China, 1650–1850*. Ann Arbor: University of Michigan Press, 1991.

Fei Xiaotong. "Basic Power Structure in Rural China." Reprinted in *China's Gentry: Essays on Rural-Urban Relations*, ed. Margaret Park Redfield. Chicago: University of Chicago Press, 1953.

Feng Erkang. *Yongzheng zhuan* (Biography of Yongzheng). Beijing: Renmin chubanshe, 1985.

Feng Yun. *Kaizhou zhi* (Kai department gazetteer). Yongzheng 5. Beijing University Library Rare Book Collection.

Fewsmith, Joseph. *Party, State, and Local Elites in Republican China: Merchant Organizations and Politics in Shanghai, 1890–1930*. Honolulu: University of Hawaii Press, 1985.

Fitzgerald, John. *Awakening China: Politics, Culture, and Class in the Nationalist Revolution*. Stanford: Stanford University Press, 1996.

Fogel, Joshua A., and Peter G. Zarrow, eds. *Imagining the People: Chinese Intellectuals and Concepts of Citizenship, 1890–1920*. Armonk, NY: M. E. Sharpe, 1997.

Foreign Broadcast Information Services Report (FBIS-CHI).

Foucault, Michel. "The Order of Discourse." In *Untying the Text*, ed. Robert Young. Boston: Routledge and Kegan Paul, 1981.

———. *Discipline and Punish: The Birth of the Prison*. Trans. by Alan Sheridan. New York: Vintage Books, 1979.

———. "Nietzsche, Genealogy, History." In *Language, Counter-memory, Practice: Selected Essays and Interviews*, ed. D. F. Bouchard. Ithaca, NY: Cornell University Press, 1977.

Fu Zhiyu. "Kangxi caizheng sixiang jiexi" (An analysis of Kangxi's ideas on public finance). *Xiandai caijing* (Modern finance and economics) 153 (November 2002).

Gao Hua. "Da jihuang yu siqing yundong de qiyuan" (The Great Famine and the origin of the Four Cleans Movement). *Ershiyi shiji* (Twenty-first century), no. 60 (October 1990): 56–68.

Geertz, Clifford. *Negara: The Theatre State in Nineteenth Century Bali*. Princeton: Princeton University Press, 1980.

Geisert, Bradley Kent. "From Conflict to Quiescence: The Kuomintang, Party Factionalism and Local Elites in Jiangsu, 1927–31." *China Quarterly* 108 (December 1986): 680–703.

Ginzburg, Carlo. *Clues, Myths, and the Historical Method*. Trans. John Tedeschi and Anne Tedeschi. Baltimore: Johns Hopkins University Press, 1986.

Goodman, Bryna. *Native Place, City, and Nation: Regional Networks and Identities in Shanghai, 1853–1937*. Berkeley: University of California Press, 1995.

Guanghan xianzhi (Guanghan county gazetteer). Chengdu: Sichuan renmin chubanshe, 1992.

Guomin zhengfu fazhibu, ed. *Guomin zhengfu xianxing fagui* (Current government laws and regulations). Shanghai, 1929.

Gupta, Akhil. "Blurred Boundaries: The Discourse of Corruption, the Culture of Politics, and the Imagined State." *American Ethnologist* 22:2 (May 1995): 375–402.

Hargett, James M. "Song Dynasty Local Gazetteers and Their Place in the History of *Difangzhi* Writing." *Harvard Journal of Asiatic Studies* 56:2 (December 1996): 405–42.

Harrison, Henrietta. *The Making of the Republican Citizen, 1911–1929.* Oxford: Oxford University Press, 2000.

Havel, Vaclav. "The Power of the Powerless." In idem, *Living in Truth.* London and Boston: Faber and Faber, 1989.

He Ruling. *Zhengdang zhengfeng jianghua* (Discussion of party and work-style rectification). Shenyang: Lianoning renmin chubanshe, 1984.

He Taoyuan. "Lun tianfu fujia" (A discussion of land tax surcharges). *Duli pinglun* (Independent commentator) 89 (February 25, 1934).

Henan Zhumadian shi shizhi bianmu weiyuanhui, ed. *Zhumadian shizhi* (Zhumadian municipal gazetteer). Zhengzhou: Henan renmin chubanshe, 1989.

Hevia, James. *Cherishing Men from Afar: Qing Guest Ritual and the Macartney Embassy of 1793.* Durham, NC: Duke University Press, 1995.

Hinton, William. *Shenfan: The Continuing Revolution in a Chinese Village.* New York: Random House, 1983.

Houn, Franklin W. *Central Government of China, 1912–1928: An Institutional Study.* Madison: University of Wisconsin Press, 1950.

Hsiao Kung-chuan. *Rural Control in Imperial China.* Seattle: University of Washington Press, 1960.

Hsu, Caroline. "Political Narratives and the Production of Legitimacy: The Case of Corruption in Post-Mao China." *Qualitative Sociology* 24:1 (June 2001): 25–54.

Hu Fusheng, ed. *Gansu shengzhi* (Gansu province gazetteer). Lanzhou: Gansu renmin chubanshe, 1991.

Hu Ji. "Jiu sifa zhidu de yixie huiyi" (A few recollections of the old judicial system). In *Facao neiwai*, ed. Fujiansheng weiyuanhui wenshi xiliao yanjiu weiyuanhui. Fuzhou: Fujian renmin chubanshe, 1989.

Huang Ang. *Xijin shi xiaolu.* Taibei: Taibei shi Wuxi tongxiang hui, 1972 [1896].

Huang Liuhong [Huang Liu-Hung]. *A Complete Book Concerning Happiness and Benevolence: A Manual for Local Magistrates in Seventeenth-century China.* Trans. and ed. Djang Chu. Tucson: University of Arizona Press, 1984.

Huang Pei. *Autocracy at Work: A Study of the Yung-cheng Period, 1723–1735.* Bloomington: Indiana University Press, 1974.

Huang Ruhai. "Guangxi nongcun shehui zhuyi jiaoyu yundong chutan" (Preliminary investigation into the Rural Socialist Education Movement in Guangxi). In *Yongding wenshi ziliao,* no. 6, ed. Yongding wenshi ziliao weiyuanhui. Nanning: Guangxi renmin chubanshe, 1989.

Huang Shumin. *The Spiral Road.* Boulder, CO: Westview Press, 1989.

Huang, Philip C. C. *Code, Custom, and Legal Practice in China: The Qing and Republic Compared*. Stanford: Stanford University Press, 2001.

———. "Class Struggle in Rural China: Representational and Objective Realities from the Land Reform to the Cultural Revolution." *Modern China* 21:1 (January 1995): 105–43.

Hunan minbao.

Hunt, Lynn. *The New Cultural History*. Berkeley: University of California Press, 1989.

Jiancha yuan gongbao. Reprinted by Nanjing: Dier lishi dang'an guan, 1989.

Jiang zongtong yanlun yanbian bianji weiyuanhui, ed. *Jiang Zongtong yanlun yanbian (yanjiang): tongyi shiqi (yi)* (President Jiang's [Jiang Jieshi] collected speeches and writings [addresses]: the period of unity [pt. I]). Taibei: Zheng-zhong shuju, 1956.

Jiao Langting, ed. *Shaanxi shengzhi* (Shaanxi province gazetteer). Xi'an: Shaanxi renmin chubanshe, 1994.

Jinqi xianzhi (Jinqi county gazetteer). Daoguang 3. Beijing University Library Rare Book Collection.

Jordan, Donald A. *The Northern Expedition: China's National Revolution of 1926–1928*. Honolulu: University of Hawaii Press, 1986.

Kai-wing Chow. *The Rise of Confucian Ritualism in Late Imperial China: Ethics, Classics, and Lineage Discourses*. Stanford: Stanford University Press, 1994.

Kraus, Richard C. *Brushes with Power: Modern Politics and the Chinese Art of Calligraphy*. Berkeley: University of California Press, 1991.

Kuhn, Philip A. *The Origins of the Modern Chinese State*. Stanford: Stanford University Press, 2002.

———. "The Development of Local Government." In *The Cambridge History of China, 1912–1949*, vol. 13, *Republican China*, pt. II, ed. John K. Fairbank and Albert Feuerwerker. Cambridge, Eng.: Cambridge University Press, 1986.

———. *Soulstealers: The Chinese Sorcery Scare of 1768*. Cambridge, MA: Harvard University Press, 1990.

———. "Local Taxation and Finance in Republican China." In *Political Leadership and Social Change at the Local Level in China from 1850 to the Present*, ed. Susan Mann Jones. Chicago: University of Chicago Press, 1979.

———. *Rebellion and Its Enemies in Late Imperial China: Militarization and Social Structure, 1796–1864*. Cambridge, MA: Harvard University Press, 1980.

Kuran, Timur. "Sparks and Prairie Fires: A Theory of Unanticipated Political Revolution." *Public Choice* 61 (1989): 41–74.

Lardy, Nicholas. "The Chinese Economy Under Stress, 1958–1965." In *The Cambridge History of China: The People's Republic*, pt. 1, ed. Denis Twitchett and John King Fairbank. Cambridge, Eng.: Cambridge University Press, 1987.

Legge, James, transl. *The Four Books*. Reprinted—Shanghai: China Book Company, 1923.

Leonard, Jane Kate, and John R. Watt. *To Achieve Security and Wealth: The Qing*

Imperial State and the Economy, 1644–1911. Ithaca, NY: East Asia Program, Cornell University, 1992.

Levy, Richard. "Corruption in Popular Culture." In *Popular China: Unofficial Culture in a Globalizing Society*, ed. Perry Link, Richard P. Madsen, and Paul G. Pickowicz. Lanham, MD: Rowman and Littlefield, 2002.

Lewis, Mark. *Writing and Authority in Early China*. Albany: State University of New York Press, 1999.

Li Jianren and Zhao Fumin. "Xiazi qu 'Siqing' yundong shimo" (The whole story of the Xiazi district's "Four Cleans"). In *Zunyi wenshi ziliao*, ed. Zhengxie Zunyi xian xuexi wenshi weiyuanhui, di wu ji. Guiyang: Guizhou renmin chubanshe, 1990.

Li Lianjiang. "Support for Anti-Corruption Campaigns in Rural China." *Journal of Contemporary China* 10:29 (November 2001): 573–86.

Li Ruojian. "Da yuejin yu kunnan shiqi de shehui dongdang yu shehui kongzhi" (Social instability and social control during the Great Leap Forward and period of difficulty). *Ershiyi shiji* (Twenty-first century), no. 60 (October 1990).

Li Tienmin. *Crisis of the Chinese Communist Regime—As Seen from the Lianjiang Documents*. Taibei: Asian People's Anti-Communist League, 1964.

Li, Victor. "The Role of Law in Communist China," *China Quarterly* 44 (October–December 1977): 66–111.

Li Zhanling et al., eds. *Pucheng xianzhi* ([Hebei] Pucheng county gazetteer). Beijing: Zhonghua shuju, 1994.

Lin Houqi. "Guomindang tongzhi shiqi de sifa gaishu" (An account of the judiciary during the period of unity under the Guomindang). In *Facao neiwai* (The ins and outs of legal cases), ed. Zhongguo renmin zhengzhi banshang huiyi Fujian-sheng weiyuanhui. Fuzhou: Wenshi ziliao yanjiu weiyuan huibian, 1989.

Lin Shantian. "Tebie xingfa" (Special penal laws). In *Zhonghua minguoshi falü zhi (chu gao)* (Legal history of the Republic of China gazette [first draft]), ed. Guoshiguan Zhonghua minguoshi falüzhi bianzhuan weiyuanhui. Xindian, Taibei: Guoshiguan, 1994.

Lin Yutang. *My Country and My People*. New York: Reynal and Hitchcock, 1935.

Linebarger, Paul. *Government in Republican China*. New York: McGraw-Hill, 1938.

Lipschutz, Ronnie D. "Terror in the Suites: Narratives of Fear and the Political Economy of Danger." *Global Society* 13:4 (October 1999): 411–39.

Liu Chuangshao. "Gongxian zhishi Shao Hongji." *Henan wenshi ziliao*, no. 24. Anyang: Henan renmin chubanshe, 1984.

Liu Yuan. *Ni suo buzhidaode Liu Shaoqi* (The Liu Shaoqi you never knew). Shijiazhuang: Henan renmin chubanshe, 1999.

Liuyang xianzhi (Liuyang county gazetteer). (Jiaqing 23). Beijing University Library Rare Book Collection.

MacAuley, Melissa. *Social Power and Legal Culture: Litigation Masters in Late Imperial China*. Stanford: Stanford University Press, 1998.

Mann, Susan. *Local Merchants and the Chinese Bureaucracy, 1750–1950.* Stanford: Stanford University Press, 1987.

Meijer, Marinus Johan. *The Introduction of Modern Criminal Law in China.* Batavia, Indonesia: De Unie, 1950.

Metzger, Thomas. *The Internal Organization of Ch'ing Bureaucracy.* Cambridge, MA: Harvard University Press, 1973.

Migdal, Joel. *Strong Societies and Weak States: State-Society Relations and State Capabilities in the Third World.* Princeton: Princeton University Press, 1988.

Miller, H. Lyman. "The Late Imperial Chinese State." In *The Modern Chinese State,* ed. David Shambaugh. Cambridge, Eng.: Cambridge University Press, 2001.

Min Tu-ki. "The Theory of Political Feudalism in the Ch'ing Period." In *National Polity and Local Power: The Transformation of Late Imperial China,* ed. Philip Kuhn and Timothy Brook. Cambridge, MA: Harvard-Yenching Institute Monograph Series, 1989.

Mitchell, Timothy. "The Limits of the State: Beyond Statist Approaches and Their Critics." *American Political Science Review* 85:1 (March 1991): 77–94.

Murata Yujiro. "Dynasty, State and Society: The Case of Modern China." In *Imagining the People: Chinese Intellectuals and Concepts of Citizenship, 1890–1920,* ed. Joshua A. Fogel and Peter G. Zarrow. Armonk, NY: M. E. Sharpe, 1997.

Neibu cankao [NBCK] (Internal reference).

Neige Tiben [NGTB] (Routine memorials of the Grand Secretariat). Includes *tanwu lei* (subheading of political corruption) and *jiucan lei* (subheading of administrative dismissals). Beijing: Number One Historical Archive.

Neizhengbu (Ministry of Personnel Archive). Number Two Historical Archive. Nanjing, PRC.

Nie Hongqin. "Qingdai qianqi de huji yu fuyi" (Census registers, taxes, and corvée during the early Qing). *Shilin* (Historic review) 2001:1.

Nye, Joseph S., Jr. "Soft Power." *Foreign Policy* 80 (1990): 153–71.

O'Brien, Kevin, and Li Lianjiang. "Campaign Nostalgia in the Chinese Countryside." *Asian Survey* 39:3 (May/June 1999): 375–93.

———. "Rightful Resistance." *World Politics* 29:1 (1996): 31–55.

Oksenberg, Michael. "Local Leaders in Rural China, 1962–65: Individual Attributes, Bureaucratic Positions, and Political Recruitment." In *Chinese Communist Politics in Action,* ed. A. Doak Barnett. Seattle: University of Washington Press, 1969.

Parish, William L., and Martin King Whyte. *Village and Family Life in Contemporary China.* Chicago: University of Chicago Press, 1978.

Park, Nancy E. "Corruption in Eighteenth-Century China." *Journal of Asian Studies* 56:4 (November 1997): 967–1005.

Perry, Elizabeth J. "Trends in the Study of Chinese Politics: State-Society Relations." *China Quarterly* 139 (September 1994): 704–13.

———. *Shanghai on Strike: The Politics of Chinese Labor.* Stanford: Stanford University Press, 1993.

———. "Collective Violence in China, 1880–1980." *Theory and Society* 13 (May 1984): 427–54.

Pipan ziliao: Zhongguo He Luxiao fu Liu Shaoqi fangeming xiuzheng zhuyi yanlun ji (Critique: the collected counter-revolutionary revisionist speeches of China's He Luxiao, spouse of Liu Shaoqi). Beijing: Renmin chubanshe, 1967.

Pomeranz, Kenneth. *The Making of a Hinterland*. Berkeley: University of California Press, 1993.

Qian Gang. "Cong *Jiefang junbao* (1956–69) kan 'jieji douzheng' yici de chuanbo" (The dissemination of the phrase *jieji douzheng* [class struggle]: a case study of *PLA Daily* [1956–1969]). *Ershiyi shiji* (Twentieth-first century), no. 77 (June 2003): 50–60.

———. "Hongse ciyu de boxing he liubian (1956–69)" (The rise and spread of red words [1956–69]). Unpublished manuscript.

Qian Ruisheng. *Minguo zhengzhi shi* (A political history of the Republic). Shanghai: Shangwu yinshuguan, 1936.

Qing Shizong shilu xuanji. Taibei: Taiwan yinhang jingji yanjiushi, 1963.

Qingyuan xianzhi (Qingyuan county gazetteer). (Guangxu reign, date incomplete). Beijing University Library Rare Book Collection.

Qiu Shi. "Jiu Luoyang xian jindai zhengquan zuzhi" (Old Luoyang county, modern political organization). In *Luoyang wenshi ziliao*, ed. Luoyang qu weiyuanhui wenshi ziliao yanjiu weiyuanhui. Anyang: Henan renmin chubanshe, 1988. 2: 100–105.

Qiu Yuqing, ed. *Fuqing shizhi* (Fuqing municipal gazetteer). Xiamen: Xiamen daxue chubanshe, 1994.

Reed, Bradley. *Talons and Teeth: County Clerks and Runners in the Qing Dynasty*. Stanford: Stanford University Press, 2000.

Remick, Elizabeth. *Building Local States: China During the Republican and Post-Mao Eras*. Cambridge, MA: Harvard University Asia Center Monograph Series, 2004.

Ren Junmo. "Yi Jiaonan xian shejiao yundong yi jiao" (A recollection of the Socialist Education Movement in [Shandong] Jiaonan County). In *Shandong wenshi ziliao, di ershiliu ji*, ed. Shandong wenshi ziliao weiyuanhui. Ji'nan: Shandong renmin chubanshe, 1989.

Renmin ribao (People's daily).

Renwen ji shehui kexue jikan (Taibei: Zhongyang yanjiuyuan Zhongshan renwen shehui kexue yanjiusuo) 7:2 (September 1995): 21–51.

Rizhou zhi (Ri department gazetteer). Qianlong 18. Beijing University Library Rare Book Collection.

Rogin, Michael. "'Make My Day!': Spectacle as Amnesia in Imperial Politics." *Representations* 29 (Winter 1990): 99–123.

Rowe, William T. *Saving the World: Chen Hong-mou and Elite Consciousness in Eighteenth-Century China*. Stanford: Stanford University Press, 2001.

Schoenhals, Michael. "'Non-people' in the People's Republic of China: A Chronicle of Terminological Ambiguity." *Indiana East Asian Working Paper Series*, no. 4 (Summer 1994).

Schoppa, R. Keith. "State, Society, and Land Reclamation on Hangzhou Bay During the Republican Era." *Modern China* 23:2 (April 1997): 246–71.

Schram, Stuart. "Classes, Old and New, in Mao Zedong's Thought." In *Class and Social Stratification in Post-Revolution China*, ed. James L. Watson. Cambridge, Eng.: Cambridge University Press, 1984.

Scott, James C. *Seeing Like a State: How Certain Schemes to Improve the Human Condition Have Failed*. New Haven and London: Yale University Press, 1998.

Selden, Mark. *The Yenan Way in Revolutionary China*. Cambridge, MA: Harvard University Press, 1971.

Shaanxi shengzhi (Shaanxi provincial gazetteer). Xi'an: Shaanxi renmin chubanshe, 1994.

Shanyin xianzhi (Shanyin county gazetteer). Jiaqing reign (date incomplete). Beijing University Library Rare Book Collection.

Shen Guoqing, ed. *Zhongwai fanfubai shiyong quanshu* (Complete practical manual of Chinese and foreign efforts to fight corruption). Beijing: Xinhua shuju, 1994.

Shen Lansheng. *Jiangnan caizheng luncong* (Collected essays on Jiangnan's fiscal administration). Shanghai: Jinglun chubanshe, 1943.

Shi Chengzhi. "Shilun 'sishi' yu 'wenge'" (Discussing the "Four Histories" and the "Cultural Revolution"). *Mingbao yuekan* (December 1971).

Shih, Chih-yu. "The Decline of a Moral Regime: China's Great Leap Forward in Retrospect." *Comparative Political Studies* 27:2 (July 1994): 272–301.

Shue, Vivienne. *The Reach of the State: Sketches of the Chinese Body Politic*. Stanford: Stanford University Press, 1988.

Skinner, G. William, ed. *The City in Late Imperial China*. Reprinted—Taibei: SMC Publishing, 1977.

Skinner, Quentin. "What Is Intellectual History?" *History Today* 35 (1985).

———. *The Foundations of Modern Political Thought*. Vol. 1. Cambridge, Eng.: Cambridge University Press, 1978.

Spence, Jonathan D. "The K'ang-hsi Reign." In *The Cambridge History of China*, vol. 9, pt. I, *The Ch'ing Empire to 1800*, ed. Williard J. Peterson. Cambridge, Eng.: Cambridge University Press, 2002.

Strauss, Julia C. *Strong Institutions in Weak Polities: State Building in Republican China, 1927–1940*. Oxford: Clarendon Press, 1998.

Sun Xiaocun. "Kejuan zashui baogao" (Report on extortionate levies and miscellaneous taxes). *Nongcun fuxing weiyuanhui huibao* (Rural Village Revitalization Committee bulletin) 12 (May 1934): 5–6.

Sun Yimin. "Ershi niandai houqi sanshi niandai chu Gong xian de san ren xianzhang (zhai chao)" (Three reigning magistrates in Gong county from the end of the 1920s through the 1930s [revised draft]). *Gongxian wenshi ziliao*, no. 3. Anyang: Henan renmin chubanshe, 1983, pp. 32–33.

Symposium "'Public Sphere'/'Civil Society' in China? Paradigmatic Issues in Chinese Studies, III," *Modern China* 19:2 (April 1993).

Tan, Chester C. *Chinese Political Thought in the Twentieth Century*. New York: Doubleday, 1971.

Tang Hongyi. "Luban 'shejiao' yundong" (Luban's Socialist Education Movement). In *Santai wenshi ziliao xuanji*, ed. Santai wenshi ziliao weiyuanhui (no. 8). Chengdu: Sichuan renmin chubanshe, 1989.

Tay, Alice. "Law in Communist China." 2 pts. *Sydney Law Review* 6:2 (1968): 153–72; 6:3 (1970): 335–70.

Teiwes, Frederick C., with Warren Sun. *China's Road to Disaster: Mao, Central Politicians, and Provincial Leaders in the Unfolding of the Great Leap Forward, 1955–1959*. New York: M. E. Sharpe, 1999.

———. "The Establishment and Consolidation of the New Regime, 1949–57." In *The Politics of China: The Eras of Mao and Deng*, ed. Roderick MacFarquhar. 2nd ed. New York: Cambridge University Press, 1997.

———. *Politics and Purges in China: Rectification and the Decline of Party Norms, 1950–1965*. New York: M. E. Sharpe, 1979.

Thornton, Patricia M. "Comrades and Collectives in Arms: Tax Resistance, Evasion and Avoidance Strategies in the Post-Mao Era." In *State and Society in 21st Century China: Contention, Crisis and Legitimation*, ed. Peter Hays Gries and Stanley Rosen. London and New York: Routledge, 2004, pp. 87–104.

———. "Beneath the Banyan Tree: Bottom-up Views of Local Taxation and the State During the Republican and Reform Eras." *Twentieth Century China* 15:1 (November 1999): 1–42.

Tien Hung-mao. *Government and Politics of Republican China, 1927–1937*. Stanford: Stanford University Press, 1972.

Tilly, Charles. *Coercion, Capital, and European States, AD 990–1992*. Cambridge, MA: Blackwell, 1990.

———. "War Making and State Making as Organized Crime." In *Bringing the State Back In*, ed. Peter B. Evans, Dietrich Rueschmeyer, and Theda Skocpol. Cambridge, Eng.: Cambridge University Press, 1985.

Tilly, Charles, ed. *The Formation of National States in Western Europe*. Princeton: Princeton University Press, 1975.

Tongxiang xianzhi (Tongxiang county gazetteer). No date. Beijing University Library Rare Book Collection.

Tsin, Michael. "Imagining 'Society' in Early Twentieth-Century China." In *Imagining the People: Chinese Intellectuals and the Concept of Citizenship, 1890–1920*, ed. Joshua Fogel and Peter Zarrow. New York: M. E. Sharpe, 1997, pp. 212–31.

Twitchett, Denis. "The Fragment of the T'ang Ordinances of the Department of Waterways Discovered at Tun-huang." *Asia Major* 6 (1957–58): 23–79.

Uhalley, Stephen, Jr. "The 'Four Histories' Movement: A Revolution in Writing China's Past." *Current Scene* 4:2 (January 15, 1966).

van de Ven, Hans J. *War and Nationalism in China, 1925–1945*. New York: Routledge Curzon, 2003.

——. "Public Finance and the Rise of Warlordism." *Modern Asian Studies* 30:4 (October 1996): 829–68.

Velde, François R. "Government Equity and Money: John Law's System in 1720 France." *Federal Reserve Bank of Chicago Working Papers*, WP-2003-31 (April 2003).

Vogel, Ezra. "Hsien (County) Organization." Unpublished paper, 1964.

Wakeman, Frederic, Jr. *Policing Shanghai, 1927–1937*. Berkeley: University of California Press, 1995.

——. "Rebellion and Revolution: The Study of Popular Movements in Chinese History." *Journal of Asian Studies* 36:2 (February 1977): 201–37.

Wakeman, Frederic, Jr., and Carolyn Grant, eds. *Conflict and Control in Late Imperial China*. Berkeley: University of California Press, 1975.

Wang Guangmei. "(Zhuanfa) 'Guangyu yige dadui de shehui zhuyi jiaoyu yundong de jingyan zongjie' de pishi" (Summary of the experiences of a production brigade in the socialist education movement) (September 1, 1964). In *Pipan ziliao: Zhongguo He Luxiao fu Liu Shaoqi fangeming xiuzheng zhuyi yanlun ji* (Critique: the collected counter-revolutionary revisionist speeches of China's He Luxiao, spouse of Liu Shaoqi). Beijing: Renmin chubanshe, 1967.

Wang Hongzhi. "Shiche bajie shi zhongquan hui jueyi, gonggu jiti jingji, fada nongye shengchan 1962)" (Implementation of the resolutions of the Tenth Plenum of the Eighth Central Committee on strengthening the collective economy and expanding agricultural production) (1962). In *Fujian Lianjiang xian feifang wenjian ji qi jiufen* (The documents of the [Communist] bandits of Fujian's Lianjiang county, with analytical notes). Taibei: Ministry of National Defense, Bureau of Intelligence, 1964.

Wang Jingqi. *Dushu tang xizheng suibi*. Reprinted—Shanghai: Shanghai guji chubanshe, 1995.

Wang Yongyin, ed. *Zhongguo lianzhengshi* (A history of honest administration in China). Zhengzhou: Zhongzhou gujie chubanshe, 1991.

Weber, Max. *Economy and Society*, vol. 2, ed. Guenther Roth and Clause Wittich. Berkeley: University of California Press, 1978.

Wedeman, Andrew. "Anticorruption Campaigns and the Intensification of Corruption in China." *Journal of Contemporary China* 14 (February 2005).

Wei, William. "Law and Order: The Role of Guomindang Security Forces in the Suppression of the Communist Bases During the Soviet Period." In *Single Sparks: China's Rural Revolutions*, ed. Kathleen Hartford and Steven M. Goldstein. New York: M. E. Sharpe, 1989.

——. *Counter-revolution in China: The Nationalists in Jiangxi During the Soviet Period*. Ann Arbor: University of Michigan Press, 1985.

Wen Lu. *Zhongguo 'zuo' wu* (China's "leftist" errors). Beijing: Chaohua chubanshe, 1993.

Weng Youwei. "Nanjing zhengfu xingzheng ducha zhuanyuan zhidu de fazhi kaocha" (Legal investigations under the Nanjing government's system of executive supervisory commissions). *Shixue yuekan* (Historiography monthly) 12 (2004): 48–59.

White, Hayden. *The Content of the Form: Narrative Discourse and Historical Representation*. Baltimore: Johns Hopkins University Press, 1987.

Whyte, Martin K. *Small Groups and Political Rituals in China*. Berkeley: University of California Press, 1974.

Wilbur, C. Martin. "The Nationalist Revolution: From Canton to Nanking, 1923–28." In *The Cambridge History of China*, vol. 12, *Republican China, 1912–1949*, pt. I, ed. John K. Fairbank and Denis Twitchett. Cambridge, Eng.: Cambridge University Press, 1983.

Wong, R. Bin. *China Transformed: Historical Change and the Limits of European Experience*. Ithaca, NY: Cornell University Press, 1997.

Wu Xiuquan. *Huiyi yu huainian* (Recollections and remembrances). Beijing: Zhonggong zhongyang dang jiao chubanshe, 1991.

Wu Zhihui. "'Quanmin geming yu guomin geming' de shangguo" (A discussion of "all people's revolution and national revolution"). In *Quanmin geming yu guomin geming* (All people's revolution and national revolution), ed. Tao Qiqing. Shanghai: Guangming shuju, 1939.

Wu, Silas. *Communication and Imperial Control in China: Evolution of the Palace Memorial System*. Cambridge, MA: Harvard University Press, 1970.

Wuchang xianzhi (Wuchang county gazetteer). Daoguang 33. Beijing University Library Rare Book Collection.

Xin Zhang. *Social Transformation in Modern China: The State and Local Elites in Henan, 1900–1937*. Cambridge, Eng.: Cambridge University Press, 2000.

Xinghua xianzhi (Xinghua county gazetteer). (Tongzhi reign, date incomplete). Beijing University Library Rare Book Collection.

Xingzhengyuan nongcun fuxing weiyuanhui, ed. *Shaanxi sheng nongcun diaocha* (Investigation of rural Shaanxi). Shanghai: Shangwu yinshu, 1934.

Yan Jinan and Bai Wenmei. "Shao Hongji er san shi" (Two or three things about Shao Hongji). *Gongxian wenshi ziliao*, no. 3. Anyang: Henan renmin chubanshe, 1983, pp. 35–36.

Yang Dali. *Calamity and Reform in China: State, Rural Society, and Institutional Change Since the Great Leap Famine*. Stanford: Stanford University Press, 1996.

Yang Xiaohong and Zhang Zongxin, eds. *Jilin shengzhi (sifa gongan zhi)* (Jilin provincial gazetteer [law and public security]). Changchun: Jilin renmin chubanshe, 1992.

Yongzheng liubu chufen zeli (Administrative punishment statutes of the Six Boards, Yongzheng reign). Taibei, Taiwan: National Library Rare Book Collection.

Yu Junxian, ed. *Guomin zhengfu jianchayuan shilu* (The veritable records of the Control Yuan) Taibei: Jianchayuan mishu chu, 1981.

Yuan Shuhe. "Liutan Guomindang zhengfu shi kejuan zaxue" (Remarks on the miscellaneous taxes and levies of the Guomindang government). In *Guangze wenshi ziliao*, ed. Fujiansheng Guangze weiyuanhui wenshi ziliao weiyuanhui. Vol. 3. Fuzhou: Fujian renmin chuban she, 1990.

Zelin, Madeleine. "The Yung-cheng Reign." In *The Cambridge History of China*, vol. 9, pt. 1, *The Ch'ing Empire to 1800*, ed. Willard J. Peterson. Cambridge, Eng.: Cambridge University Press, 2002.

———. *The Magistrate's Tael: Rationalizing Fiscal Reform in Eighteenth-Century Ch'ing China*. Berkeley: University of California Press, 1984.

Zeng Jijun. "Shishi xunzheng yu junzheng jianshe" (The implementation of tutelage and the establishment of military rule). In *Zhonghua Minguo jianguo shi* (The history of the founding of the Chinese Republic), ed. Jiaoyubu zhupian (Ministry of Education). Taibei: Guoli bianyiguan, 1989, vol. 3.

Zeng Xianghu, ed. *Hunan shengzhi zhengfa zhi* (Hunan provincial political and legal gazetteer). Changsha: Hunan chubanshe, 1995.

Zhang Hao. "Minguo shiqi xiangcun zizhi tuixing zhi qianyin houguo—cong *Minguo xiangcun zizhi wenti yanjiu* tanqi" (The ins and outs of implementing rural self-government during the Republican period—a discussion of *Research into the Problems of Rural Self-Government During the Republic*). *Shixue yuekan* (Historiography monthly) 5 (2003): 73–78.

Zhang Jianxing. *Luoding xianzhi* (Luoding county gazetteer). Guangdong: Guangdong renmin chubanshe, 1994.

Zhang Yihui, ed. *Jiandong xianzhi* (Jiandong county gazetteer). Shanghai: Shanghai renmin chubanshe, 1991.

Zhao Chen, ed. *Xingfa fenze shiyong* (Applied penal statutes). Chongqing: Dadong shuju, 1946.

Zhejiang Tongxiang Lushi zongpu (Zhejiang Tongxiang Lu clan genealogy). Qianlong 54. Beijing University Library Rare Book Collection.

Zheng Jingyi. *Falu daci shu* (*Zengding zhongyin*) (Dictionary of law [enlarged and reprinted]). Taibei: Shangwu yinshuguan, 1972.

Zhong Sheng and Tan Senshu. "Shilun Nanjing zhengfu xunzheng qianqi (1928–1937) de difang dangzheng de jiufen" (On party-state disputes during the Nanjing government's early tutelage period [1928–1937]). *Shixue yuekan* (Historiography monthly), no. 2 (1999).

Zhonggong Fujiansheng Lianjiang xian weiyuanhui (zhuanfa), ed. *Fujian Lianjiang xian feifang wenjian ji qi yanxi* (Documents and analysis from the bandit area of Fujian Lianjiang county). Taibei: Ministry of National Defense, Bureau of Intelligence, 1964.

Zhongguo Guomindang dangshi weiyuanhui, ed. *Zhongguo Guomindang xuanyanji* (Declarations of the Nationalist Party). Taibei: Jingxiaochu Zhongyang wenwu gongyingshe, 1976.

Zhongguo Guomindang zhongyang weiyuanhui dangshi weiyuanhui (Central Committee of the Nationalist Party's Committee on Party History), ed. *Guofu quanji* (Complete works of our founding father). Taibei: Dangshi hui, 1973.

Zhongguo renmin daxue Qingshi yanjiusuo, ed. *Kang Yong Qian shiqi chengxiang renmin fankang douzheng ziliao* (The resistance struggles of urban and rural peoples during the Kangxi, Yongzheng, and Qianlong reign periods). Beijing: Zhonghua shuju, 1979.

Zhongyang ribao.

Zhu Qihan. *Zhongguo nongcun jingjide xiushi* (Perspectives on China's rural economy). Shanghai: Zhongguo yanjiu shudian chuban, 1936.

Zhu, Ying. "*Yongzheng Dynasty* and Chinese Primetime Television Drama." *Cinema Journal* 44:4 (Summer 2005): 3–17.

Zito, Angela. *Of Body and Brush: Grand Sacrifice as Text/Performance in Eighteenth-Century China.* Chicago: University of Chicago Press, 1997.

Zou Fang. "Zhongguo tianfu fujia de zhonglei" (Types of surcharges on China's land tax). *Dongfang zazhi* (Eastern miscellany) 31:14 (July 1934).

Zuigao renmin jianchayuan (Supreme People's Procuracy), ed. *Jianguo yilai fanfubai huilu fagui ziliao xuanbian* (Anthology of anti-corruption and bribery laws and regulations since the founding of the People's Republic). Beijing: Zhongguo xiancha chubanshe, 1991.

Index

Harvard East Asian Monographs
(*out-of-print)

42. Ezra Vogel, Margie Sargent, Vivienne B. Shue, Thomas Jay Mathews, and Deborah S. Davis, *The Cultural Revolution in the Provinces*

43. Sidney A. Forsythe, *An American Missionary Community in China, 1895–1905*

*44. Benjamin I. Schwartz, ed., *Reflections on the May Fourth Movement.: A Symposium*

*45. Ching Young Choe, *The Rule of the Taewŏngun, 1864–1873: Restoration in Yi Korea*

46. W. P. J. Hall, *A Bibliographical Guide to Japanese Research on the Chinese Economy, 1958–1970*

47. Jack J. Gerson, *Horatio Nelson Lay and Sino-British Relations, 1854–1864*

48. Paul Richard Bohr, *Famine and the Missionary: Timothy Richard as Relief Administrator and Advocate of National Reform*

49. Endymion Wilkinson, *The History of Imperial China: A Research Guide*

50. Britten Dean, *China and Great Britain: The Diplomacy of Commercial Relations, 1860–1864*

51. Ellsworth C. Carlson, *The Foochow Missionaries, 1847–1880*

52. Yeh-chien Wang, *An Estimate of the Land-Tax Collection in China, 1753 and 1908*

53. Richard M. Pfeffer, *Understanding Business Contracts in China, 1949–1963*

*54. Han-sheng Chuan and Richard Kraus, *Mid-Ching Rice Markets and Trade: An Essay in Price History*

55. Ranbir Vohra, *Lao She and the Chinese Revolution*

56. Liang-lin Hsiao, *China's Foreign Trade Statistics, 1864–1949*

*57. Lee-hsia Hsu Ting, *Government Control of the Press in Modern China, 1900–1949*

*58. Edward W. Wagner, *The Literati Purges: Political Conflict in Early Yi Korea*

*59. Joungwon A. Kim, *Divided Korea: The Politics of Development, 1945–1972*

60. Noriko Kamachi, John K. Fairbank, and Chūzō Ichiko, *Japanese Studies of Modern China Since 1953: A Bibliographical Guide to Historical and Social-Science Research on the Nineteenth and Twentieth Centuries, Supplementary Volume for 1953–1969*

61. Donald A. Gibbs and Yun-chen Li, *A Bibliography of Studies and Translations of Modern Chinese Literature, 1918–1942*

62. Robert H. Silin, *Leadership and Values: The Organization of Large-Scale Taiwanese Enterprises*

63. David Pong, *A Critical Guide to the Kwangtung Provincial Archives Deposited at the Public Record Office of London*

*64. Fred W. Drake, *China Charts the World: Hsu Chi-yü and His Geography of 1848*

89. Sung Hwan Ban, Pal Yong Moon, and Dwight H. Perkins, *Rural Development*

*90. Noel F. McGinn, Donald R. Snodgrass, Yung Bong Kim, Shin-Bok Kim, and Quee-Young Kim, *Education and Development in Korea*

*91. Leroy P. Jones and Il SaKong, *Government, Business, and Entrepreneurship in Economic Development: The Korean Case*

92. Edward S. Mason, Dwight H. Perkins, Kwang Suk Kim, David C. Cole, Mahn Je Kim et al., *The Economic and Social Modernization of the Republic of Korea*

93. Robert Repetto, Tai Hwan Kwon, Son-Ung Kim, Dae Young Kim, John E. Sloboda, and Peter J. Donaldson, *Economic Development, Population Policy, and Demographic Transition in the Republic of Korea*

94. Parks M. Coble, Jr., *The Shanghai Capitalists and the Nationalist Government, 1927–1937*

95. Noriko Kamachi, *Reform in China: Huang Tsun-hsien and the Japanese Model*

96. Richard Wich, *Sino-Soviet Crisis Politics: A Study of Political Change and Communication*

97. Lillian M. Li, *China's Silk Trade: Traditional Industry in the Modern World, 1842–1937*

98. R. David Arkush, *Fei Xiaotong and Sociology in Revolutionary China*

*99. Kenneth Alan Grossberg, *Japan's Renaissance: The Politics of the Muromachi Bakufu*

100. James Reeve Pusey, *China and Charles Darwin*

101. Hoyt Cleveland Tillman, *Utilitarian Confucianism: Chen Liang's Challenge to Chu Hsi*

102. Thomas A. Stanley, *Ōsugi Sakae, Anarchist in Taishō Japan: The Creativity of the Ego*

103. Jonathan K. Ocko, *Bureaucratic Reform in Provincial China: Ting Jih-ch'ang in Restoration Kiangsu, 1867–1870*

104. James Reed, *The Missionary Mind and American East Asia Policy, 1911–1915*

105. Neil L. Waters, *Japan's Local Pragmatists: The Transition from Bakumatsu to Meiji in the Kawasaki Region*

106. David C. Cole and Yung Chul Park, *Financial Development in Korea, 1945–1978*

107. Roy Bahl, Chuk Kyo Kim, and Chong Kee Park, *Public Finances During the Korean Modernization Process*

108. William D. Wray, *Mitsubishi and the N.Y.K., 1870–1914: Business Strategy in the Japanese Shipping Industry*

109. Ralph William Huenemann, *The Dragon and the Iron Horse: The Economics of Railroads in China, 1876–1937*

*110. Benjamin A. Elman, *From Philosophy to Philology: Intellectual and Social Aspects of Change in Late Imperial China*

111. Jane Kate Leonard, *Wei Yüan and China's Rediscovery of the Maritime World*

112. Luke S. K. Kwong, *A Mosaic of the Hundred Days:. Personalities, Politics, and Ideas of 1898*

*113. John E. Wills, Jr., *Embassies and Illusions: Dutch and Portuguese Envoys to K'ang-hsi, 1666–1687*

114. Joshua A. Fogel, *Politics and Sinology: The Case of Naitō Konan (1866–1934)*

*115. Jeffrey C. Kinkley, ed., *After Mao: Chinese Literature and Society, 1978–1981*

116. C. Andrew Gerstle, *Circles of Fantasy: Convention in the Plays of Chikamatsu*

117. Andrew Gordon, *The Evolution of Labor Relations in Japan: Heavy Industry, 1853–1955*

*118. Daniel K. Gardner, *Chu Hsi and the "Ta Hsueh": Neo-Confucian Reflection on the Confucian Canon*

119. Christine Guth Kanda, *Shinzō: Hachiman Imagery and Its Development*

*120. Robert Borgen, *Sugawara no Michizane and the Early Heian Court*

121. Chang-tai Hung, *Going to the People: Chinese Intellectual and Folk Literature, 1918–1937*

*122. Michael A. Cusumano, *The Japanese Automobile Industry: Technology and Management at Nissan and Toyota*

123. Richard von Glahn, *The Country of Streams and Grottoes: Expansion, Settlement, and the Civilizing of the Sichuan Frontier in Song Times*

124. Steven D. Carter, *The Road to Komatsubara: A Classical Reading of the Renga Hyakuin*

125. Katherine F. Bruner, John K. Fairbank, and Richard T. Smith, *Entering China's Service: Robert Hart's Journals, 1854–1863*

126. Bob Tadashi Wakabayashi, *Anti-Foreignism and Western Learning in Early-Modern Japan: The "New Theses" of 1825*

127. Atsuko Hirai, *Individualism and Socialism: The Life and Thought of Kawai Eijirō (1891–1944)*

128. Ellen Widmer, *The Margins of Utopia: "Shui-hu hou-chuan" and the Literature of Ming Loyalism*

129. R. Kent Guy, *The Emperor's Four Treasuries: Scholars and the State in the Late Chien-lung Era*

130. Peter C. Perdue, *Exhausting the Earth: State and Peasant in Hunan, 1500–1850*

131. Susan Chan Egan, *A Latterday Confucian: Reminiscences of William Hung (1893–1980)*

155. Richard J. Smith, John K. Fairbank, and Katherine F. Bruner, *Robert Hart and China's Early Modernization: His Journals, 1863–1866*

156. George J. Tanabe, Jr., *Myōe the Dreamkeeper: Fantasy and Knowledge in Kamakura Buddhism*

157. William Wayne Farris, *Heavenly Warriors: The Evolution of Japan's Military, 500–1300*

158. Yu-ming Shaw, *An American Missionary in China: John Leighton Stuart and Chinese-American Relations*

159. James B. Palais, *Politics and Policy in Traditional Korea*

*160. Douglas Reynolds, *China, 1898–1912: The Xinzheng Revolution and Japan*

161. Roger R. Thompson, *China's Local Councils in the Age of Constitutional Reform, 1898–1911*

162. William Johnston, *The Modern Epidemic: History of Tuberculosis in Japan*

163. Constantine Nomikos Vaporis, *Breaking Barriers: Travel and the State in Early Modern Japan*

164. Irmela Hijiya-Kirschnereit, *Rituals of Self-Revelation: Shishōsetsu as Literary Genre and Socio-Cultural Phenomenon*

165. James C. Baxter, *The Meiji Unification Through the Lens of Ishikawa Prefecture*

166. Thomas R. H. Havens, *Architects of Affluence: The Tsutsumi Family and the Seibu-Saison Enterprises in Twentieth-Century Japan*

167. Anthony Hood Chambers, *The Secret Window: Ideal Worlds in Tanizaki's Fiction*

168. Steven J. Ericson, *The Sound of the Whistle: Railroads and the State in Meiji Japan*

169. Andrew Edmund Goble, *Kenmu: Go-Daigo's Revolution*

170. Denise Potrzeba Lett, *In Pursuit of Status: The Making of South Korea's "New" Urban Middle Class*

171. Mimi Hall Yiengpruksawan, *Hiraizumi: Buddhist Art and Regional Politics in Twelfth-Century Japan*

172. Charles Shirō Inouye, *The Similitude of Blossoms: A Critical Biography of Izumi Kyōka (1873–1939), Japanese Novelist and Playwright*

173. Aviad E. Raz, *Riding the Black Ship: Japan and Tokyo Disneyland*

174. Deborah J. Milly, *Poverty, Equality, and Growth: The Politics of Economic Need in Postwar Japan*

175. See Heng Teow, *Japan's Cultural Policy Toward China, 1918–1931: A Comparative Perspective*

176. Michael A. Fuller, *An Introduction to Literary Chinese*

177. Frederick R. Dickinson, *War and National Reinvention: Japan in the Great War, 1914–1919*